Anonymous

Indiana Historical Society Publications

Anonymous

Indiana Historical Society Publications

ISBN/EAN: 9783337307905

Printed in Europe, USA, Canada, Australia, Japan

Cover: Foto ©ninafisch / pixelio.de

More available books at **www.hansebooks.com**

Indiana Historical Society

PUBLICATIONS

VOLUME I

INDIANAPOLIS
THE BOWEN-MERRILL COMPANY
1897

TABLE OF CONTENTS.

No. 1. Proceedings of the Society, 1830–1886.
No. 2. Northwest Territory.
    Letter of Nathan Dane concerning the Ordinance of 1787.
    Gov. Patrick Henry's Secret Letter of Instruction to George Rogers Clark.
No. 3. The Uses of History. By President Andrew Wylie, D. D.
No. 4. The National Decline of the Miami Indians. By John B. Dillon.
No. 5. Early History of Indianapolis and Central Indiana. By Nathaniel Bolton.
No. 6. Joseph G. Marshall. By Prof. John L. Campbell.
No. 7. Judge John Law. By Charles Denby.
No. 8. Archæology of Indiana. By Prof. E. T. Cox.

APPENDIX.

No. 9. The Early Settlement of the Miami Country. By Dr. Ezra Ferris.

INDIANA HISTORICAL SOCIETY PUBLICATIONS

VOLUME I　　　　　　　　NUMBER I

PROCEEDINGS

OF THE

INDIANA HISTORICAL SOCIETY

1830–1886

INDIANAPOLIS
THE BOWEN-MERRILL COMPANY
1897

PREFACE.

The Indiana Historical Society came into existence on December 11, 1830. Its existence has been very quiet—so quiet at times as to suggest death. And yet in the course of its long and varied career, throughout its suspensions and reorganizations, it has gathered and published a large amount of valuable material. That collected since the last reorganization of the society, in 1886, has been published in Vol. 2 of the society's collections, and in some pamphlets which will appear in Vol. 3. It is the object of this volume to preserve in permanent form all of the publications that appeared prior to 1886. With these are included the minutes of the proceedings of the society, and for their better understanding it has been deemed proper to prefix a sketch of the history of the society and its work.

The organization of the society was chiefly due to the efforts of John H. Farnham, the first corresponding secretary of the society, who was efficiently aided by Benjamin Parke, the first president, Bethuel F. Morris, the first recording secretary, and James Blake, the first treasurer. These four were the incorporators of the society. The movement was a popular one. Nearly all the prominent men of the state became members, and for five years a marked activity was shown in the work. Mr. Farnham was especially active in his office, and in the course of his correspondence with honorary members secured the letter from Nathan Dane concerning the history of the ordinance of 1787, which has become known to the world as one of the authoritative documents on that question. He also secured a number of donations of books, which are still preserved, and himself added a set of the earlier house and senate journals of the state, which make the society's collection of these documents the most complete in existence.

From 1835 to 1842 the society was inactive. One meeting was held in 1842, at which nothing of importance occurred, and the society again relapsed until 1848. In 1848 a more determined effort was made to maintain the society, the most active spirit being John B. Dillon, who was at that time state librarian. Some work was accomplished, but after 1853 the condition of inaction was reached again, and lasted until 1859. In 1859 the society was "reorganized and placed on a permanent basis," and that was its last appearance on the stage before the civil war. In this reorganization a new minute book was used, and owing to its subsequent loss the history of the society has had to be gathered piecemeal. In 1863 Mr. Dillon was appointed to a position in Washington, and resided there most of the time until 1875. He was in Indianapolis for a time in the fall of 1873, when the society was again revived and lasted through a few meetings. He found that the books and papers of the society which had been left in the old state bank building had been removed to new quarters in the county court-house, and that in the removal a number of valuable documents had been lost, including the new minute book of 1859.

In 1877 the society was once more revivified and held several meetings, after which nothing was done until after Mr. Dillon's death on February 27, 1879. One meeting was then held at which Gen. W. H. H. Terrell was elected to fill Mr. Dillon's place, and no more meetings occurred until the present organization. In fact the existence of the society had become almost forgotten except by the former members then surviving.

In 1886 several gentlemen of Indianapolis agreed to unite for the purpose of preserving historical material pertaining to the state. Among those asked to join was Major Jonathan W. Gordon, who had been a member of the society, and who suggested its reorganization. This plan was adopted. A meeting of the surviving members of the society was called, new members were elected, and the society was once more put in motion. Since then meetings have been held regularly, and the work of the society has been prosecuted with persistence if not with vigor.

A large part of the work has consisted in the recovery of the material included in the present volume, which was felt to be a matter of duty by the members. Fortunately the original minute-book of the society was preserved, and this gave a clue to its work for the first twenty-eight years. But a part of the papers read before the society had never been printed in pamphlet form, and at the time of the reorganization of 1886 no paper read before the society was in its possession in any form. The search for these was long and trying. For example, years passed before any trace could be found of Mr. Dillon's paper on the National Decline of the Miami Indians. There was a tradition that it had been printed in some Cincinnati paper, but a search of files for six months after its delivery failed to reveal it. At length, by chance, Mr. English came into possession of a fragment of the address as published, but without any date or the name of the paper. The type, however, corresponded to that of the Cincinnati Gazette, and after careful investigation there was found on the back of the slip, where the columns slightly overlapped, the letters "t 28," which were guessed to be the remnants of a date line, and could mean, of course, nothing but August 28. By this clue the article was easily found as printed some fifteen months after its delivery.

The remaining thirty-seven years of the society's history prior to the last reorganization had to be gathered piecemeal from newspaper accounts and a few chance sources of information. As a matter of necessity this character of work does not admit of absolute certainty as to the perfection of the record obtained, but it is confidently believed that every paper read before the society has been recovered, and that the minutes are complete with the exception of two or three unimportant meetings. It is therefore felt that the record is practically so complete that the society is justified in publishing it without further delay, and that if hereafter any omitted matter of importance should be discovered the public will understand that its omission was not due to any lack of effort on the part of the society in the ten years that this investigation has been in progress.

MINUTES

OF THE

INDIANA HISTORICAL SOCIETY.

INDIANAPOLIS, December 11, 1830.

At a large and respectable meeting of the members of the general assembly and citizens of the state and town of Indianapolis, convened at the court-house on Saturday evening, the 11th of December, 1830, for the purpose of taking into consideration the expediency of forming an historical society for the state of Indiana, Mr. Wm. Graham, of Jackson county, was invited to the chair, and Mr. H. P. Thornton, of Washington county, appointed secretary.

Mr. John H. Farnham, of Washington county, having in a few appropriate remarks stated the object of the meeting, presented the following resolutions for consideration:

WHEREAS, This meeting is fully impressed with the importance and necessity of collecting and preserving the materials for a comprehensive and accurate history of our country, natural, civil and political, many of which are of an ephemeral and transitory nature, and in the absence of well directed efforts to preserve them are rapidly passing into oblivion; and whereas, the establishment of safe depositories for the keeping of natural curiosities, manuscripts, public documents, etc., in the custody of intelligent guardians interested in their accumulation and preservation, has ever been found promotive of the public good and auxiliary to the advancement of science and literature; therefore,

Resolved, As the sense of this meeting, that it is expedient to form ourselves into a society to be known and designated by the name of the "HISTORICAL SOCIETY OF INDIANA."

Resolved, That a committee of seven gentlemen be appointed for the purpose of drafting a constitution for the government of said society to be submitted to the approbation of the meeting.

Which were read and unanimously adopted.

The following gentlemen were appointed a committee in pursuance of the second resolution, viz.: Messrs. John H. Farnham, Jesse L. Holman, Jeremiah Sullivan, Isaac Blackford, William C. Linton, James Whitcomb and David Wallace.

After a retirement of a few minutes, Mr. Farnham, from said committee, reported a draft of a constitution, which, after receiving sundry amendments, was adopted, as follows, viz.:

THE CONSTITUTION OF THE HISTORICAL SOCIETY OF INDIANA.

Article I. This society shall be called the Historical Society of Indiana.

Article II. The objects of this society shall be the collection of all materials calculated to shed light on the natural, civil, and political history of Indiana, the promotion of useful knowledge, and the friendly and profitable intercourse of such citizens of the state as are disposed to promote the aforesaid objects.

Article III. Meetings of the society shall be held semi-annually at the court-house in Indianapolis on the second days of the sessions of the supreme court, and there shall be an annual meeting of the same on the first Saturday succeeding the meeting of the general assembly.

Article IV. The officers of said society shall be:

1st. A president, who shall preside and preserve order at all meetings of the society.

2d. Three vice-presidents, one of whom, in the order of appointment, shall preside at all meetings in the absence of the president.

3d A corresponding secretary, who shall be charged with all the correspondence required by the affairs of the said society.

4th. A recording secretary, who shall record and preserve the minutes of the society.

5th. A treasurer, who shall receive all moneys due the society and hold the same subject to its order and make an annual report of all receipts and disbursements.

6th. An executive committee of five members, any three of whom shall constitute a quorum, whose duty it shall be to meet on the day upon which the society holds its session or as soon thereafter as practicable, to select subjects for public lectures and appoint the individuals by whom the same shall be delivered at the annual and semi-annual meetings of the society. It shall also be their duty to attend to the publication of such lectures and communications made to the society as they may deem expedient; to take charge of all books, papers, specimens, models, curiosities, etc., belonging to the society, and to submit at each annual meeting a detailed report of their proceedings to the inspection of the society. They shall have power to make by-laws not inconsistent with the constitution, to direct and superintend all disbursements, and generally to carry into effect all measures not otherwise provided for.

Article V. The president, vice-president, secretaries and

treasurer shall have the privilege of sitting with the executive committee and voting on all matters that come before them.

Article VI. The signature of the constitution and the payment of the annual contribution shall constitute membership.

Article VII. The officers of said society shall be elected by ballot at the annual meeting, and shall continue in office for one year and until the election of their successors.

Article VIII. Each member shall pay into the hands of the treasurer one dollar, to be paid at the annual meeting, and a failure to pay such annual contribution as aforesaid shall suspend the right of membership.

Article IX. Any member of said society shall at any time have the right of withdrawing upon filing with the secretary a notice in writing of such intention, accompanied with the treasurer's receipts in full for all dues.

Article X. The constitution shall be subject to amendment at any annual meeting by a vote of two-thirds of the members present.

LIST OF SIGNERS OF THE CONSTITUTION.

(This does not include all the members, but only those whose names are affixed to the constitution.)

B. PARKE
JAMES SCOTT
JOHN OWENS
DENNIS PENNINGTON
JAMES BLAIR
WM. POLKE
PHILIP SWEETSER
N. B. PALMER
JOSEPH ORR
JAMES BLAKE
GEO. H. DUNN
MILTON STAPP

JESSE L. HOLMAN
J. H. FARNHAM
S. C. STEVENS
A. W. MORRIS
CALVIN FLETCHER
H. GREGG
J. P. DRAKE
N. NOBLE
H. P. COBURN
SAMUEL HALL
E. M. HUNTINGTON
J. T. MCKINNEY

INDIANA HISTORICAL SOCIETY.

Albt. S. White
Charles Dewey
I. T. Canby
Wm. B. Slaughter
A. Kinney
Wm. McPherson
E. B. Martin
Saml. Merrill
Jas. M. Ray
Obed Foote
Wm. W. Wick
T. A. Howard
Wm. Connor
Benjamin Adams
David Wallace
Elias Murray
E. N. Elliott
Samuel Newberry
John H. Thompson
Danl. D. Pratt
Chas. W. Cady
T. L. Sullivan
Th. H. Sharpe
Jer. Sullivan
James Whitcomb
Wm. C. Linton
Isaac N. Heylin
Samuel Frisbie
Isaac Howk
Amos Lane
Isaac Blackford
John Law
Ezra Ferris
Saml. Henderson
James Morrison
John R. Porter
H. P. Thornton

Wm. Sheets
James Rariden
Wm. Marshall
H. Hurst
Isaac Coe
H. Bradley
John DePauw
D. Maguire
John Cain
A. W. Harrison
Hiram Brown
W. Quarles
Allen Hamilton
John J. Neely
Joseph M. Hayes
O. H. Smith
W. E. Dunbar
James P. Foley
E. Brown
Abner T. Ellis
H. W. Beecher
John B. Dillon
Jno. D. Defrees
John M. Frazee
A. St. Clair
Saml. Judah
B. F. Morris
Sam Smith
Saml. G. Mitchell
John Tipton
James Farrington
C. G. Hassey
Enoch McCarty
I. Naylor
C. I. Battell
And. Ch. Griffith
F. W. Hunt

R. C. Talbott
J. F. D. Lanier
J. L. Mothershead
Wm. B. Beach
J. H. Hager
A. L. Roache
Saml. E. Perkins
Aaron Wood
Geo. W. Lane
J. F. Stevens
Wm. Mitchell
Oliver B. Torbet
Daniel Mace
Saml. Hannah
J. W. Gordon
Hamilton Smith
William T. Otto
H. S. Lane
Ballard Smith
G. D. Wagner
Jacob B. McChesney
Saml. Osbourne
Wm. F. Reynolds
J. G. Marshall
Abel C. Pepper
Gordon Tanner
Ashbel P. Willard
William A. Holliday
Ebenezer Dumont
Samuel Grimes
Wm. J. Burns
S. B. Gookins

H. Lasselle, Jr.
Geo. W. Mears
James W. Borden
E. L. Beard
W. M. McCarty
Robt. W. Underhill
Joseph A. Wright
John Coburn
George Upfold
J. R. Bryant
R. H. Milroy
Jas. W. Dunn
T. R. Cressy
E. R. Ames
Solomon Blair
Jno. W. Dawson
Saml. Hanna
Wm. S. Holman
R. T. Brown
Jesse L. Williams
A. M. Higgins
C. L. Dunham
Paris C. Dunning
James D. Conner
Thos. Dowling
A. B. Line
S. Fisher
E. W. H Ellis
James H. Stewart
Samuel L. Rugg
D. E. Snyder.

(At this point a new record was put in use, but it was afterward lost. The foregoing are the signers prior to 1860.)

October 7, 1873.

F. C. Holliday
T. M. Stevens, M. D.
Daniel Hough
James A. Wildman
Lawson Abbett
S. Yandes
Dr. Delany Wiley
Hanford A. Edson
H. W. Clark
Alfred H. Clark
T. A. Hendricks
J. B. Julian
Henry D. Pierce
Charles B. Lizius
Samuel Morrison
George W. Sloan
Brainard Rorison

W. W. Curry
Barton D. Jones
George Brown, U. S. N.
P. D. Hammond
Morris M. Ross
John S. Simonson
Thomas H. Lynch
John Collett
John L. Campbell
Charles N. Todd
D. H. Oliver
M. D. Manson
P. L. Kennedy
Henry B. Carrington
Henry F. Keenan
John Love

November 26, 1873.

David S. Gooding
S. C. Willson
John W. Blake
Levi Ritter
George L. Curtiss
E. T. Cox
E. C. Tuttle
J. M. Ridenour
Jo. Poole
G. M. Levette
Charles Evans
George P. Brown
Henry Day
David Gibson
Henry Coburn

Temple C. Harrison
Charles H. Test
Wm. M. Blake
George W. Carr
M. C. Kerr
E. E. Bassett
Samuel V. Morris
Joseph F. Daugherty
George W. Julian
Charles H. Raymond
George Hasty
R. B. Duncan
J. P. C. Shanks
L. F. Walker
W. H. H. Terrell

FEBRUARY 6, 1877.

JOHN J. CUMMINS
W. H. FOGG
DANIEL THOMAS
THOS. J. LOGAN
G. M. BALLARD
F. J. VAN VORHIS
JAMES MILLISON

J. F. GOOKINS
W. W. WOOLLEN
W. A. BELL
PETER H. LEMON
J. A. MINICH
WILLARD H. HINKLEY

APRIL 8, 1886.

WM. H. ENGLISH
JOHN R. WILSON
W. DEM. HOOPER

J. P. DUNN, JR.
DANIEL WAIT HOWE

INDIANAPOLIS, December 15, 1830. At an adjourned meeting of the Historical Society of Indiana held at the court-house in Indianapolis on Wednesday evening the 15th of December, 1830, Milton Stapp was called to the chair and Henry P. Thornton continued to act as secretary.

By direction of the chairman the constitution as engrossed was read.

And on motion of Mr. Law the society proceeded to the election of its officers, and Messrs. Howk and Farnham were appointed tellers.

Mr. Farnham nominated the Hon. Benjamin Parke as a suitable person to fill the office as president, and on counting the ballots the Hon. Benjamin Parke was declared to be unanimously elected president of the society.

Mr. Law nominated Messrs. Scott, Holman and Blackford as suitable persons to fill the offices of first, second and third vice-presidents and on counting the ballots Isaac Blackford was declared to be elected first vice-president, Jesse L. Holman was declared to be elected second vice-president and James Scott was declared to be elected third vice-president.

On motion the society proceeded to the election of a corresponding secretary, and on counting the ballots John H. Farnham was declared duly elected.

On motion the society proceeded to the election of a recording secretary, and on counting the ballots B. F. Morris was declared elected.

On motion the society proceeded to the election of a treasurer, and on counting the ballots James Blake was declared to be elected.

On motion the society proceeded to the election of an executive committee, and on counting the ballots Samuel Merrill, George H. Dunn, Isaac Howk, James Whitcomb and John Law were elected.

On motion of Mr. Farnham the sixth article of the constitution was reconsidered and amended by striking out the residue of the article after the word "membership."

On motion of Mr. Sullivan the following was added to the constitution as an additional article:

"Honorary members may be elected at the annual meeting by the votes of a majority of the members present."

On motion of Mr. Holman it was

Resolved, That the executive committee be requested to procure the delivery of lectures at the annual and semi-annual meetings of the society or the communication of disquisitions on the following subjects:

1. The history of the Indian tribes within the state.
2. The civil and political history of the state from its earliest settlement.
3. Ancient remains and natural curiosities within the state.
4. The natural history of the state embracing its geology, mineralogy and botany, its soil, productions and climate, its animals, birds and fishes.

On motion of Mr. Morrison it was

Resolved, That the executive committee be requested to draft and present to the general assembly a respectful memorial requesting the passage of a law incorporating the present society by the name of the Historical Society of Indiana and that the gentlemen this evening elected be recommended to be named in the contemplated act of incorporation as the first officers of said society; that the said memorial respectfully request the general assembly to remember the said society in the annual distribution of the laws, journals and public documents of this state, and that the secretary of state be authorized to deliver to said society two boxes of books now in the executive department addressed to the Historical Society.

The following gentlemen were elected honorary members of the society:

Lewis Cass, Michigan Territory.
William Henry Harrison, of Ohio.
Edward Coles, of Illinois.
William McClure, of New Harmony, Indiana.
Andrew Wylie, of Bloomington, Indiana.
James Hall, of Vandalia, Illinois.
John Baddolet.
Francis Vigo, of Knox county, Indiana.

And on motion the corresponding secretary is directed to acquaint the above-named gentlemen with their election and solicit such information and assistance in furtherance of the objects of the society as it may be in their power to make.

And the society adjourned *sine die*.

INDIANAPOLIS, December 18, 1830.

At a meeting of the executive committee of the Historical Society of Indiana, held at Indianapolis on the 18th day of December, 1830, present Samuel Merrill, John Law, James

Whitcomb and George H. Dunn, members of said committee, and Isaac Blackford, Jesse L. Holman and James Scott, vice-presidents, and John H. Farnham, corresponding secretary.

Mr. Merrill was called to the chair and George H. Dunn appointed secretary for the evening.

On motion of Mr. Law it was

Resolved, That the president of this society be requested to deliver at the semi-annual meeting in May a discourse on the civil and political history of this state from its earliest settlement.

The following resolutions were moved and adopted by Mr. Whitcomb:

1. *Resolved*, That the corresponding secretary address communications accompanied by a copy of the constitution and the names of the officers of this society to the different historical societies in the United States and also to some of the most distinguished friends of science in this and our sister states, soliciting such aid, information and occasional communications as they may be disposed to furnish in furtherance of the important objects of this society.

2. *Resolved*, That the treasurer be authorized to cause a sufficient number of copies of the constitution and of our proceedings, together with the names of the officers, to be printed on letter paper for the purpose of enabling the corresponding secretary to carry into effect the preceding resolution.

3. *Resolved*, That the corresponding secretary address our senators and representatives in congress enclosing a copy of this constitution and of such act of incorporation as may be obtained and soliciting such patronage from the general government as it is customary for it to bestow on similar societies.

4. *Resolved*, That the corresponding secretary be further instructed to communicate a copy of the constitution of the society and such act of incorporation as may be obtained to the executive department of the several states and territories,

soliciting from their respective state and territorial governments a copy of their respective codes and public documents and such aid and patronage as it has been customary for them to give similar societies.

5. *Resolved*, That the executive committee, in conjunction with the officers of this society, will act as a committee to receive donations to the society or deposits of such curiosities, books, manuscripts, etc., upon such terms and conditions as the owners of such articles shall think proper to annex thereto.

On motion of Mr. Law it was

Resolved, That the corresponding secretary be requested to obtain from such individuals in the different counties of this state as may feel disposed to furnish the information, the history of their respective counties as well as of their county seats and other towns in such county, the names of individuals first locating themselves in the limits of the county, the first settlement of the county seats, the names of the first proprietors and settlers, and all such other information with regard to the first settlement of the different counties and county seats, their rise and progress, as may be useful to the society or serve as memoranda for a future history of Indiana.

On motion of Mr. Farnham it was

Resolved, That the Rev. Isaac McCoy and Dr. Benjamin Adams be requested to deliver a lecture or send a dissertation to this society at its next annual meeting on the ancient remains of the aborigines and natural curiosities in the state; that the corresponding secretary furnish Dr. Adams with a copy of this resolution and of the constitution of the society, and respectfully request the aid and co-operation of Dr. Adams in promoting the objects of the society.

2. That Dr. Andrew Wylie be respectfully requested to deliver a public discourse at the next annual meeting of the society on the value and importance of historical societies and on such correlative matters in aid of the objects of this society

as he shall deem proper; that the corresponding secretary acquaint Dr. Wylie of the adoption of this resolution and solicit his compliance with this request.

3. *Resolved*, That the treasurer cause four hundred copies of the constitution to be printed for the use of the society, one of which shall be transmitted to each member.

And the meeting adjourned.

G. H. DUNN, *Secretary*.

CIRCULAR OF 1830-1.

INDIANA HISTORICAL SOCIETY.

On the 11th of December, 1830, a number of citizens of Indiana convened from various parts of the state at the seat of government, formed themselves into an association under the name of the "Indiana Historical Society," and adopted a constitution from which the following articles are extracted:

"Art. 2. The objects of the society shall be the collection and preservation of all materials calculated to shed light on the natural, civil and political history of Indiana, the promotion of useful knowledge, and the friendly and profitable intercourse of such citizens of the state as are disposed to promote the aforesaid objects."

"Art. 4. The officers of the society shall be a president, who shall preside and preserve order at all meetings of the society; three vice-presidents, one of whom, in the order of appointment, shall preside at all meetings in the absence of the president; a corresponding secretary, who shall be charged with all the correspondence required by the officers of the society; a recording secretary, who shall record and preserve the minutes of the society; a treasurer, who shall receive all moneys due the society, and hold the same subject to its order, and make an annual report of all receipts and disbursements; an executive committee of five members, any three of whom shall constitute a quorum, whose duty it shall be to meet upon the day on which the society holds its sessions, or as soon thereafter as practicable, to select subjects for public lectures, and the individuals by whom they shall be delivered at the annual or semi-annual meetings of the society. It shall also be their duty to attend to the publication of such lectures and communications made to the society as they may deem expedient, to take charge of all books, papers, specimens, models, curiosities, etc., belonging to the society. They shall have power to make by-laws not inconsistent with the constitution, to direct and superintend all disbursements, and generally to carry into effect all measures not otherwise provided for.''

Pursuant to the provisions of the constitution, the following gentlemen were elected officers of the society, viz. :

Hon. Benjamin Parke, of Salem, president; Hon. Isaac Blackford, of Vincennes, first vice-president; Hon. Jesse L. Holman, of Aurora, second vice-president; Hon Jas. Scott, of Charlestown, third vice-president; John H. Farnham, of Salem, corresponding secretary; Bethuel F. Morris, of Indianapolis, recording secretary; James Blake, of Indianapolis, George H. Dunn, of Lawrenceburgh, Isaac Howk, of Charlestown, James Whitcomb, of Bloomington, and John Law, of Vincennes, the executive committee.

At the same general meeting, the following resolution was adopted:

Resolved, That the executive committee be requested to procure the delivery of lectures, or the communications of disquisitions at the annual and semi-annual meetings of the society, on the following subjects:

1st. The history of the Indian tribes within this state.

2dly. The civil and political history of the state from the earliest settlements.

3dly. The ancient remains and natural curiosities within the same.

4thly. Its natural history, embracing its geology, mineralogy and botany, its soil, productions and climate, its animals, birds, fishes, etc.

On Saturday evening the 18th inst. the executive committee of the Historical Society assembled at the chamber of the supreme judges: Present, Samuel Merrill, George H. Dunn, Isaac Howk, James Whitcomb and John Law, also the three vice-presidents, corresponding secretary and treasurer.

Mr. Merrill was appointed chairman, and Mr. Dunn secretary of the committee.

On motion of Mr. Law the following resolution was adopted:

Resolved, That the president of this society be requested to deliver, at the semi-annual meeting in May next, a discourse on the civil and political history of the state from its earliest settlement.

On motion of Mr. Whitcomb:

Resolved, That the corresponding secretary address communications, accompanied by a copy of the constitution and the names of the officers of the society, to the different historical societies in the United States, and also to some of the most distinguished friends of science in this and our sister states, soliciting such aid, information, and occasional communications as they may be disposed to furnish, in furtherance of the important objects of this society.

Resolved, That the corresponding secretary address our senators and representatives, enclosing a copy of the constitution and of such act of incorporation as may be obtained, and solicit such patronage from the general government as it is customary for it to bestow on similar societies.

Resolved, That the corresponding secretary be further instructed to communicate a copy of the constitution of the society to the executive department of the several states and territories, soliciting from the respective state governments and territories a copy of their respective codes and public documents, and such aid and patronage as it has been customary for them to give similar societies.

Resolved, That the executive committee, in conjunction with the officers of the society, will act as a committee to receive donations to the society and deposits of such curiosities, books, manuscripts, etc., upon such terms as the owners of such articles shall think proper to annex thereto.

The following is the act of incorporation passed by the general assembly of Indiana:

"AN ACT to incorporate the Indiana Historical Society, approved January 10, 1831:

"Sec. 1. Be it enacted by the general assembly of the state of Indiana, That Benjamin Parke, John H. Farnham, Bethuel F. Morris, and James Blake, with their associates, are hereby created and constituted a body politic and corporate, by the name and style of 'The Indiana Historical Society,' and by such name may have perpetual succession, hold, purchase, receive, enjoy and transfer any property real and personal, have and use a common seal, sue and be sued, plead and be impleaded, defend and be defended in all courts of judicature.

"Sec. 2. There shall be an annual meeting of the members of said society at the time and place appointed by their constitution, at which time and place the officers of said society named in said constitution shall be elected, who shall continue in office until the next annual meeting, and until their successors are elected. The members of said society at such meetings may alter and amend their constitution, change the time of the annual meeting, and frame such laws for the government of said society as they shall think proper, the same not being inconsistent with the constitution and laws of this state.

"Sec. 3. The officers of said society may make such rules for their own government and for carrying into effect the objects of the society, not inconsistent with its constitution, as they shall think proper, all of which, together with their receipts and disbursements, shall be reported to the annual meeting of the society.

"Sec. 4. The secretary of state shall deliver to the officers of said society one copy of the laws of this state and one copy of the journals of the senate and house of representatives, which may hereafter be published, and also copies of the laws and journals of former years, where more than five copies of the same for any one year remain in his office. The secretary shall also deliver to the officers of said society all books and other articles which may have been or may hereafter be transmitted to his office for the use of said society."

INDIANAPOLIS, ——— 1831.

MY DEAR SIR—The preceding abstract from the constitution and proceedings of the "Indiana Historical Society," exhibits an index of its character and will, it is hoped, attract your favorable regard. In pursuance of the general objects of the society, and in obedience to its resolutions, the corresponding secretary has the honor to address you, respectfully soliciting such aid, information, and patronage as it may be in your power to afford. All communications addressed to the undersigned at Salem, Washington county, Indiana, will be gratefully received, and, whenever necessary, promptly acknowledged. I have the honor to remain, with sentiments of respect, Your ob't servant,

JOHN H. FARNHAM,
Corresponding Secretary.

INDIANAPOLIS, May, 1831.

At a semi-annual meeting of the Historical Society of Indiana, held at Indianapolis on Tuesday, the third day of May, 1831, and adjourned until Wednesday evening, the 4th of May, 1831, the Hon. Benjamin Parke, president of the society, took the chair and called the meeting to order.

Mr. Blake informed the meeting that Dr. Isaac Heylin, of Philadelphia, had placed in his hands as a donation to the society a copy of the "Annals of Philadelphia."

And therefore it was

Resolved, That the thanks of this society be tendered to the said Dr. I. Heylin for his valuable present.

And the meeting adjourned.

B. F. MORRIS, *R. S.*

INDIANAPOLIS, Nov. 8, 1831.

At a semi-annual meeting of the Historical Society of Indiana held at Indianapolis on the 8th of November, 1831, the Hon. Benjamin Parke took the chair and Austin W. Morris was appointed recording secretary *pro tem*.

The corresponding secretary informed the society that since the last meeting he had received sundry communications from gentlemen in various parts of the United States, and particularly from those gentlemen who had been elected honorary members of the society, returning their acknowledgments for the honor conferred. Some of these communications were, on motion, read, particularly a letter from the Hon. Nathan Dane, of Beverly, communicating a history of the ordinance of 1787 for the government of the Northwestern Territory, and presenting to the society his "Abridgment of American Law" in nine volumes.

After the reading of Mr. Dane's letter, on the motion of Mr. Merrill, it was unanimously

Resolved, That the thanks of this society be presented to

the Hon. Nathan Dane, of Beverly, Massachusetts, for his valuable and interesting history of the ordinance of 1787, and that the same be deposited in the archives of the society and printed for the use of the members under the superintendence of the executive committee.

Resolved, further, That we gratefully acknowledge the kindness and liberality of the venerable author of the Ordinance of 1787 in presenting this society with a copy of his "Abridgment of American Law" in nine volumes.

Resolved, That the corresponding secretary transmit to Mr. Dane a copy of the foregoing resolutions.

The corresponding secretary further informed the society that since the last meeting he had received from the Hon. Edward Everett, of Massachusetts, as a donation to this society, copies of several orations and addresses of which Mr. Everett was the author, and from the Hon. Jonathan Jennings, of this state, four volumes of the Journals of Congress, commencing with the American Revolution and ending in 1788.

Also from the same gentleman a copy of the Journal of the Federal Convention in 1787.

On motion of Mr. Wick it was

Resolved, That the corresponding secretary return the thanks of this society to the Hon. Jonathan Jennings and to such other gentlemen as have made, or may hereafter make, donations to this society.

On motion of Mr. Whitcomb,

Resolved, That the executive committee be authorized to publish such correspondence as they may deem of sufficient importance.

And the meeting adjourned.

AUSTIN W. MORRIS, *Rec. Sec.*

NOVEMBER 8, 1831.

At a meeting of the executive committee of the Historical Society of Indiana the Hon. Benjamin Parke, president of the society, took the chair and A. W. Morris was appointed recording secretary *pro tem*.

On motion of Mr. Law

Resolved, That the president of the society be requested to open a correspondence with the Right Rev. Bishop Flaget and the pastor of the Catholic church in Vincennes for the purpose of endeavoring to procure copies of such manuscript records of or in the Catholic church in Vincennes as will throw any light upon the early history of the state.

On motion of Mr. Merrill

Resolved, That the treasurer procure a suitable case for the books of the society.

On motion of Mr. Dunn

Resolved, That Messrs. Farnham and Whitcomb be requested to deliver each an address at the annual meeting upon such subjects as they may severally select.

And the meeting adjourned.

INDIANAPOLIS, Dec. 10, 1831.

At the first annual meeting of the Indiana Historical Society, held at Indianapolis on the 10th of December, A. D. 1831, the president of the society being absent, the chair was taken and the meeting called to order by the Hon. Isaac Blackford, first vice-president of the society.

The Rev. A Wylie, in compliance with the request of the executive committee, addressed the society on the value and importance of historical societies

And thereupon, on motion of Mr. Farnham, it was

Resolved, Unanimously, that the thanks of this society be presented to the Rev. A. Wylie for his appropriate and eloquent discourse, and that he be requested to furnish a copy of the same for publication by the society, and that a committee be appointed to carry into effect the objects of this resolution.

Messrs. Farnham and B. F. Morris were appointed that committee.

And the society adjourned until the 17th inst.

ADJOURNED MEETING, 17TH DEC., 1831.

Present, Isaac Blackford, first vice-president, who, in the absence of the president, took the chair.

The following gentlemen were unanimously elected honorary members of the society, viz.: Nathan Dane, Joseph Story, Daniel A. White, Edward Everett, Thomas L. Winthrop, Orville Dewey, Jared Sparks, John Quincy Adams and Francis C. Gray of Massachusetts; Nathan Guilford and Timothy Flint of Ohio, Samuel Gilman of South Carolina, Rowland Heylin of Pennsylvania, William Gibbes Hunt of Tennessee, James Kent of New York, and Edward Livingston of Louisiana.

INDIANAPOLIS, Dec. 16, 1835.

At the annual meeting of the Indiana Historical Society, held at the court house in the town of Indianapolis, December 16, 1835, Isaac Blackford, second vice-president, took the chair and George H. Dunn was appointed recording secretary *pro tem*.

The members present then proceeded to elect the officers for the ensuing year, and Samuel Merrill was unanimously elected president, Jeremiah Sullivan first vice-president, Charles I. Battel second vice-president, Abner T. Ellis third vice-president, Isaac Blackford corresponding secretary, James Blake treasurer, and G. H. Dunn recording secretary.

Mr. Merrill and Mr. Ellis were appointed to deliver addresses at the next annual meeting of the society.

H. P. Coburn, James Farrington, Charles Dewey, James McKinney and James M. Ray were appointed the executive committee.

Simon Gabriel Bruté of Vincennes, Robert Dale Owen of New Harmony, Dr. James Blythe of New Hanover, and Elihu Baldwin of Crawfordsville, were elected honorary members, and the meeting adjourned.

G. H. DUNN, *Rec. Sect.*

INDIANAPOLIS, Dec. 30, 1842.

At the annual meeting of the Indiana Historical Society held at the supreme court room in Indianapolis, December 30, 1842, Samuel Merrill, president of the society, took the chair and William Sheets was appointed recording secretary *pro tem.*

The election of officers of the society was then gone into, which resulted in the choice of

SAMUEL MERRILL for President.
JEREMIAH SULLIVAN, First Vice-President.
CHARLES DEWEY, Second Vice-President.
ISAAC BLACKFORD, Third Vice-President.
JOHN LAW, Corresponding Secretary.
WILLIAM SHEETS, Recording Secretary.
CHARLES W. CADY, Treasurer.
HENRY P. COBURN
JAMES M. RAY,
HENRY W. BEECHER, } Executive Committee.
GEO. H. DUNN,
DOUGLASS MAGUIRE,

On motion of Mr. Law the constitution was so amended as to require the payment of fifty cents instead of one dollar as the annual contribution of members, and also that the place of meeting should be changed to the supreme court room.

On motion of Judge Dewey all arrearages against members were canceled.

John B. Dillon, of Logansport, George Bancroft, of Boston, John McLean, of Cincinnati, William H. Prescott, Boston, John L. Stephens, of Central America, Calvin E. Stowe, Cincinnati, Doct. Lyman Beecher, Cincinnati, Salma Hale, Keene, N. H., John L. Blake, New York City, and Doct. Daniel Drake, of Louisville, were unanimously elected honorary members of the society, and then the society adjourned.

WM. SHEETS, *R. S.*

CIRCULAR ADDRESS PRINTED IN THE INDIANA JOURNAL—
INDIANA HISTORICAL SOCIETY.

At the annual meeting of said society, holden at the supreme court room on the 30th December, 1842, the following officers were chosen, viz.:

SAMUEL MERRILL, President.
JEREMIAH SULLIVAN, First Vice-President.
CHARLES DEWEY, Second Vice-President.
ISAAC BLACKFORD, Third Vice-President.
JOHN LAW, Corresponding Secretary.
WILLIAM SHEETS, Recording Secretary.
CHARLES W. CADY, Treasurer.

HENRY P. COBURN,
JAMES M. RAY,
HENRY W. BEECHER, } Executive Committee.
GEORGE H. DUNN,
DOUGLASS MAGUIRE,

Under the sanction of the official appointment above announced, the undersigned begs leave to call the attention of the citizens of the state to the objects of its historical society, believing that this course is the one most proper for him to pursue in order to give energy to the department assigned to him. Without some pecuniary aid it will be impossible to accomplish with any tolerable efficiency the particular objects which the society proposes for the action of its members; and the most earnest hopes are indulged that in the present reorganization of the society, under the auspices of several of her most distinguished sons, every citizen of Indiana will hail its success as a matter of personal pride and effort. If every citizen of moderate means would contribute his half-dollar fee for membership, how much could be done in a few years for the honor, interest and good repute of the state? How many traditions of binding force, "secrets of dark antiquity," now mouldering away with the decaying energies of our aged pioneers, might be snatched from "oblivion's night" and converted to the useful purpose of adorning and illustrating the moral, civil and political history of this commonwealth! Now is the critical period for citizens to aid in the efforts begun by a few public-spirited individuals to rekindle that lively interest in the past circumstances and history of the state which is so necessary to a just and general appreciation of her past career and probable future destiny. The results of those efforts must be wrought out from the scattered materials of the rapidly receding past, and their influences—forming a part of that aggregated glory and renown which are so justly the pride of every intelligent and free people—must be faithfully transmitted to the future. The general objects which the society hopes to accomplish through the medium of its present organization are most intimately connected with the welfare and fame of the state; and impartial history—the materials for which the society intends to collect—will make that welfare and fame of sterling value in the estimation of posterity, for whose approval and example the society would fain labor with its might while labor promises a rich reward.

The general objects of the society are:

1st. The collection of materials calculated to shed light on the natural, civil, and political history of Indiana.

2d. The promotion of useful knowledge, and the friendly and profitable intercourse of such citizens as are disposed to unite in such a cause.

3d. The history and present condition of the Indian tribes within the state.

4th. The collection and description of ancient remains and natural curiosities; the formation of geological, mineralogical, and botanical cabinets; full descriptions of the soil, climate and productions of the state; and in fine, the collection of every fact and thing that can be made subservient to the use of the society.

It will be seen, therefore, that some money will be needed to defray the expense of publishing the society's transactions and collections; of postages; the transportation of such books and other articles as may be presented from abroad; and of fitting up a suitable room for the library and collections. Such citizens as wish to become members will be duly recognized as such upon the payment of fifty cents, the annual subscription fee. The undersigned very respectfully suggests that a number can unite their subscriptions and remit per mail at the risk and expense of the society; and he would urgently beg of gentlemen in different towns in the state their aid in calling general attention to the objects and wants of the society. In a work of this kind they will see that now is not, can not be, the day of their reward, but that like all philanthropic and patriotic laborers they must needs "cast their bread upon the waters." One question needs only to be asked, "Shall Indiana, whose importance is not least in comparison with that of her sister states, be the last to appreciate the utility of collecting and preserving the materials for her just history?"

Donations in money, books, pamphlets, manuscripts, specimens and other articles, may be addressed to either of the executive committee, or to the undersigned.

CHAS. W. CADY, *Treasurer*.

INDIANAPOLIS, March 1, 1843.

Publishers of papers throughout the state are very respectfully desired, in behalf of the society, to publish the above in their respective publications.

INDIANAPOLIS, January 22, 1848.

At a meeting of the Indiana Historical Society held at the supreme court room in Indianapolis, January 22d, 1848, the Hon. Isaac Blackford, being one of the vice-presidents of the society (the president being absent), took the chair. Whereupon George H. Dunn was appointed secretary *pro tem*.

On motion of Mr. Law the proceedings of the last meeting were read.

On motion of Governor Whitcomb it was

Resolved, That a committee be appointed by the chair to apply to the general assembly for authority for the society to use one of the committee rooms in the state-house for the keeping of their books and transacting of the business of the society.

Governor Whitcomb and James M. Ray were appointed the committee.

On motion James M. Ray was appointed treasurer for the ensuing year and until his successor is appointed.

On motion of Mr. Blake

Resolved, That a committee be appointed by the chair to nominate officers for the ensuing year.

Messrs. Blake, Cady and Law were appointed.

On motion of Mr. Cady

Resolved, That the annual contribution of members shall hereafter be one dollar.

The nominating committee now reported the following persons for office:

ISAAC BLACKFORD, President.
GEORGE H. DUNN,
JOHN LAW,   } Vice-Presidents.
JEREMIAH SULLIVAN,
CHARLES W. CADY, Corresponding Secretary.
JAMES M. RAY, Treasurer.
THOMAS L. SULLIVAN, Recording Secretary.
JAMES WHITCOMB,
JAMES BLAKE,
GEO. W. MEARS,   } Executive Committee.
H. P. COBURN,
JNO. B. DILLON,

And on ballot said persons were unanimously elected to said offices.

On motion of Mr. Ray

Resolved, That the executive committee be requested to appoint a sub-committee or take other measures to ensure a speedy collection of funds and of additional subscribers to the society.

Whereupon the society adjourned until next semi-annual meeting or until called together by order of the executive committee.   GEO. H. DUNN, *Sec. pro tem.*

INDIANAPOLIS, January 22, 1848.

At a meeting of the executive committee held on the 22d day of January: Present Isaac Blackford, president; G. H. Dunn, John Law, vice-presidents; C. W. Cady, corresponding secretary; J. M. Ray, treasurer; James Whitcomb, Jas. Blake, H. P. Coburn, Jno. B. Dillon. Gov. Whitcomb in the chair.

On motion Geo. H. Dunn was appointed secretary *pro tem.*

On motion Jno. B. Dillon was requested to deliver an address to the society at the next semi-annual meeting.

Also Mr. Law was requested to deliver an address at the next annual meeting.

Mr. Dillon was appointed librarian.

On motion Mr. Blake, Mr. Cady and Mr. Dillon were appointed a sub-committee who shall take such measures as may be deemed necessary to further the interests of the society by publishing the constitution of the society, calling attention of the public to the same, solicit subscriptions and payments thereof.

Whereupon, on motion of Mr. Blake, the above resolution and appointment was considered.

Ordered that a meeting of the society be held at this place on next Saturday evening.

Whereupon committee adjourned.

G. H. DUNN, *Sec'y pro tem*.

INDIANAPOLIS, January 29, 1848.

At an adjourned meeting of the Indiana Historical Society held at the supreme court room in Indianapolis, Saturday evening, January 29, 1848, Hon. Isaac Blackford, president, took the chair.

On motion of Mr. Ray the following resolution was adopted:

Resolved, That all old subscribers to the society be released from all past arrearages by the payment of one dollar, which shall be credited for 1848 if paid in the month of January or February, 1848, and that the corresponding secretary be requested to give notice hereof and also to invite subscriptions generally.

On motion of Gov. Whitcomb, the following resolution was adopted after remarks in its favor by Messrs. Whitcomb, Law, Stapp and Blake, viz.:

Resolved, That measures be taken as far as practicable by

the executive committee, librarian and corresponding secretary, to rescue from oblivion the fading recollections of the early history of the different counties and towns of Indiana, and that the aid of those who favor the objects of the society, and especially of the earlier surviving inhabitants of the state, is respectfully invoked for that purpose.

On motion of Dr. George W. Mears, Hon. Elihu Stout, of Vincennes, was duly elected an honorary member of this society.

On motion the meeting adjourned.

Attest: CHAS. W. CADY,
Rec. Sec'y pro tem.

INDIANAPOLIS, May 23, 1848.

The society met at its first semi-annual session for the year 1848 at Wesley Chapel, the Hon. Isaac Blackford, president of the society, in the chair.

John B. Dillon, Esq., then, in pursuance of the request of the executive committee, addressed the society on "The National Decline of the Miami Indians."

And whereupon, on motion of Jeremiah Sullivan, the thanks of this society were unanimously tendered to Mr. Dillon for his able and eloquent address, and the executive committee authorized and instructed to request a copy of the same for publication.

Whereupon, on motion, the society adjourned to meet at the supreme court room in Indianapolis on the second day of the next session of the supreme court of Indiana.

Attest: T. L. SULLIVAN,
Rec. Secretary.

MONDAY EVENING, Jan. 31, 1853.

The society and guests assembled in the hall of the house of representatives, the Hon. Isaac Blackford, president of the society, in the chair.

Nathaniel Bolton, state librarian, addressed the society on the early history of Indianapolis and central Indiana.

On motion of William J. Brown the thanks of the society were returned to the speaker and a copy of the address was requested for publication.

Feb. 23, 1859.

The society met at the state capital.

The report of the committee on reorganization was heard and adopted.

Officers for the ensuing year were elected as follows:

President—Hon. JOHN LAW, of Evansville.

First Vice-President—Hon. A. B. LINE, of Franklin Co.

Second Vice-President—Rt. Rev. GEORGE UPFOLD, of Indianapolis.

Third Vice-President—Hon. HAMILTON SMITH, of Cannelton.

Treasurer—JAMES M. RAY, Indianapolis.

Secretary—JOHN B. DILLON, Indianapolis.

Executive Committee—CALVIN FLETCHER, Dr. GEORGE W. MEARS, JOHN COBURN, A. L. ROACHE, HENRY S. LANE.

CIRCULAR OF 1859.

INDIANAPOLIS, IND., March 24, 1859.

SIR—At a meeting held at the state-house at Indianapolis on the 23d of February, 1859, the Indiana Historical Society, which was incorporated in 1831, was reorganized and placed on a permanent basis. The officers of the society for the year 1859 are:

President—Hon JOHN LAW, of Evansville.

Vice-Presidents—Hon. A. B. LINE, of Franklin county; Rev. BISHOP UPFOLD, of Indianapolis; Hon. HAMILTON SMITH, of Cannelton, Perry county.

Executive Committee—CALVIN FLETCHER, Esq., of Indianapolis; Dr. GEORGE W. MEARS, of Indianapolis; JOHN COBURN, Esq., of Indianapolis; Hon. A. L. ROACHE, of Parke county; Hon. HENRY S. LANE, of Montgomery county.

Treasurer—JAMES M. RAY, Esq., Indianapolis.
Secretary—JOHN B. DILLON, Indianapolis.

The legislature of Indiana has made a liberal appropriation of means to aid the Indiana Historical Society in making purchases of books, maps, manuscripts, and such other materials as may be calculated to throw light upon the manners, customs, pursuits, and condition of the pioneer settlers of the region now included within the boundaries of the state. The executive committee have made provisions for the securing and fitting up of suitable rooms for the reception, proper arrangement and preservation of such materials of history as may be added to the collection of the society, by purchase or by donation.

With a view to enlarge the number, and to increase the value and the interest of its collections, the Indiana Historical Society is making preparations to receive as donations, or on deposit, or by purchase, any kind of rare, interesting or valuable materials of western history—such as books, pamphlets, autograph letters, manuscripts, maps, paintings or daguerreotypes of soldiers, legislators, jurists, or pioneer settlers of Indiana, authentic drawings or engravings of Indiana scenery—drawings and descriptions of old forts, blockhouses, Indian mounds, old dwelling-houses, and old public edifices—plans of towns and accounts of general and local improvements—files or single copies of old newspapers published in the west—statistical information, &c., &c.

The executive committee of the Indiana Historical Society entertain the hope that, by means of this circular, they will be able to obtain at an early day, from authentic sources—

Information in relation to the origin of the names of the

several counties of Indiana, and short biographical notices of the persons after whom the counties were named.

Brief notices of the first settlement of the several counties of the state.

Biographical notices of the early settlers of each county, including names and biographical sketches of the first preachers of the Gospel, first schoolmasters, the men who built the first churches and the first school-houses, the men who first planted nurseries and set out orchards, the proprietors of towns, the publishers of the first newspapers, and the first county and township officers.

Any authentic information that you may think proper to communicate to the undersigned with respect to these subjects (especially so far as such information shall relate to the county in which you reside), will be very thankfully received and carefully arranged and preserved among the collections of the society.

Communications addressed to the secretary at Indianapolis will receive attention, and all freight or express charges on donations will be paid by the society.

JOHN B. DILLON, *Secretary*.

(The following is the appropriation law referred to in the preceding circular.)

AN ACT providing for the appropriation of a sum not exceeding five hundred dollars, from the state treasury, to aid the Indiana Historical Society.

(Approved March 4, 1859.)

Section 1. Be it enacted by the general assembly of the state of Indiana, That a sum not exceeding five hundred dollars be, and the same is hereby appropriated from the state treasury, to be paid out under the same rules and regulations as are now provided for by law for the payment of moneys from the state treasury, to aid the Indiana Historical Society in the purchase of the different kinds of transcripts, papers, manuscripts, documents, etc., as are calculated to shed light on the early civil, social and political history of the state of Indiana: *Provided, however*, that no warrant shall be issued authorizing the drawing of said sum, or any part thereof, from the state treasury until there shall be a certificate presented, signed by the president and countersigned by the secretary, that said Indiana Historical Society is duly organized, according to the rules and regulations for the organization of the same.

Sec. 2. Said amount of five hundred dollars, or any part thereof may be paid over to said society on the order of the executive committee, signed by the president and countersigned by the secretary of said society.

Sec. 3. The amount hereby appropriated, or any part thereof, shall only be paid out by said Indiana Historical Society, or its officers, for the purpose of purchasing papers, manuscripts, transcripts and documents, with such other matter as is calculated to shed light on the early history of the state of Indiana, and for the transit of the same to the capital of the state.

Sec. 4. The secretary of the society shall present to the next session of the general assembly, or to either branch thereof, an exhibit of the number of members belonging to said society, the amount of funds received from members or by donation, and the amount received from the state treasury, the amount expended, and for what purpose, and such other matters as may advise the legislature of the doings of the society.

Sec. 5. It is hereby declared that an emergency exists for the passage of this act; it is therefore to take effect and be in force from and after its passage.

OCTOBER 7, 1873.

In pursuance of a notice published by the executive committee of the Indiana Historical Society, a number of the members of the society, together with other citizens, met in the hall of the house of representatives at 2 o'clock on Tuesday, October 7, 1873, for the purpose of adopting measures calculated to place the society in a condition which will enable it to carry into effect the important purposes for which it was organized.

On motion of Hon. A. L. Roache, Hon. Henry S. Lane was called by an unanimous vote to preside over the meeting. On taking the chair Mr. Lane delivered an interesting and eloquent address in reference to the history and objects of the society.

On motion of F. C. Holliday, D. D., John B. Dillon was appointed secretary.

At the request of Messrs. Coburn and Roache the secretary read the first constitution of the society and made a statement in reference to the former proceedings of the association, and to the present condition of its collections.

Gen. John Coburn made some interesting remarks on the origin and progress of the society and on the necessity of increasing its usefulness, and read letters addressed to him by James M. Ray, Esq., and W. S. Holman.

Judge Roache addressed the meeting on the importance of reorganizing the society, and hoped that all present would sign the constitution.

On motion of Gen. Coburn, it was resolved that the citizens present who were not members of the society be requested to sign the constitution and participate in the proceedings of the meeting. A number of gentlemen thereupon added their names to the roll of members of the society.

Rev. Dr. Holliday presented to the society a handsomely

bound copy of his work entitled "Indiana Methodism," for which donation he received a vote of thanks.

Brief addresses were made relative to the interests of the Indiana Historical Society by Rev. Dr. T. H. Lynch, Governor Hendricks, Gen. Henry B. Carrington, Prof. John Collett (who exhibited two Indian medals), Rev. Dr. Holliday, Prof. John L. Campbell, of Wabash College, J. B. Julian, Esq., Prof. Daniel Hough, Hon. W. W. Curry, and others.

Henry F. Keenan, Esq., editor of the Indianapolis Sentinel, proffered a copy of that paper for the files of the society from this date, for which, on motion of the Rev. Dr. Holliday, the unanimous thanks of the society were tendered to the Sentinel Company.

Prof. John L. Campbell presented the society copies of the journal and proceedings of the United States Centennial Commission.

On motion of Mr. Curry a committee was appointed to examine the charter of the society and revise its constitution and by-laws. Messrs. Curry, Yandes and Hough were selected to act as such committee.

On motion of Gen. Coburn a committee of five was appointed to make arrangements for conducting the business of the next meeting of the society. The president appointed Gen. Coburn, Judge Roache, Dr. Holliday, Hon. W. W. Curry and John B. Dillon to constitute said committee.

The society then adjourned to meet at 2 o'clock on Wednesday the 26th of November next.

NOVEMBER 26, 1873, 3 P. M.

The Indiana Historical Society met at the Supreme Court room.

The following named gentlemen were present: John B. Dillon, Samuel Morrison, of Dearborn county, Simon Yandes, H. W. Clark, of Hamilton county, C. Clemens, Kosciusko county, A. L. Roache, Prof. Hough, Secretary Curry, Dr. Holliday, Prof. Campbell, of Wabash College, Geo. W. Mears, Prof. Cox, Geo. W. Julian, Rev. G. L. Curtis, Alfred M. Clark, Dr. C. B. Lizius, W. H. L. Noble, Dr. Levi Ritter, Judge S. C. Wilson and Joseph Poole. In the course of the meeting some others dropped in. On motion of Mr. Dillon, Judge Roache was called to the chair, and Mr. Dillon was asked to state the order of the meeting. He announced that, under the program of the committee, Mr. Carr was to have made the first address, but as that gentleman was not present, that it would be well to attend first to business matters and postpone address until evening. Prof. Campbell said that the paper which he had prepared was designed rather for the society than a public meeting, and he would prefer to present it at that time. Dr. Holliday moved that Prof. Campbell be heard. It was suggested, however, that the minutes of the meeting be first read by the secretary, Mr. Dillon. Mr. Curry asked if any list of the officers of the society last elected were in existence. Mr. Dillon gave the names of the officers and of those yet living. Mr. Curry stated that his object in asking was to ascertain the legal status of the society, as the committee on reorganization meet with legal difficulties in their work. He had procured a copy of the original act of incorporation, and read some of its provisions as to the time of holding regular meetings. Mr. Dillon said that an amended constitution had been made, but was not now to be found. He thought it unnecessary to raise a question of legal power at this point, as whatever the society should determine upon would doubtless be accepted without question. Dr. Holliday thought that as this meeting was in the line of true apostolic succession it had jurisdiction in the absence of the lost record. Mr. Curry said that the committee were prepared with a report, which he read, as follows:

INDIANAPOLIS, Nov. 26, 1873.

To The Indiana Historical Society:

Gentlemen—Your committee, to whom was referred the question of a revision of the constitution and by-laws of the society, would respectfully report that they have had the same under consideration and find:

1. That the society was incorporated by an act of the general assembly, approved January 10, 1831, so liberal in its provisions as not to need any change.

2. That the said act authorizes changes in the constitution, such changes to be made at each annual meeting to be held on "the first Saturday succeeding the meeting of the general assembly." It is, therefore, doubtful whether any change can lawfully be made at this time.

3. That the following changes of the constitution are recommended as desirable: In article iii as follows: "An annual meeting of the society shall be held at Indianapolis on the second Tuesday in January in each year, and such other meetings from time to time as the society may vote or as the executive committee may call." In article iv strike out the third paragraph relating to a corresponding secretary and change the fourth paragraph so as to read: "Third, a secretary, who shall record the proceedings of the society, and of its executive committee, have charge of its books, manuscripts and literary effects, and discharge all other usual or assigned duties." Change the fifth paragraph to the fourth. Change the sixth paragraph as follows: "Fifth, an executive committee of five members, who, with the elective officer, shall have power to carry into effect all the purposes and orders of the society within the limits of its constitution and laws, and to make all necessary arrangements for its meetings."

4. As there is now no annual meeting of the general assembly, we are of the opinion that the proper construction of the organic law will be "the time each year set for its meet-

INDIANAPOLIS, Nov. 26, 1873.
To The Indiana Historical Society:

Gentlemen—Your committee, to whom was referred the question of a revision of the constitution and by-laws of the society, would respectfully report that they have had the same under consideration and find:

1. That the society was incorporated by an act of the general assembly, approved January 10, 1831, so liberal in its provisions as not to need any change.

2. That the said act authorizes changes in the constitution, such changes to be made at each annual meeting to be held on "the first Saturday succeeding the meeting of the general assembly." It is, therefore, doubtful whether any change can lawfully be made at this time.

3. That the following changes of the constitution are recommended as desirable: In article iii as follows: "An annual meeting of the society shall be held at Indianapolis on the second Tuesday in January in each year, and such other meetings from time to time as the society may vote or as the executive committee may call." In article iv strike out the third paragraph relating to a corresponding secretary and change the fourth paragraph so as to read: "Third, a secretary, who shall record the proceedings of the society, and of its executive committee, have charge of its books, manuscripts and literary effects, and discharge all other usual or assigned duties." Change the fifth paragraph to the fourth. Change the sixth paragraph as follows: "Fifth, an executive committee of five members, who, with the elective officer, shall have power to carry into effect all the purposes and orders of the society within the limits of its constitution and laws, and to make all necessary arrangements for its meetings."

4. As there is now no annual meeting of the general assembly, we are of the opinion that the proper construction of the organic law will be "the time each year set for its meet-

ings"; consequently that the proper time for an annual meeting to elect officers and act on proposed constitutional changes will be the Saturday after the first Monday in January, next, or the 10th day of that month.

All of which is respectfully submitted.

W. W. CURRY,
DANIEL HOUGH,
SIMON YANDES,
Committee.

On motion of Dr. Holliday, the report of the committee was adopted.

On motion of Prof. Campbell, the committee on reorganization was continued, with instructions to report a code of by-laws at the next regular meeting.

Prof. Campbell then read a memorial paper upon the late Joseph G. Marshall. [No. 6.]

Dr. Holliday moved that the thanks of the society be returned to Prof. Campbell, and that the article be placed on file. At the suggestion of Mr. Curry, the opportunity was given and improved by several present to sign the constitution as members of the society. Dr. Holliday called for the reading of certain resolutions. The first presented was by Gen. Coburn, asking the legislature to provide for the gathering of statistics of historical value.

Dr. Holliday supported the resolution in a short speech. Mr. Curry asked if the society meant business and really wished its influence to go to the legislature as expressed. Being answered in the affirmative by several he proceeded to give the history of a bill which was passed except a final vote at the last session. The resolution was passed and Mr. Curry and Judge Roache appointed to follow it up in the next legislature. Mr. Dillon presented the following, which was adopted:

Resolved, That in the opinion of the Indiana Historical

Society a monthly paper devoted especially to the collection of facts which relate to the antiquities and scientific interests of Indiana and the early local history of the several counties, would be worthy of popular favor and a very general circulation among the people of the state.

Mr. Dillon read the following resolutions presented by Mr. Henry F. Keenan:

Resolved, That the Historical Society of Indiana observe with satisfaction an effort toward the restoration to this state of the remains of its first governor, General and President William Henry Harrison, and that cordially sympathizing with that effort, this society lends its voice and influence to the support of that undertaking.

Resolved, further, That his excellency, Governor Hendricks, be memorialized to procure authoritative action from those who have power in the matter, and that a committee of this society take the matter into consideration and report such action as seems necessary, and co-operate with such action as his excellency, the governor, may designate.

Resolved, further, A committee of seven be appointed to correspond with the family of President Harrison, and that the governor be appointed chairman of said committee.

A lively discussion was called out in favor of this resolution by Col. S. C. Wilson, of Crawfordsville, Dr. Holliday and Secretary Curry. The last gentleman was certain that the people, both of this state and Kentucky, would heartily co-operate in the building of a monument to the fallen heroes who lie buried on the field of Tippecanoe, and if the friends of President Harrison would consent, there was no doubt that all would agree in the removal of his remains to the same spot. Col. Wilson had talked with John Scott Harrison and other members of the family and was confident that the Hon. John Scott Harrison and other members of the family would endorse the plan. The resolution was passed unanimously and with an emphasis. Mr. Dillon presented a resolution of his own in these words:

WHEREAS, It is assumed to be expedient and practicable to publish in the year 1876 a great national work to be entitled "Annals of the First Century of the Government of the United States of America," and

WHEREAS, It will be essential to the credit and utility of such a work that it shall in all respects be commenced and carried on and completed under auspices which will make it worthy of the national approbation and encouragement, and place it as an interesting and imperishable memorial among those which will mark the commemoration of the close of the first century of the existence of the government of the United States; therefore

Resolved, That in the opinion of the Indiana Historical Society the desirable popular approval of such a great national work will be obtained if the work shall be prepared for publication by editors and compilers who shall have been selected by the joint action of the authorities of the Smithsonian Institution and a committee of the United States Centennial Commission.

Resolved, That copies of this preamble and resolution be forwarded to the president of the centennial commission, and also to Prof. Henry, secretary of the Smithsonian Institution.

The resolution was discussed by Prof. Campbell, Mr. Dillon, Dr. Holliday and Dr. Mears. The latter moved that the chairman be authorized to appoint a historian to carry out the resolution. Prof. Cox said that we had two histories of Indiana, and good ones, one written by Mr. Dillon he knew to be good. Mr. Dillon urged the resolution as it stood, for the committee named therein to control the writing of this history. He should doubt the qualifications of any man who would wish to write a history of Indiana. Mr. Poole saw no objection to each state society making a historical contribution to the work proposed. Prof. Campbell withdrew his amendment. Mr. Dillon spoke of the distinction between a general and local history. The resolution of Mr. Dillon was then passed. In the meantime the chair appointed a committee to correspond and take charge of the removal of President Harrison's remains to Indiana. The committee consists of Governor Hendricks, ex-Governor Conrad Baker, the Hon. Henry S. Lane, Mr. H. F. Keenan, Col. Samuel C. Wilson, Prof. E. T. Cox, the Hon. George W. Julian and the Hon. A. L. Roache. The chairman then presented a manuscript biographical notice of the late Judge John Law, prepared by Judge C. Denby, of Evansville, which, he stated, was so complete that he asked to present it instead of the paper that he was expected to prepare. It was so accepted, with the thanks of the society to Judge Denby, and a request that he would revise and adapt it to the records of the society. [See No. 7.]

Judge Roache said that he, in common with the society, had become tired of the stereotyped forms of resolutions of condolence, and they desired to place on the records of the historical society a memorial which should express as fully as possible the estimation in which Judge Law was held by the society. With this view the paper had been prepared, which he would read, as follows:

MEMORIAL ON JOHN LAW.

The Historical Society of Indiana, upon the announcement of the death of its chief presiding officer, desires at this, its first regular meeting since his decease, to signalize their sense of his merits, and to express their sentiments of the excellences and virtues which adorned his character, by placing this memorial upon their records: John Law, although not a native of Indiana, cast his lot among the early pioneers who devoted themselves to subduing the then wilderness of Indiana. Arriving in the state a few days before obtaining his majority, and within a year of its admission into the Federal Union, the whole of his long active life was coeval with its history. He found a wilderness with a sparse population, with the legal attributes of a state, but with all its institutions in their unformed infancy. He was one of that band of superior men, who, amid the toils, privations and struggles of the pioneer, laid the foundation, deeply and wisely, of that matchless prosperity and admirable social and political system which constitute the glory and greatness of the state. Through a long and busy life here of more than fifty years, he did his full share of the labor of forming and perfecting these institutions. In the full fruition of the advantages and blessings of a perfected system of government and a highly enlightened and cultivated social organization, it becomes us not to forget how much we owe to the generation that precedes us. Let it be borne in mind that in all this toil and privation, John Law bore his full share. In all the varied relations he sustained to the community in his long and active life as a private member of society, as a legislator in the state and federal councils, and as the presiding judge of the circuit court, he filled the full measure of honorable usefulness and has left an example to which the youth of this generation may be safely and profitably pointed. This society owes much to his early and continuous zeal for its interests. He gave much time and labor to perfecting its organization and extending its usefulness and set its members an example it is to be hoped will inspire them, of patiently gathering up and putting into a permanent form the traditions of the early pioneers, which constitute the very charm of history. We desire to give this public expression of the profound sympathy of the members of this society with his surviving members; but while with them we deplore his loss, we and they have the consolation of knowing that he went down to the grave in the fullness of years after a long life of useful labors and that the world is wiser and happier and better for his having lived.

A resolution by Prof. Hough was adopted, as follows:

Resolved, That we earnestly invite all cities, colleges, universities or other educational corporate bodies in this state that have issued catalogue or educational reports, to present complete files of the same to this society.

The following resolution by Prof. Cox was referred to the January meeting:

In view of the fact that the subjects of the Indiana Historical Society and those of the Indianapolis Academy of Sciences are in some respects identical; be it

Resolved, That we deem it advisable that the two societies be united under the name of the Indiana Historical and Natural History Society.

Prof. Cox supported his resolution in a brief and earnest address, when the meeting adjourned until evening.

NOVEMBER 26, 1873, 8 P. M.

The Indiana Historical Society met at the Meridian street church. The audience, though small, manifested much interest in the experiences that were given. Judge Roache introduced the Hon. George W. Carr, one of the speakers previously announced, in a very complimentary manner. He said that Mr. Carr was one of the few men of his age, natives of Indiana, who have held many prominent positions in the state. He had occupied a place in the legislature and was president of the constitutional convention that had framed the present constitution. Mr. Carr, who is a man of probably three score and ten, came forward and was pleasantly received by the audience. He regretted that one better qualified than he to entertain his hearers and do justice to the subject had not been called upon. He happened to be one of the early natives of the state, not one of the early settlers; he did not claim to be one of them, as he had been born in the state. Other men deserved the credit of coming to Indiana and commencing its improvement. The early settlers of Indiana encountered hardships, privations and perils to a greater degree than it happens to the first settlers of new countries generally. In the southern part of the state, especially, they had to encounter heavy forests in addition to their other difficulties. His father had come to Indiana territory from Mercer county, Ky., in March, 1804, and settled in Clark's grant, where he was born in the year 1807; he therefore did not deserve the credit of coming. A few years after the territory commenced settling, before his recollection, there was no trouble with the Indians, and but very little until about 1811, a year, perhaps, in advance of the declaration of war against Great Britain. He recollected some of the early scenes of the troubles with the Indians. He recollected the building of forts. When the Indians became troublesome it became necessary for settlers at some central point in the neighborhood to build a fort, or block-house, where they repaired and lived in order to defend themselves against the attacks of the savages. These forts were built of round logs, and were usually two stories high. The logs of the upper story were cut about two feet longer than those of the lower one, thus forming an aperture all around the structure from which they could use their rifles upon their antagonists outside. Port-holes were in the wall of the upper story sufficient in size to shoot rifle balls from them, which would strike the ground at an angle. At a certain distance from the fort, timbers were stuck in the ground about nine feet high. This enclosure was made of different sizes to suit the demands of the defenders; frequently an angle of the fort formed the block-house. Everything that was required to be secured from the depredation of the savages was brought inside of this picket fence, and the gate was strongly barred up.

The first Indian difficulty that he recollected was the massacre of the "Pigeon Roost," which was so named from the fact that pigeons many years before that time had roosted there upon the trees in vast numbers, breaking down a large portion of the timber. The land was cleared there by the settlers, who gave the settlement the name of "Pigeon Roost," which was several miles in extent. They took no measures to defend themselves against the attacks of the Indians. A man by the name of Norris went to the settlement on business and was staying over night with Mr. Collins, who lived there, expecting to return back home the next day. He wanted to know of Mr. Collins if he was not afraid to live there in that unprotected condition, without any fort or means of defense. Collins replied that he was not afraid; that he felt just as safe as if he were inside of Philadelphia. A few moments after that, before the conversation ended, Captain Norris looked in a certain direction and saw the Indians approaching. He told Mr. Collins about the Indians and asked him what they should do. Collins told him to come into the cabin, and they would fight till they died. They did so, and with two or three rifles they manged to keep the savages at bay until after night. Mr. Collins' family at the time consisted of two daughters. They agreed upon a plan. Norris was to take one of the daughters and go first to some corn that was standing a few steps from the cabin. He and the girl arrived safely to the corn after being fired upon by the Indians. Collins was to follow with the other daughter, and altogether were to make their way to the nearest fort. Collins and his daughter were attacked while on their way, but at length, after a fierce battle with the enemy, the entire party arrived at the fort with safety. This was the first attack he remembered by the Indians upon the settlers. The last one was made within a few hundred yards from the town of Leesville, upon an old man named Flint and his son and son-in-law. The two young men were disabled—one of them mortally wounded—and the old man was taken prisoner. He, however, escaped some time afterward and returned to his family. Other incidents of the depredations of the savages were related, most of which are familiar to those fond of hearing stories of western adventures.

When the Indian troubles closed, the improvement of the country began, and the tide of emigration set in more rapidly. The first mill they ever had in Jackson county was built by the citizens, and his father was one of those who helped to do it. The mill stones were quarried out of a bluff and hauled to the point where they expected to build the mill, which, when constructed, was little better than the old hand mill. The early settlers were no ordinary class of men. They were a brave, resolute and determined set of men, that came here after having counted the cost, and who knew the difficulties, privations and hardships they had to encounter. In that day, and for many years afterwards, there was a fraternal feeling existing among the old settlers. They sympathized with each other, and, as a general thing, each took a sincere interest in the welfare of his neighbors. Without this kind of feeling the improvements of the country could never have been made at that time. Logs could never have been rolled or houses have been raised. The country was all green woods in those times; there were no prairies in all that region. The plan was for a man to cut down all the timber he could, cut it up into logs about twelve feet long, and then call on his neighbors in the spring of the year to help him roll them by hand. In this way they cleared the land. They assisted each other in building their houses and at corn-husking. The speaker had served a regular apprenticeship at rolling logs, and had the ambition that no man should excel him in the art of lifting. A corn-husking was described. It came off at night and every one went at it with a will, and there was often a strife to see who could husk the most. The ladies were very seldom called upon to take part at these huskings, but while the men were husking out the corn, the mother and the daughters were engaged in preparing a good substantial supper, which was partaken of with a zest at about ten or eleven o'clock. Everything the settlers wore or used was manufactured by themselves. It was a common thing in the early days that the women had spinnings, to which all the young girls and married ladies of the neighborhood brought their spinning wheels, and while the father and sons were at their logs they were at their spinning wheels. When the log-rolling or house-raising was over, then they sometimes played "Sister Phebe" until nine or ten o'clock at night. Whisky or liquor was used at all those log-rollings, house-raisings and corn-huskings generally, but it should not be inferred from that that it was a dissipating or drinking community. There was but little of it used except on those occasions, and what they did use was not of that vicious character that is now used. It did not take a man down and use him up within seventy-five yards of where he drank it. The speaker was twenty-five or thirty years old before he saw a case of delirium tremens.

The character of the schools and school-houses of those times was spoken of. All the school they had in those times was generally three months of school in the winter season. The teacher was some man of the neighborhood that was prevailed upon to take the school. The books they used were Webster's spelling book, Pike's reader and a small dictionary. The school-houses were log cabins built by the voluntary labor of the men of the neighborhood and were warmed by a large fire-place at one end. The seats and furniture were made of split logs, the writing desks occupying the sides of the room next the windows. The speaker said he was rejoiced to see Indiana developing as she has been, but he thought she was in her infancy still. He was proud that he was a native of Indiana. He had witnessed her growth since he was large enough to notice anything, and rejoiced in her prosperity. On taking his seat the audience applauded him earnestly.

On motion of Governor Hendricks, the society tendered Mr. Carr a vote of thanks for his entertaining and instructive address.

Mr. F. C. Holliday was then called for, and came forward and offered the following tribute to the memory of Captain Calvin Fletcher:

MEMORIAL ON CALVIN FLETCHER.

Calvin Fletcher, Esq., one of the originators of this society, and at the time of his death a member of its executive committee, having died during the temporary suspension of the active working of the society it is due alike to him and to the Indiana Historical Society that a suitable minute be made of his death, and a record of the society's appreciation of his life and character be filed with its proceedings. Calvin Fletcher was in many respects a model man. His energy and self-reliance fitted him for leadership, especially in a new country. His courage and preseverance enabled him to conquer difficulties from which less resolute natures would have shrunk. In him the genius of hard work was fully developed. He rarely failed in any enterprise that he undertook, and never through want of suitable effort. His success in acquiring knowledge, accumulating property, mastering the profession of law, inaugurating new enterprises for the public good, receiving and maintaining the confidence of his fellow citizens of all shades of political and religious sentiments, and above all his high moral and religious character, present him as a model worthy of the emulation of the young men of our state. His success in business is the history of a life of hopeful labor, pure integrity, genial benevolence, steady caution, and untiring application, all guided by a rather more than ordinary share of practical sense; in which great results were attained, not by brilliant strokes of adventure or any dependence upon fortune, but by those plainer and less obtrusive methods which are within the reach of the great majority of men, and furnishes a lesson both of hope and warning. Of hope to the upright, diligent and frugal, and of warning to the reckless and idle who wait upon fortune. Mere success in worldly aims, however high and honorable, was not the controlling inspiration of his career; his vigilant and generous attention to every call of benevolence; his patient care of all wholesome means of public improvement; the amount of labor bestowed in fostering Sabbath-schools and in personally teaching in them; his consistent and avowed interest in the imperial claims of religion, moral and general education; and his admirable success in securing the happiness and promoting the culture of a large family, show clearly that whatever importance he attached to the acquisition of wealth, he never lost sight of his responsibility to God nor of his dependence upon the divine blessing and approbation for his success and happiness in life. Mr. Fletcher was a strong man physically, morally and intellectually. In the earlier years of his pioneer life, physical courage and strength were in high repute and not unfrequently in demand; and while he was a man of peace, genial and gentlemanly in his bearing, he gave sufficient proof both of his strength and courage, to command the respect of those who held such qualities in highest regard, and secure his person from the assaults of insolent braggarts. And his moral courage was never doubted. He was a friend and patron of learning, not merely as taught in the schools, but in the diffusion of popular literature among the people. He did much to promote agriculture and retained an unabated interest in practical farming till the close of life. He was a great lover of nature, and seemed in full sympathy with the animal kingdom. He took a decided interest in ornithology. He made himself familiar with the habits, characteristics and instincts of birds. He was fond of natural science in all its departments. He esteemed positive knowledge more highly than mere opinions, and hence he was pre-eminently a man of facts. Perhaps no man in Indiana had at the time of his death, in addition to his law library and his well selected library of general literature, so large a collection of large histories in the form of pamphlets, magazines and files of newspapers as Calvin Fletcher.

Mr. Fletcher's religious character partook of the same solid and comprehensive qualities that marked his general course through life. While the Methodist Episcopal church was his religious home, he was in full sympathy with all true Christians, and heartily co-operated with all Evangelical churches. His hand was open to their assistance, and his contribution aided in the erection of the churches of all denominations.

Mr. Fletcher came to Indianapolis in the fall of 1821, and thenceforth he was closely identified with the interests of Indiana, and especially of Indianapolis, till the close of his life. He was appointed states attorney of the fifth judicial circuit in 1825; his circuit embracing twelve or fifteen counties. He resigned this office before the close of the year, having been elected to the state senate, in which capacity he represented his county for seven years. In 1834 he was appointed by the legislature, with three others, to organize a state bank, and to act as sinking fund commissioner. He held this office also seven years. From 1843 till 1859 he acted as president of the branch of the State Bank at Indianapolis till the expiration of the bank charter.

Mr. Fletcher was born in the state of Vermont, February 4, 1798. His father was a Revolutionary soldier, had a large family and was unable to give them any better education than such as they could get in the district school during a few months in each year. Mr. Fletcher left home when 17 years of age. In 1818 we find him in the vicinity of Urbana, O., where he taught a country school, finally studied law, and from there came to Indianapolis, where he took and maintained a first rank among the leading men of the state throughout the remainder of his life.

Mr. Fletcher's life is a striking illustration of the possibilities that lie before the young men of our free country. His industry, energy and high moral integrity were prominent throughout his whole life.

Mr. Fletcher died at his residence in Indianapolis on the 26th of May, 1866, aged 68 years.

The Indianapolis Historical Society, appreciating the character and services of Calvin Fletcher, Esq., one of its founders and active members, orders that the foregoing be adopted as a part of its proceedings.

A vote of thanks was tendered Mr. Holliday for the paper just read, and the same was ordered to be placed on the records of the society.

Judge Test was called for and arose in his seat. He said he would be glad to comply with the wishes of the society, but insisted on being excused on the occasion. He hoped to have been able to present a few thoughts on paper of the early men who laid the foundations of the improvement and progress of the state, but business had been such as to prevent him from doing so. He thought at some future time he would lay before the society a few thoughts upon those concerned in the early history of the state. He had lived some sixty-three years in Indiana and it gave him pleasure to think of some of the men who, in the early times, figured in the state. The state has not been destitute of men of great talent, of peculiar genius in all departments, in the law, in the medicine, in the fine arts and even in the pulpit. He recollected one instance, that of John P. Durbin, who had acquired eminence in the pulpit. If living in Indiana, he did not know that he would have much character, but he went away from here, and occasionally we hear of him. Not long ago they had heard that he was the head of some institution, one of the greatest men that lived in that vicinity. He referred to another incident. It was that of a young man who had no particular character in this state, and that man was Beecher. He could when here command a very respectable congregation; but now he is one of the greatest preachers in the world, and commands a salary almost equal to that of the president of the United States. There was another man from this state named Simpson, a self-made man, a man of high character. He said that he almost regretted sometimes that they didn't live in Kentucky, because there they kept their great men and helped them along; so it was in Virginia and New England. But a kind of rivalship involves a great man, until he gets away from here. He spoke of this to show that they had men in early days who were men of eminence—men of great powers. If George G. Dunn had lived anywhere but in Indiana, he believed he would have become one of the great men of the nation; so of Joseph Marshall. He was sorry for this, and hoped it would be remedied in the future.

On motion, Judge Test was requested to deliver an address before the society at the next annual meeting, on the 10th of January next.

The society then adjourned.

INDIANAPOLIS, Jan. 6, 1877.

Pursuant to public notice a meeting of the Indiana Historical Society was held at the state-house in the agricultural room, on Saturday evening, January 6, 1877.

On motion, Hon. Charles H. Test was called to the chair.

Hon. John Coburn moved to take up the amendments to the constitution of the society, which were reported by a committee on the 26th of November, 1873, and informally adopted at that time. The motion was agreed to, and the said amendments to the constitution of the society unanimously adopted.

On motion of Mr. Coburn it was resolved that a committee of five members of the society be appointed whose duty it shall be to request the board of county commissioners to set apart for the use of the Indiana Historical Society a room in the new court-house at Indianapolis.

The chairman appointed the following named members to act as said committee, viz.: Messrs. John Coburn, Thomas A. Hendricks, Addison L. Roache, John B. Dillon and Jonathan M. Ridenour.

The society then adjourned to meet on the first Tuesday in February, 1877.

JOHN. B. DILLON, *Secretary*.

INDIANAPOLIS, Feb. 6, 1877.

Pursuant to an adjournment of the 6th ultimo, the Indiana Historical Society met in the grand jury room of the United States court, Hon. Charles H. Test in the chair.

Mr. Coburn made a favorable report from the committee appointed at the last meeting to request the board of county commissioners to set apart in the new court-house a room for the use of the Indiana Historical Society. The report was accepted, and on motion of Mr. Duncan the committee was continued.

On motion of Mr. Ridenour, the secretary read the constitution, by-laws and act of incorporation of the society.

In the course of the meeting the constitution was signed by the following named gentlemen, viz.: R. B. Duncan, E. E. Bassett, John P. C. Shanks, Sam V. Morris, L. F Walker, Joseph F. Daugherty, and W. H. H. Terrell.

Gen. Terrell offered the use of the United States court room in the post-office building for meetings of the society until the completion of the new court-house, and on motion the thanks of the society were tendered to Gen. Terrell.

Suggestions in reference to the interests of the society were made by Gen. Coburn, Gen. Terrell, J. M. Ridenour, Esq., R. B. Duncan, Esq., Col. John W. Blake, and the secretary.

Gen. Terrell moved that a committee be appointed to devise a plan to promote the interests of the society and to report at the next meeting. The motion was agreed to and the chair appointed a committee composed of the members whose names follow, viz.: Messrs. Terrell, Duncan, Ridenour, Blake, Evans and Dillon.

Mr. Blake moved that Prof. Cox, state geologist, be invited to deliver an address on archæology before the society at such time as may suit his convenience, and that the state officers and members of the general assembly be invited to be present at the delivery of such address. Adopted.

The society then adjourned to meet on Tuesday evening, February 20, 1877.   JOHN B. DILLON, *Secy*.

INDIANAPOLIS, Friday, Feb. 9, 1877.

The executive committee met, present, Messrs. Terrell, Ridenour, Evans, Blake and Dillon.

Gen. Terrell submitted a report on the subject of the condition and future action of the society. The report was discussed, agreed to, and ordered to be submitted to the society at its meeting on the 20th instant.

JOHN B. DILLON, *Secy*.

INDIANAPOLIS, Wednesday, Feb. 14, 1877.

The society assembled in special session, and in conformity with an invitation from the society Prof. E. T. Cox delivered an address on the Archæology of Indiana.

Judge C. H. Test occupied the chair and made some interesting remarks on the early history of Indiana. He invited members of the legislature and others to become members of the society.

The society adjourned to Tuesday evening, February 20, 1877.   JOHN B. DILLON, *Secy*.

INDIANAPOLIS, Tuesday Evening, Feb. 20, 1877.

An adjourned meeting of the Indiana Historical Society was held in the United States court room, Hon. Charles H. Test in the chair.

Mr. Ridenour presented a letter from Gen. Terrell relating to the death of his relative, Hon. David C. Branham, and requesting that the report on the reorganization of the society be postponed till the next meeting. The request was agreed to.

On motion of Mr. Ridenour, the chair appointed a committee composed of Mr. Ridenour, W. H. H. Terrell, and another person to be selected by them, to prepare for the use of the society a biographical sketch of the Hon. David C. Branham, late state senator from Jefferson county, and to communicate to the bereaved family of the deceased senator the sincere sympathy of the members of the Indiana Historical Society.

On motion of Gen. Coburn, the thanks of the society were tendered to Prof. E. T. Cox for his able and interesting address on the Archæology of Indiana, and Prof. Cox was requested to furnish a copy of the address for the use of the society.

Remarks bearing on the interests of the society were made by Messrs. Cox, Test, Blake, Coburn and Hinkley.
Adjourned to meet Wednesday evening, February 28, 1877.　　　　　　　　　　　　　　J. B. D., *Secy*.

INDIANAPOLIS, Feb. 28, 1877.

At an adjourned meeting of the Indiana Historical Society, held in the post-office building, Hon. Charles H. Test in the chair, no quorum being present the meeting adjourned to meet at the same place on next Wednesday evening, March 7, 1877.　　　　　　　　　　　　　　J. B. D., *Secy*.

INDIANAPOLIS, July 8, 1879.

In pursuance of due public notice, a special meeting of the Indiana Historical Society was held on Tuesday evening, July 8, 1879, at the United States court room in the city of Indianapolis. The Hon. Charles H. Test, president of the society, took the chair and explained the object of the meeting to be the election of a secretary to fill the vacancy occasioned by the death of the Hon. John B. Dillon, and for the transaction of other necessary business.

Appropriate remarks on the life and character of the late Mr. Dillon were made by President Test and other members, and on motion of Col. John W. Blake a committee of three, consisting of Col. Blake, W. W. Woollen and W. H. H. Terrell, was appointed to prepare and present at the next meeting a suitable memorial commemorative of the life and public services of the late secretary.

On motion Col. Blake was appointed temporary secretary of the present meeting.

A motion to proceed to the election of a secretary, vice Dillon, was adopted.

Thereupon a ballot to fill the vacancy was had, which resulted in the election of W. H. H. Terrell unanimously.

A committee was appointed consisting of Woollen, Blake and the secretary, to which the president was afterwards added, to memorialize the board of commissioners of Marion county to assign and set apart a suitable and convenient room, free of rent, in the Marion county court-house, for the permanent use of the society, the room heretofore designated by said board for said purpose being unsuited on account of inaccessibility.

Said committee was instructed to report at the next meeting. W. H. H. TERRELL, *Sec*.

(There were no other meetings of the society until the reorganization of 1886.)

5

INDIANA HISTORICAL SOCIETY PUBLICATIONS

VOLUME I   NUMBER II

NORTHWEST TERRITORY

LETTER OF NATHAN DANE CONCERNING THE ORDINANCE OF 1787

AND

PATRICK HENRY'S SECRET LETTER OF INSTRUCTION TO GEORGE ROGERS CLARK

INDIANAPOLIS
THE BOWEN-MERRILL COMPANY
1897

NORTHWEST TERRITORY.

LETTER OF NATHAN DANE.

(The original of this letter is not now in the possession of the society, and it is not known in what form it was originally published. It was sent to the *New York Tribune* in 1875 by John D. Defrees, and published in that paper on June 18.)

BEVERLY, MASS., May 12, 1831.

DEAR SIR: A few days ago I received your letter of April 12, 1831, inclosing the printed constitution and circular of the Indiana Historical Society. It is truly gratifying to observe the rapid, the respectable, and the substantial manner in which the Northwestern Territory is settled. In your letter you say: "We have been accustomed in Indiana to regard you as the author and supporter of the ordinance of 1787; that was the opinion until a senator from Missouri (Col. Benton) in the senate, session '29 and '30, denied your agency," etc. As you express a strong desire "to receive an authentic history of the *Magna Charta* of no less than three states, to be deposited in the archives of your society, I send inclosed the printed note 'A' as the best concise account extant of the ordinance and its formation. The note is a part of an appendix to the ninth volume of my General Abridgment of American Law, with occasional notes and comments.

As to the article excluding slavery, an important one, though perhaps not more so than the provision against impairing contracts, two questions arise: Who first thought of excluding slavery from the Northwestern Territory? Who caused the article to be made a part of the ordinance? The committee that reported the plan of April, 1784, including an article against slavery, very imperfect (as stated in the printed note), consisted of Mr. Jefferson, Mr. Chase, of Maryland, and Mr. Howell, of Rhode Island. As Mr. Howell was from a non-slave-holding state, an active and able member, might he not more probably first think of excluding slavery? Be that as it may, the slave article in the plan of 1784 was very deficient, and the plan being adopted and the slave article rejected, there was an end of it. The next year, '85, Mr. King, of Massachusetts, moved to add a slave article, better in words, but imperfect in substance; this being only committed, a slave article was no longer proposed by any committee. When the ordinance of '87 was reported to congress, and under consideration, from what I had heard, I concluded that a slave article might be adopted, and I moved the article as it is in the ordinance. It was added, and unanimously agreed to, I thought to the great honor of the slave-holding states.

As it may be asked, how does this motion appear, it is proper to add: In the Missouri debate (as stated in the note) expressions were used that made it proper to inquire in whose handwriting the ordinance was. Mr. Otis, then in the senate, caused inquiry to be made, and received from Daniel Brent a certificate, of which the following is a copy:

"I have the pleasure to send you a printed copy of the ordinance of 1787, found among the old papers of congress, with the draft in manuscript of the sixth article introduced into that ordinance. We can find nowhere the report of the committee upon which the ordinance was founded, but I presume the handwriting of the amendment will be sufficient for your purpose."

Mr. Otis, in his letter to me, says that the amendment (the slave article) was in my handwriting. These facts show who caused the slave article to be made a part of the ordinance. In fact, the plan of 1784 was so very imperfect that it could not be amended to answer any purpose, nor could materials be found in it to form a thirteenth part of the ordinance of July 13, 1787. Your obedient servant,

N. DANE.

JOHN H. FARNHAM, Salem, Indiana.

(Inclosure.)

"A"

As, after a lapse of 43 years, some, for the first time, claim the ordinance of July 13, 1787, as a Virginian production, in substance Mr. Jefferson's, it is material to compare it with his plan or resolve (not ordinance) of April, 1784, in order to show how very groundless the assertion of Senator Benton is, that the ordinance of '87 was "chiefly copied" from his plan. To those who make the comparison not a word need be said to refute his assertion. On the face of them the difference is so visible and essential; but thousands read his speeches, extensively published, where one will make this comparison. It is surprising that at this late day this claim is made for Virginia, and never made by herself.

As but few possess the journals of the old congress, in which Mr. Jefferson's plan of '84, and the ordinance of '87, formed by the author (Mr. Dane), are recorded, it is proper here, concisely, to point out the material difference between them:

First. The plan of '84 is contained in two and a half pages; the ordinance of '87 in eight pages.

Second. The first page in the plan or resolve of '84 is entirely omitted in the ordinance of '87.

Third. From the remaining page and a half of the plan there appears to be transferred to the ordinance, in substance, these provisions, to wit: (1) "The said territory, and the states which may be formed therein, shall ever remain a part of this Confederacy of the United States of America, subject to the articles of confederation." (2) "To all the acts and ordinances of the United States in congress assembled, conformable thereto." (3) "The inhabitants and settlers in the said territory shall be subject to pay their part of the federal debts contracted, or to be contracted, to be apportioned on them by congress, according to the same common rule and measures by which apportionments thereof shall be made on the other states." (4) "The legislatures of these districts or new states shall never interfere with the primary disposal of the soil by the United States in congress assembled, nor with any regulations congress may find necessary for securing the title to such soil to the *bona fide* purchasers." (5) "No tax shall be imposed on lands the property of the United States." (6) "And in no case shall non-resident proprietors be taxed higher than residents."

It will be observed that provisions 4, 5 and 6, some now view as oppressive to the west, were taken from Mr. Jefferson's plan. The residue of the ordinance of '87 consists of two descriptions, one original, as the provisions to prevent legislatures enacting laws to impair contracts previously made, to secure the Indians their rights and property, part of the titles to property made more purely republican and more completely divested of feudality than any other titles in the Union were in July, '87. The temporary organization was new—no part of it was in the plan of '84. The other description was selected mainly from the constitution and laws of Massachusetts, as any one may see who knows what American law was in 1787, as: 1. Titles to property by will, by deed, by descent, and by delivery, cited verbatim in the 7th volume of this abridgment, pages 389–390. Here it may be observed that titles to land once taking root are important, as they are usually permanent; in this case they were planted in 400,000 square miles of territory and took root as was intended. 2. All the fundamental, perpetual articles of compact, except as below, as, first, securing forever religious liberty; second, the essential parts of a bill of rights declaring that religion, morality, and knowledge, being necessary to good government and the happiness of mankind, schools and the means of education shall forever be encouraged. These selections from the code of Massachusetts, as also the titles to property, have created for her an extensive and lasting influence in the west, and of the most republican, liberal, and beneficial kind.

The organization, providing officers to select or make, to decide on and execute, laws, being temporary was not deemed an important part of the ordinance of '87. Mr. Charles Pinckney assisted in striking out a part of this in 1786.

The sixth article of compact, the slave article, is imperfectly understood. Its history is: In 1784 a committee, consisting of Mr. Jefferson, Mr. Chase and Mr. Howell, reported it, as a part of the plan of 1784. This congress struck out; only two members south of Pennsylvania supported it; all north of Maryland voted to preserve it, so as to exclude slavery. It was imperfect, first, as it admitted slavery until 1800; second, it admitted slavery in very considerable parts of the territory forever, which will appear on a critical examination, especially in the parts owned for ages by French, Canadian, and other inhabitants, as their property, provided for only in the ordinance of 1787. In the ordinance of 1787 slavery is excluded from its date and forever from every part of this whole territory of the United States northwest of the River Ohio, over all which the ordinance established government.

The amended slave article, as it is in the ordinance of '87, was added on the author's motion, and, as the journals show, was not reported from the committee. On the whole, if there be any praise or any blame in this ordinance, especially in the titles to property, and in the permanent parts, as the most important, it belongs to Massachusetts, as one of her members formed it and furnished the matter, with the exceptions following:

First: He was assisted by Mr. C. Pinckney, who did so little that he felt himself at liberty to condemn it in debate.

Second: The author took from Mr. Jefferson's resolution of 1784, in substance, the said six provisions in the fourth article of compact, as above stated.

Third: He took the words of the slave article from Mr. King's motion made in 1785, and extended its operation as to time and extent of territory as above mentioned; as to matter his invention furnished the provision respecting impairing contracts and the Indian security and some smaller matters. The residue, no doubt, he selected from existing laws.

(The Appendix "A" as printed in the Abridgment is somewhat longer than as given here. Whether this was cut by Mr. Defrees, or the other rewritten, is not known.)

CLARK'S LETTER OF INSTRUCTION.

(How the original of this secret letter of instruction from Governor Patrick Henry, of Virginia, to George Rogers Clark came into possession of the Indiana Historical Society is not now known. It was published by the society in *fac-simile*, copies of the publication being often mistaken for the original.)

Virginia—Sct.

IN COUNCIL, W^{ms}BURG, Jany. 2^d, 1778.

Lieu. Colonel George Rogers Clark:

You are to proceed with all convenient speed to raise seven companies of soldiers to consist of fifty men each, officered in the usual manner & armed most properly for the Enterprize, & with this Force attack the British post at Kaskasky.

It is conjectured that there are many pieces of cannon &

military stores to considerable amount at that place, the taking and preservation of which would be a valuable acquisition to the state. If you are so fortunate therefore as to succeed in your Expedition, you will take every possible Measure to secure the artillery & stores & whatever may advantage the state.

For the Transportation of the Troops, provisions, &c., down the Ohio, you are to apply to the Commanding officer at Fort Pitt for Boats, & during the whole Transaction you are to take especial care to keep the true Destination of your Force secret. Its success depends upon this. Orders are therefore given to Captn Smith to secure the two men from Kaskasky. Similar conduct will be proper in similar cases. It is earnestly desired that you show Humanity to such British subjects and other persons as fall in your hands. If the white Inhabitants of that post & the neighbourhood will give undoubted Evidence of their attachment to this State (for it is certain they live within its limits) by taking the Test prescribed by Law & by every other way & means in their power, Let them be treated as fellow citizens & their persons & property duly secured. Assistance & protection against all Enemies whatever shall be afforded them & the Commonwealth of Virginia is pledged to accomplish it. But if these people will not accede to these reasonable Demands they must feel the miseries of war under the direction of that Humanity that has hitherto distinguished Americans & which it is expected you will ever consider as the Rule of your Conduct & from which you are in no instance to depart.

The Corps you are to command are to receive the pay & allowance of Militia & to act under the Laws & Regulations of this state now in force. The Inhabitants at this Post will be informed by you that in case they accede to the offers of becoming Citizens of this Commonwealth a proper garrison will be maintained among them & every attention bestowed to render their commerce beneficial, the fairest prospects being opened to the Dominions of both France & Spain.

It is in contemplation to establish a post near the Mouth of Ohio. Cannon will be wanted to fortify it. Part of those at Kaskasky will be easily brought thither or otherwise secured as circumstances will make necessary.

You are to apply to General Hand for powder & lead necessary for this Expedition. If he can't supply it the person who has that which Capt. Lynn bro' from Orleans can. Lead was sent to Hampshire by my orders & that may be delivered you. Wishing you success, I am.

    Sir,
      Your hble. ser.,
        P. HENRY.

INDIANA HISTORICAL SOCIETY PUBLICATIONS

VOLUME I   NUMBER III

THE USES OF HISTORY

BY

PRES. ANDREW WYLIE, D. D.

INDIANAPOLIS
THE BOWEN-MERRILL COMPANY
1897

A DISCOURSE

DELIVERED BEFORE THE

INDIANA HISTORICAL SOCIETY

IN THE HALL OF THE HOUSE OF REPRESENTATIVES
AT ITS ANNUAL MEETING, ON SATURDAY,
11TH DECEMBER, 1831

BY ANDREW WYLIE, D. D.,

PRESIDENT OF INDIANA COLLEGE

PUBLISHED BY REQUEST OF THE SOCIETY

INDIANAPOLIS
A. F. MORRISON, PRINTER
1831

At a meeting of the Indiana Historical Society, on Saturday evening, 11th December, the following resolution was unanimously adopted:

Resolved, That the thanks of this society be presented to the Rev. Dr. Wylie, for the appropriate and eloquent discourse delivered this evening at their request, and that he be respectfully solicited to furnish a copy of the same for publication.

ORDERED, That Mr. Farnham and Judge Morris be a committee to communicate to Dr. Wylie the foregoing resolution.

DISCOURSE.

The wisdom of those provisions, moral and intellectual, which the author of nature has employed in connecting the successive generations of the human race, demands an attentive and profound consideration. It is not bare existence that is transmitted, but existence with accumulating good or evil. Nor is it from the times immediately preceding their own that the people of any generation are thus affected; the good or evil may come upon them from periods of the most remote antiquity. As far back as the current of events can be traced, it is seen to have been directed in its course by the agency of men, who, long since, have been withdrawn from the busy scenes of life. In the universe, so far, at least, as our knowledge extends, nothing is insulated. Moral, no less than physical nature is, indeed, divided into individuals, but these are collected into systems, and, as from every orb that revolves in unlimited space there proceeds an influence which reaches to every other, however remote, so in the aggregate of human beings, there is not an individual whose condition and character may not be affected by every other. The same law may forcibly pervade the intelligent universe. The human race, coming into existence in succession, the stream of influence is in the same direction with the course of time; the past controls the present, and the present the future. But there is also an influence in a reverse order, of the future upon the present, and there is no man, whose sentiments are in conformity with nature, who is not determined in his course of conduct by motives, drawn from a regard to those who are to come after him.

Moral causes procure their effects by a slow and secret, but sure process, like that of vegetation. The earth has completed three-fourths of her annual revolution before the the seed deposited in her bosom produces its fruit. So it often happens that the appropriate consequences of human actions do not take place till late in the life of the individual, sometimes not till life is ended;.yet, we believe, he will find them in that unknown world whither death conveys him. But, as nations have a more permanent existence on earth, the results of moral causes, so far as they are concerned, are disclosed in this world, not always, nor even usually, in the course of one generation, or two, but for the most part, within a period sufficiently brief to be illustrated by the lights of history. So that, it is to history that the world is, in a great degree, indebted for whatever sense of morality prevails in it. The tendency of actions is the criterion by which mankind generally judge of their moral nature. The philosopher and the Christian have a better test; but the many will never be persuaded to condemn that course of conduct which they see to be prosperous. The mass of mankind would never agree with Lucan in weighing the opinion of Cato against the decision of the gods: "*Victrix causa Diis placuit, sed Victa, Catoni.*" "The successful cause of Gods approved, the unsuccessful Cato."

It is of the utmost importance, therefore, that they should be accustomed to view things as they appear on the extended scale of their causes and consequences. It is often in the power of bad men to show instances in which wicked men seem to be successful. The immediate consequences of vice are often in reality, and always considered, by those who practice it, to be advantageous. In this, indeed consists the nature of the present state as a state of trial. For there could be no trial without temptation, and no temptation, if no immediate advantage appeared on the side of vice. One reason why temptations to a profligate course are frequently so successful in youth, arises from the inexperience that belongs to that interesting but dangerous stage of life. The young are apt to be delighted with the free and careless gayety, the false honor, the unrestrained indulgence and appearance of generous feeling, with which certain vices seem to be connected. They are captivated by what appears to them the manly and honorable carriage and deportment of the gallant and high spirited young gentleman, who, out of pure friendship, would lead them to participate in his licentious pleasures. They partake, and are undone. But could they see, at first, what a few short years will reveal the same individual, now the object of their inconsiderate admiration, besotted, corrupted, debased in body and mind, poor, forsaken, shunned, despised and abhorred, and sinking into an untimely grave, the charm would be broken, and they would fly from his company as from the solicitations of an infernal demon. But they do not see these things, for they are hidden in the future. How important, then, that they be taught to see them in the past, which is a sample of the future. "The thing that has been is that which shall be, and there is nothing new under the sun." It is thus that biography, which is a species of history, even the biography of "evil men and seducers," may be consulted by the young with so much advantage. In fact, young people, whose minds have been seasonably imbued with the wholesome influence of good reading, seldom, if ever, turn out profligates in after life. And what biography is to individuals, general history is to nations. The incidents which make the ground work of the latter are not, indeed, noted by the same historian; but some by one, and some by another, in long succession, till at length all the testimony respecting the actors and events of the period to be illustrated are, by some competent hand, collected, compared and embodied in the form of a continued narrative. A history of this kind may be compared to a series of astronomical observations, continued through successive ages. Some of the heavenly bodies move in orbits so extended that their course can not be determined in the lifetime of one observer. But he takes his observations, his successor does the same, and so on, till, by taking the whole together, some future astronomer is enabled to determine the location of the track in which the ethereal traveler performs his appointed journey through the heavens. So is the course which nations pursue marked by the notices of history; and its influence in this respect has been great and salutary on the policy of the civilized world.

There are principles implanted in our hearts by the hand of nature, intended to be the guards and auxiliaries of virtue, which, as they operate in a degree independent of reason and will, may be either strengthened or impaired, but not utterly extirpated. Among these, a regard to character holds a chief place. Over such as live in obscurity, its influence is, perhaps, inconsiderable. But with those who occupy conspicuous stations in society this is not the case. Knowing that their actions undergo the scrutiny of the public, they can not feel at ease while conscious that they merit censure. They even anticipate the condemnation of posterity, and the reproaches of their own minds seem to be re-echoed by millions of voices, issuing not only from the circle of surrounding contemporaries, but from the indignant ranks of future generations. The power of this sentiment is even more sensibly felt in anticipation of the future than in view of the present. Those among whom we live may be biased by interest or blinded by passion. Conscious integrity may therefore scorn their censures. A tyrant, on the other hand, may find means to corrupt or mislead the public sentiment, and the stings of guilt may be soothed by the flattery of parasites. The press may be shackled or bought, and the murmurs of the multitude will be suppressed while the iron mace of power is held over them. But in the meanwhile, a tribunal is preparing under the auspices of history, when the voice of truth will be heard, when impartial justice will preside; passion, and prejudice, and fear, having died away, time, that great revealer of secrets, having brought everything to light, fame with her hundred tongues stands ready to proclaim the sentence to all nations. Instances there are, in the shape of men who can persuade themselves that, at death, they shall cease to exist; but it may be doubted whether there ever lived a man, so much a monster, as to reconcile his feelings to the idea of anticipated infamy. It is usual, indeed, to say of a man when he is dead that he is beyond the reach of censure, but this avails not, since he dreads it while living, and that, though the sentence which involves it may not be pronounced till long after his bones have mouldered into dust.

A sensibility to character is not less powerful, and is certainly more lovely, when it manifests itself in pursuing what is praiseworthy, than when it deters from vice by the fear of reproach. And the circumstances in which, under the former of these modifications, it appears to the best advantage, are precisely those in which the weakness of human virtue renders its assistance the most necessary. There is something childish, to say the least, in the conduct of a man who is always looking to popularity, and who goes with reluctance to the performance of a noble action, unless he can be paid in hand by present applause. But when we see one holding fast his integrity, though surrounded with opposition, and acting for the public good, while the public impeach his motives and detract from his services, aware that, when the enmity of rivals, the envy of inferiors and the malice of calumniators shall be quelled in death, a generation will arise to enjoy the benefit of his labors and to bless his memory, we not only love him for his goodness, but revere and venerate him for his magnanimity. Two, the most splendid examples which history furnishes, to illustrate the excellence of this lofty character (I except, of course, the Author of Christianity, whom it would be impious to mention in connection with any imperfect mortal, however exalted in virtue), were men who lived in ages and countries the most remote from each other, but between whom, not only as it respects their moral qualities, but the incidents of their lives, there exists a considerable resemblance, both distinguished for heroic virtue, both chosen instruments in the hand of God of delivering nations from bondage, both tried with the incessant murmurings of the envious and pusillanimous, and both removed from the earth before they had seen the people whom they liberated quietly settled in the land of their inheritance—Moses and George Washington.

He certainly fulfills an office gratifying to the best feelings of the human heart who employs the powers of history in rearing a monument to the honor of such illustrious men, causing them to live again in the memory of distant ages. Our sense of justice is consoled for the sufferings and ill-treatment they once endured, while we imagine—and surely it is not a vain imagination—that, though invisible to mortal eyes, they still exist, and, from the high sphere to which they are exalted, look down with delight upon the effects which their labors have produced on the state of that world which they have left, and on the benefited and grateful multitudes who love to cherish the remembrance of their exalted worth. We kindle into emulation while we read the story of their virtuous deeds, and are encouraged in the race that is set before us by seeing in the success of their example how difficulties may be overcome by perseverance. The recital of their troubles and perplexities awakens our sympathy, and we glow with admiration at the firmness of their principles. We are better reconciled with the world, on account of their virtue, by which its darkness has been broken; and our despondency for its future destinies is relieved by those triumphs in the good cause which they have achieved. Disgusted, as we must often be, with the vices and vulgarities of common life, it is delightful to seek, in converse with the wise and good of former ages, to whose company the historian introduces us, refreshment and relief to our spirits, and we are even put in better humor with our nature and with all who partake in it, by seeing in those specimens of excellence which it has from time to time exhibited that it is not, by any law of invincible necessity, doomed to the baseness of undistinguished and hopeless reprobation. Our reasoning powers are immensely aided and improved by gathering up, here a little and there a little, of those sublime instructions which experience has strewed around the track along which the human race have been for so many ages moving; and the rays of those burning and shining lights which, at distant periods, and in different countries, have stood alone amidst the surrounding darkness, being collected and arranged by the magic power of historical genius, shed abroad a cheering light upon the pathway of life.

An acquaintance with history will not, indeed, inspire in man the love of virtue. A special influence from above can alone effect this. Yet it deserves our notice that the author of this influence has connected it with truth, and that history is one of the forms in which He himself has condescended to communicate the truth to mankind. Historical truth is one of the pillars of Christianity. And whoever will lay aside prejudice, and divesting himself of all those prepossessions, on one side or the other, arising from the artful attacks of the enemies of divine revelation, or the awkward and unhappy defenses of its friends, will take up the Old Testament, as he would a new book, and peruse it as a book of its pretensions ought to be perused, and in the exercise of such a temper as an ignorant sinner ought to feel, and then will go through its sequel in the New, in the same manner, can not fail to rise from the perusal a wiser and a better man, if not a confirmed believer in the truth of the Christian system. Even profane history will not be without its use in this respect, as it tends to impress the conviction that the world is under the control of a moral governor. A proper belief of this truth must dispose the mind favorably towards the inspired volume, wherein it is so clearly exhibited and illustrated. Besides, everyone acquainted with history and with the bible must see that the principles of moral government contained in the latter coincide with the tenor of human experience unfolded in the former. That some of the most celebrated historians have been opposed to Christianity affords no grounds of objection to what has been alleged. No amount of truth, not demonstration itself, will compel belief. Gibbon and Hume were infidels, yet the great work of the former, notwithstanding the sly innuendoes and studied irony with which it abounds, might be recommended as containing as much matter of fact, inconsistent with the infidelity of the author, and in support of the cause which he so plainly hated, as can be found in almost any other book of equal extent. Let any man read, for instance—I mean not a fool, who is prepared to swallow without examination whatever comes from such a source—but a man of sense, who will reflect on what he reads—let any man of this character read the causes which this ingenious writer has assigned for the rapid spread of Christianity, and he will find, if he is an infidel, not a little to shake his opinion. The doctrine of a moral government has been sadly misunderstood. Yet the practice, sometimes to be found among professing Christians, and common with all ignorant and superstitious people, of putting an interpretation to suit themselves on every passing event, arises from a deplorable misapplication of a very sound principle. The wheels on which the affairs of men, and especially of nations, revolve, are so large, that a minute portion of their circumference, such as falls under the observation of an individual in the course of a single life, is insufficient to justify a judgment respecting the whole. The designs of God can not be seen till the whole train of events which they contemplate has passed before us. We should be careful, therefore, to "judge nothing before the time." Yet, that the Almighty has connected natural evil with moral —that suffering is, according to the settled order of things, the fruit of transgression, and that "righteousness exalteth a nation," are truths which history teaches in the most impressive manner. These, and a variety of other maxims favorable to the cause of virtue and human happiness, which the experience of a few years very imperfectly illustrates, are made clear in the events of a more extended period. For, while the great drama, in which nations are concerned is in progress, both the actors and spectators are insensibly changed, the individuals of one generation retiring while others are coming in their place; so that no one can judge of what is before him till the whole scheme, and the connexion and tendency of every part, is laid open by the catastrophe.

In reviewing the past, we are often surprised to find incidents, trifling in themselves and apparently fortuitous, turning the whole course of events, the plans and works of men tending to results exactly the reverse of what they had in view, accidental discoveries in nature, deemed of no importance at first, changing insensibly the entire face of society, and strange coincidences of circumstances, each in itself inert, but deriving power, from their junction at the critical moment, to shake the world. Observations such as these, which the attentive reader of history can not fail to make, must indicate to his views a wise and controlling agency at the helm of all human affairs.

History gives us an insight into our own nature. In the past ages of the world, man has been placed in almost every possible condition that the nature of earthly things can furnish. The power of all sorts of institutions, of all sorts of systems and forms of government—of every conceivable religious and philosophical creed, and of every possible combination of circumstances, has been, at one time or another, tried upon him—and truly he has occasionally exhibited strange phases of character, and been seen ranging the scale of qualities from the point where he affronts the brute up to that which shows him on the confines of angelic nature. Whatever be his tendencies and capacities, his powers and frailties, we shall find them in history; for they have been all developed. Among them we find, it is true, a capability of indefinite improvement, and therefore it would be unreasonable to conclude that he will always be what he now is. But, I am afraid the doctrine of his perfectibility is a fiction. Of one thing I am quite certain, that the same spirit which, in modern days, has advanced the doctrine, will never verify it, and that, if perfection is ever to be his lot on earth, it will not be attained by an overweening confidence in his own powers, for the past has shown this of him, that, when he thinks himself strong, he is then the weakest, and the most a fool when he boasts of his wisdom. The most discouraging thing in his history, perhaps, is this, that he never has been able to unite religion and philosophy; but, when he seeks to be religious he forsakes his reason, and when he professes to consult his reason he forgets his dependence on his Maker.

Considering man in reference to that relation which subsists between his capacities of enjoyment and the things of this world, and in view of the question so often asked and variously answered, What is the chief good? history gives at least a negative answer, which, were it seriously regarded, might save us from much extravagance and folly, as well as pain and disappointment. There is no road to earthly good, real or imaginary, in which some of mankind have not pursued it, with all the ardor and energy of which their nature was susceptible. They have heaped up wealth, courted honor, grasped at power, sought for pleasure in every way and by all expedients. The scepter, the miter, the sword, art, nature, solitude, society, everything has been tried, and man has come away from them all, dissatisfied. Those things which, usually, men most intensely covet, have been found by experience to be supremely worthless. One seeks to be prime minister of a great nation, obtains the office, and stabs himself. Another, weary of royalty, renounces it, and then goes to war to recover what he had voluntarily resigned. A third aims at universal empire, spends years of restlessness and sheds oceans of blood to obtain it, and dies, chained to a rock. "What do you intend," said Cyneas to Pyrrhus, preparing for an expedition into Italy, "when you have subdued the Romans?" "Pass into Sicily." "What then?" "Conquer the Carthaginians." "And what next?" "Return home and enjoy ourselves." "And why," said the sensible minister, "can not we do the last, even now?"

The instructions of the bible relative to human happiness may be summed up in two words, "Godliness and contentment." And history teaches the same: the latter by showing us the perplexing causes and sad reverses to which those in high stations are exposed, and the former (I comprise in my remarks sacred as well as secular history), by recommending to our imitation the wisdom of those who feeling themselves to be "pilgrims and strangers on earth, sought a better country even an heavenly, and a city which hath foundations, whose builder and maker is God." Among the various uses of history, the rational amusement it affords should not be entirely overlooked. The mind requires occasionally to be relieved from the severer studies and cares of life, not by positive inaction, but by some employment calculated to give a gentle exercise to its faculties, and to soothe its sensibilities by the delightful play of imagination. History in a high degree answers these purposes, while at the same time it conveys useful instruction. Its incidents are no less striking than those which occur in works of fiction, with the additional advantage that they do not mislead the understanding, nor corrupt the taste by exhibiting a false representation of human life. What can give a more agreeable excitement to our feelings than to follow the narrative of the historian, while he brings up to view the characters and pursuits of those who once acted and suffered on this earth as we now do, who felt and exhibited all the variety of passion which the changeful scenes of life are calculated to elicit, and whom we recognize, as they pass before us, as partakers of a common nature with ourselves. What can be more gratifying to a rational curiosity than to watch the movements of the human heart, in trying and critical situations, and in conditions of life dissimilar among themselves, as well as different from any with which we have been conversant. What so entertaining to the fancy as to transport ourselves to distant ages, review customs and modes of thought and seats of empires which the hand of time has changed, and mark the effects produced upon the human character by institutions which have passed away, to be revived no more—to sit, as it were, on the brink of the stream of time, and gaze upon the various objects, great and small—kings and conquerors, mighty cities and empires, philosophers and their systems, statesmen and their schemes of policy, and an endless flotilla of minor things—as they are borne along by the swift current towards that boundless ocean to which all that is earthly tends. Who, whether man or woman, young or old, that has any capacity for reflection, would turn away from the position where he can indulge in a reverie, at once so instructive and delightful, to follow the *ignis fatuus* of fiction through a land of specters and furies, obscene phantoms and "goblins damned."

An acquaintance with history, useful to all, is most important to men in public stations. The injuries which mankind have suffered from those entrusted with the management of their affairs have been so grievous as to give to the very name of office a malignant signification. The sentiment has become prevalent among the people of all nations, that no sooner is a man elevated to power than he may be expected to use it with a special eye to his own private interests, regardless of the public. Authority and patriotism are thought incompatible. That there has been given, in fact, too much ground for such a sentiment, is undeniable. Yet, every candid judge of human nature and of the course of events must give, I apprehend, more credit to public men for patriotic intentions than they generally have received. Why should rulers hate their subjects? Why should we suspect a man of the design to wreck the vessel the moment he is honored with a station at the helm? The people surely ought at least to have the credit of being faithful to themselves, and of honestly endeavoring to promote their own interests. Yet, this is more, a great deal, than could be fairly allowed them, were they to be judged by the tendency of their measures. The truth is, that rulers have inflicted injury upon their subjects, and the people upon themselves, rather through error than design; and they have been in error because ignorant of history. The interests of nations depend on the joint operation of so many different causes, and the effect of public measures is often so entirely opposite to what could reasonably have been anticipated, as to render the business of government in the highest degree complicated and difficult. All, whether rulers or people, are apt to have in view the immediate effects of any proposed scheme of policy, rather than its remote consequences, though the former may be inconsiderable compared with the latter. Few, indeed, are capable of viewing remote consequences at all, and none, without the light derived from experience, the only safe guide in everything concerning the government, trade and policy of nations. Theories of government formed on reasonings *a priori* are sure to be fallacious, if not wild and visionary, however wise the heads in which they originate. Those of Plato, Sir Thomas More, Harrington and Locke, are striking examples. Those constitutions and forms of policy which have proved salutary in their operation have not been the offspring of human wisdom employed in laborious thoughts to give them birth, but have been formed gradually, one piece being suggested after another, by some pressing exigency, and retained or rejected afterwards as found useful or otherwise on sufficient experiment.

A prudent regard to history is, however, as widely different from submission to the authority of precedent as it is from the presumptuous spirit of inconsiderate innovation. The great advantage to be derived, by the statesman, from consulting the experience of the past, would be lost, if he were not permitted to reject what is faulty, as well as to adopt what is good, in the practice of preceding generations, and also to modify what he adopts so as to suit the changes which time and human improvements may have effected in the state of society. It was on these principles that the sages proceeded who framed the constitution of our government; they retained whatever was found to be expedient in the government of other nations, accommodating it at the same time to the end in view, and to whatever was peculiar in our condition in this new world. They did not extend their views further back than to those periods of the world to which English history reaches, nor, for the purpose, was it necessary.

Yet, in many things interesting to our policy and prosperity as a nation, much useful information might be derived from the writings of more remote antiquity. The field of remark which here opens is too large to be explored in the most general and cursory manner, on the present occasion. Yet, I can not pass it by without remarking the great similarity in their modes of warfare that there is between some ancient nations and the savages which at different times committed such ravages upon the infant settlements of this country. It has often painfully occurred to me that had those who conducted military operations against them been acquainted with what Xenophon has written on the modes of war among Greeks and Persians, it had been well for themselves and the brave men whom they commanded. They never would have suffered themselves to be surprised, at least in their encampments.

Lest, however, among my praises of history, it should occur to some who hear me that there is one piece of ancient history that I have not read, the story of Hannibal and Phormio, and as my pursuits in life have not made me much acquainted with the undesirable business of carnal warfare, I would only say, on the subject in general, that if our fellow-citizens were but tolerably acquainted with the terribly instructive lessons on the subject of war with which history so much abounds they would try to have as little to do with it as possible, and especially with civil war, which concentrates in itself the sum and essence of all earthly calamities. History, it is probable, had not its origin in any foresight of the advantages to which it is subservient, but in a wise provision which nature has made in the instinctive propensities of the human mind for the transmission of knowledge. Old age is communicative and youth inquisitive; and the happy junction of these opposite qualities forms a channel through which the experience of the past is made to flow into and enrich the future. One who has spent the vigor of his days among great and important transactions feels a peculiar gratification in the decline of life in calling them up again to his remembrance. The scenes with which he was conversant, while yet his energies were unimpaired, are more intimately present to him than those with which he is now surrounded. The illusions of imagination which brighten the prospects of youth have furnished a delightful theme to the poet and the philosopher; they are probably no less attendant upon the retrospect of the past, which serves to cheer the evening of life. Anxiety always mars our enjoyment of the present; but, when what was doubtful in the undertaking has become certain in the event, we look back upon it with pleasure. Time gives to things the mellow coloring and gentle outline of a distant landscape. What was painful is either forgotten or becomes pleasant in the remembrance; and though it has often been remarked, and perhaps truly, that few have been so happy as to wish to live their lives over again, yet none are ever tired of reverting to past scenes, except the guilty. When the haven is in view the weather-beaten mariner delights to recount the toils he has endured and the dangers he has escaped. Nor do the young attend with emotions less delightful to the narratives of the old. How often have our youthful fancies been thrown into a delirium of ecstasy while we listened to the recital of the incidents of the revolutionary war—the perils, the sufferings, and the triumphs of that eventful period.

The first essays of history consisted, doubtless, in oral narratives of this kind, and before the invention of written language there was no other way to distinguish the terms employed in the rehearsal of some great event, the memory of which the narrator wished to go down to after ages, than by giving them an arrangement and pronunciation different from those employed in ordinary discourse. This was poetry.

One of the most lofty pieces of poetical composition, as well as the most ancient, is an historical commemoration of the passage of the Israelites over the Red Sea, and the destruction of their pursuers beneath its returning waves, composed by Moses and sung on that great occasion. The Iliad is the recital of a series of achievements performed by a band of heroes confederated for the accomplishment of a particular purpose, and it is said to have been preserved in the memory of ancient bards for about five hundred years before it was committed to writing. But the transmission of facts by oral tradition, at best uncertain, became still more so by being associated with poetry. For the poet, finding that his power to give pleasure depended less upon the facts embodied in his narrative than on the effect of regular numbers upon the ear, and the charms of an highly ornamental style upon the imagination, was under the constant temptation of adding to it new embellishments, till, at length, his facts were lost in the mass of surrounding fiction. Thus the muses, the daughters of memory, by degrees forsook the service of their venerable parent, and found a more pleasing employment under the indulgent rule of imagination. Poetry now fell into discredit as a voucher of past transactions; and monuments, medals and anniversary ceremonies were resorted to as the means of commemorating events. Of these, the latter are the most effectual, and their use has been consecrated by religion. But they are all exceedingly imperfect, compared with the art of letters, an art which makes of "the grey goose quill" an instrument more powerful than the sculptor's chisel, and converts a heap of rags into a monument more noble than the pyramid.

The first history, both in point of time and importance, which the world possesses, records, not the actions of men, but the doings of Omnipotence. The Pentateuch of Moses!

If it is not inspired, it is a prodigy more stupendous than any or all the miracles which it relates. Herodotus, who flourished about the middle of the fifth century before the Christian era, Thucydides, who succeeded him, and Xenophon, who wrote about the beginning of the fourth century before Christ, have handed down to us nearly all that we know of ancient times, except what comes to us from the pen of inspiration. The works of the latter of these historians connect the early periods of Grecian history, which are evidently obscured by fable, with the times when the extension of the Roman power and the cultivation of letters in Italy prepared the way for a freer and more perfect intercourse among the nations who were merged in that great empire; and thus the means of procuring authentic information were greatly multiplied. From the commencement of the second century before the Christian era, history assumes a character of comparative certainty and increasing interest. In this period the stubborn contest between Rome and her great rival was terminated in the destruction of the latter; and the splendor of the former was increased by introducing into it the literature and arts of conquered Greece. The century which at its close introduced the Savior into the world was illuminated throughout by a constellation of the most illustrious characters. Within the three succeeding centuries was effected the greatest revolution in the state of the world which ever yet has taken place. Christianity, without the support of any of those causes which recommend new opinions to the acceptance of mankind, and making its way in opposition to the wealth and power of pagan Rome, after sustaining the shock of ten successive and bloody persecutions, obtained, under Constantine the Great, an establishment on the throne of the Cæsars. The Roman empire, at this period, extended in breadth upwards of two thousand miles from the extreme limits of Dacia on the north to the Tropic of Cancer, and in length more than three thousand, from the western ocean to the Euphrates, covering the finest part of the temperate zone, and estimated to contain upwards of sixteen hundred thousand square miles. The strength of this immense empire, it is generally supposed, was weakened by the transfer of its seat from Rome to Constantinople, an event which took place early in the third century. But a considerable time previous to this had commenced the incursions of the northern barbarians, who, though often defeated, and often, by the wretched policy of the times, hired by the payment of immense sums to retire from the countries they had overrun, as often returned again, in augmented numbers, till, at length, the imperial city was taken and sacked by the Goths, under Alaric, in the beginning of the fifth century; and, at its close, the different barbarian tribes were in possession of Italy, France, Spain, and the countries in Africa bordering on the Mediterranean. The early part of the sixth century is distinguished by the rise of the Mahometan imposture, which overspread Arabia in the lifetime of its author, and continued to extend, under his successors, till nearly the whole of the eastern and a considerable portion of the western empire submitted to their dominion. On the 29th day of May, 1453, Mahomet the Second took by storm the city of Constantinople, which from that time became the seat of a power which at one period threatened the whole of Christendom with subjugation, and which, notwithstanding its recent humiliation, still maintains a formidable position on the map of nations. The honor of opposing a barrier to its progress in the west belongs to the famous Charles Martel the Second, of the Carlovingian dynasty, who, in a great battle fought in the heart of France, defeated the Saracens with great slaughter, and drove them across the Pyrenees. These general facts have been mentioned for the purpose of turning your attention to certain institutions which they served to introduce, and which have had, and still continue to exert, a most powerful influence on the state of the world.

The rise of the Romish Hierarchy is one of the most wonderful and instructive themes of history. In the time of the Apostles, converts to the Christian faith were organized into churches, under the care of the most experienced men of their number, who were called elders, of whom one presided in their deliberations and took the lead in giving instruction. The addition of great numbers to their communion, which often took place in a little time, especially in cities, made it convenient to constitute several churches, still under the superintendence of the presiding elder, or presbyter of the original church, who in consequence assumed a place of permanent superiority over his associates in office, with the title of bishop or overseer. Example propagates itself; and in this way, even in the early part of the second century, the Christian world presented the aspect of numerous clusters of congregations, attached to the jurisdiction of as many bishops, each possessing subordinate officers of its own. Such a cluster was called a diocese. Different dioceses, in order to keep up a correspondence and harmony with each other, constituted and held annual, sometimes semi-annual meetings. The metropolis of the province was the place of meeting, and its limits the boundaries of their associated dioceses. This was natural, but the custom gave to the bishop of the metropolis a superiority of influence, and at length a permanent ascendency over his brethren. This ascendancy was denoted by a name, and metropolitan became a title, which, by the aid of management and favorable circumstances, conferred power. The same reasons which rendered it convenient for all, and desirable for the ambitious, that the churches of one district should be united in one diocese, and the dioceses of a province united under the metropolitan, rendered it expedient that the dioceses and churches of a kingdom should be united under one council, and that this council should have its patriarch. This system, carried a degree higher, completed the ecclesiastical pyramid, and the bishop of Rome, with the title of universal, or Catholic, became the apex. The concentration of power proceeded with the formation of the system, and by much the same means which ambition always employs to attain its object, especially where superstition benumbs the faculties of the understanding. One of these, as it casts light of the genius of the ages in which this astonishing system of spiritual domination was reared, deserves notice. It consisted in the following piece of logic: Peter was the chief of the Apostles, because the Savior had said, "Thou art Peter, and on this rock will I build my church," and had committed to him the keys of His kingdom, and the power of the sword. But Peter had founded the church at Rome, and therefore the bishops of that city, as his successors, inherited his authority. This dialectic skill of the bishop of Rome and his votaries would not have availed, however, were it not that the logic suited the circumstances, and obtained, in the superior dignity of the imperial city, the prodigious influx of wealth which fanaticism poured into the treasury of the church of St. Peter, and the vigilant policy of her officers, substantial support. How the spirit which actuated that policy could have derived its origin from the doctrines and example of Christ, to which it is so diametrically opposite, seems, at first view, utterly unaccountable. In tracing its progress we shall see a striking example of the subtle and stealthy manner in which corruption proceeds.

Paul, in his epistle to the converts at Corinth, a city whose commerce and wealth gave great occasion to litigation, had directed them to submit their disputes about secular matters to the arbitration of some of their own brethren rather than to go to law about them before a heathen magistrate. The direction was excellent, and was adopted not only by them but by the primitive Christians generally. It was natural that pastors of churches, who, in times of primitive purity, were, on account of their integrity and prudence, competent, and, among a rude and ignorant people, almost the only competent persons to decide in such cases, should be, in many instances, chosen to arbitrate. The happy effects at first observed to result from this method made it a custom. Custom at length conferred a right, and the right was easily and grossly abused. Yet this abuse could not have been general, or of long continuance, so long as the custom stood on its ancient footing. But when Constantine had provided by law that the decision of the bishop should be final, and executed by the civil magistrate, and that either party to a suit pending before a civil magistrate might, in any stage of the process, carry it by appeal to the tribunal of the bishop, the principle of the bishop's adjudication was essentially and fatally changed. Before, his decision could be respected only when just; now, it was compulsory and needed not justice to support it. The emperor Valens increased still further this arbitrary jurisdiction of the bishop; and, in general, it may be remarked, that as the civil magistrate was weak, and needed the countenance of the church to any of his measures, or superstitious, and in awe of its censure, he was ready to confer power and privilege upon its ministers. Besides this, an ignorant and superstitious people were easily taught to believe that, in all the contests of their priests and dignitaries with the secular authority, their cause was the cause of God; and it may give us some idea of the adroitness and success with which these sources of influence and wealth were managed if we reflect that in little less than half a century after the church of Rome had emerged from a bloody persecution she arose, by the munificence of the emperors and other opulent proselytes, to the summit of earthly grandeur. Her power was yet in its infancy. When full grown it prostrated everything before it, and trampled in the dust, not only the scepters of kings and emperors, but the reason and conscience, the hopes and fears and the very senses of mankind.

On reflecting upon that corruption of Christianity which took the form of that tremendous institution which has passed under our notice, it is obvious that two powerful causes cooperated in its production; the first, the divisions of the barbarous nations which settled down in the territories of the Roman empire, and which rendered some strong influence necessary to unite them; and second, that singular temper which characterized them, compounded of ignorance, superstition, ardor of feeling and wildness of imagination.

The monastic institutions, subordinate and cognate branches of the same great system, and deriving their growth from the same principles, will, if properly examined, confirm still further the truth of these remarks. In the primitive times of persecution, many pious Christians fled, some alone, and others with their families, into desert places, to shun temptations to apostacy, and enjoy the pleasures of devotion unmolested by the world. The practice continued when the motives to it had ceased, and men secluded themselves from society, not to escape persecution but to recommend themselves to God by voluntary poverty and penance, chastity and prayer. A reputation for superior sanctity was thus acquired, and multitudes forsook cities, colleges and the abodes of industry, to seek it in the desert. The desert was a desert no longer. Monasteries and nunneries were erected and liberally endowed by donations and bequests from infatuated mortals, many of whom, after a life of profligacy and rapine, thought by this means to purchase heaven. The monks assumed a peculiar dress and called each other friars—this is brothers—thus indicating their exclusive regard for themselves. The world readily gave in to their absurd pretensions, and many an atrocious villain has, when at the point of death, ordered himself to be dressed in the monkish garb, as a protection against the expected attack of the evil one.

In the monastic communities superstition obtained a monstrous growth, which yielded a powerful support to the church of Rome. Their inmates, who, on account of the various rules of sanctity to which they bound themselves by oath, were called regulars, were the steady adherents of a power which, in its turn, supported their pretensions and employed them as its ministers and emissaries. Yet, in the monastic institutions there was some good mixed with the predominating evil. The morals of those who resorted to them continued for a considerable time after their first establishment comparatively pure. They not only supported themselves by their industry, but procured the means of relief for the indigent and helpless. Their sacred character enabled them to afford a sanctuary to the oppressed, which even the lawless violence of the barbarous ages dared not violate. Their seclusion from the world gave them leisure for mutual improvement, and whatever of learning escaped the inundation of barbarism that rolled over the Roman empire was preserved during the dark ages by their means. Even the piety which they cherished, though in all cases deeply tinged with superstition, and in some degenerating into downright hypocrisy, was, upon the whole, greatly preferable to the profligacy and brutal manners which everywhere else prevailed. And, it deserves to be noticed, that though the different monastic orders obtained, one after another, exemption from the jurisdiction of the secular clergy and became immediately dependent on the see of Rome, and might, therefore, have been expected to be, as in general they actually were, blindly devoted to its interests, yet the spirit of resistance to the overgrown prerogatives of the Romish hierarchy which led the way to the glorious reformation was enkindled in the cloister. The observation may appear strange but it is nevertheless true, that the same causes which gave rise to monarchism originated an institution in many respects totally dissimilar—I mean chivalry. The same spirit, though under different modifications, pervaded them both.

The barbarians, who, under various names, overran the Roman empire, were a military people, fierce, hardy, bold, ardent and adventurous. The chieftains, whose steps they followed from the inhospitable regions of the north, had, in general, no other authority over them than that which is created by the possession of those qualities of mind and body which impress with awe the minds of a rude people—personal prowess, intrepidity in danger, sagacity in council and conduct in action. Fortune is the divinity of the unthinking, and the savage hordes who had so often fought under the victorious banners of their chosen leader, yielded to his dictates a more ready submission, for the most part, than in civilized communities is given to the decisions of law. A partition of the districts which their arms had subdued was made on the same principles which had secured subordination in the camp. The general was the sole proprietor; his subordinate officers held lands under him, which they subdivided among their particular followers. The rent, if so it may be called, which was to be paid for land, was not money or produce, but military service. Such, briefly, was the feudal system, which, on the dissolution of the Roman empire, was established all over Europe—a hateful system of military aristocracy—from which the nations of the old world are not yet emancipated.

The officers, holding immediately from the crown, were called barons, and under these again were ranked counts, viscounts, vavassors, capitains, etc. These were the nobility. Those below the rank of nobility were either first, freemen, who possessed allodial estates; or second, villeins, a sort of renters, but transferable with the soil which they cultivated, or thirdly, slaves, a numerous class, who had no rights, and whom their masters might put to death at pleasure, without judge or jury. The military tenant, of whatever rank, was called a vassal. He paid no tribute but service in arms. He was the companion of his lord in his sports in the field, in the feasts of his hall, and on the tribunal of judgment. He fought mounted and equipped in coat of mail. One of the most wonderful facts to be found in the history of the middle ages, and which may give us some idea of the turbulence and insecurity of those wretched times, is that free men, holding allodial estates, should be found willing to exchange their condition for that of a vassal or even a villein. Yet nothing was more common. Under William, duke of Normandy, it was done by the whole body of the landed proprietors in Great Britain. In accepting a feudal grant, or benefice, the vassal, with his head uncovered, his belt ungirt and his sword and spear removed, kneeled, and placing his hands between those of his lord, promised to become his man thenceforward; to serve him with life and limb and worldly honor; and in conclusion of the ceremony received from his lord a kiss. This was called doing homage, a thing very different, in our apprehensions, from acting the man, which the word signifies. Besides this, the vassal took an oath of fidelity, or, as it was called, swore fealty to his lord, by which he bound himself to maintain the honor of his lord and of his family, to lend him his horse in battle, if he should be dismounted, to go into captivity for him as an hostage if he were taken prisoner, and to do for him all sorts of deferential service. Besides the great duties of fealty and service, the vassal was bound to render others that were incidental. He paid a relief, that is, a premium on taking possession of his estate, and a fine upon alienation, that is, a premium when he sold it. His estate was subject to escheat; in other words it reverted to the lord in default of heirs, and it was liable to forfeiture upon the violation of fealty, of which the lord was to be the judge. Aids or contributions were levied by the lord on his vassal on any urgent occasions. In England these were reduced by Magna Charta to three, when the lord's oldest son was to be knighted, his oldest daughter married, or himself redeemed from prison. During his minority the vassal was under wardship to his lord, to be educated, or rather trained to arms, under his direction, the lord being in the meantime entitled to the profits of his ward's estate.

Another feudal right respected his female vassals, the exercise of which, however, they would not, in all cases, regard as an intolerable grievance; it consisted in providing them with husbands whom they were not at liberty to reject, but by the payment of a fine or a *bona fide* declaration that they were above sixty years of age. We are surprised to find that the condition of a vassal, encumbered as it was by all these burdens, should have been preferred to that of a free man or allodial proprietor. But our surprise will cease when we consider that in those times of military ascendancy the independent proprietor was always exposed to the rapacity of men in power, over whom laws had no control and who had under them hordes of savage vassals as rapacious as themselves; that his possessions were liable to be pillaged, sometimes by a foreign enemy, but more frequently by the partisans of private warfare, and that, surrounded continually by a host of miscreants who esteemed war as pastime and plunder as lawful gain, he had no resource but in the protection of some neighboring castle which, of course, he could not obtain but on condition of vassalage to its proprietor. In those times of violence many were compelled to become slaves. Urged by famine, which frequently prevailed, many sold their liberty for bread; others lost it by debt, some by crime, and more in war. Many were reduced to this sad condition by failing to attend upon military expeditions of the king, the penalty of which was a fine called heriban, with the alternative of perpetual servitude.

The mode of deciding controversies under this horrible system was of a piece with the rest. To determine what was just and right, by a careful examining of witnesses and sifting out the truth from a mass of conflicting testimony, and by a reference to statute books, or the dictates of natural justice, was a manner of proceeding that did not comport with the genius of the feudal system. The arrogance of brute force and the stupidity of superstition suggested a shorter, easier, and, as was supposed, a more infallible method, the judicial combat. The parties fought, and the overthrow or death of one or the other made known the decision of God. A party to the cause might challenge a witness to combat before his testimony was delivered, or he might challenge and fight the judges, or the first one of their number who should decide against him; and if virtuous, the decision was in his favor, and in those cases none dared to refuse the challenge. The aged, the infirm and the female sex, it is obvious, would have to submit to every species of outrage and injury from the strong and those who were expert in the use of weapons. These were allowed therefore to contend by proxy and to employ champions—an odd sort of lawyers—to maintain their rights. To ecclesiastics the same privilege was granted. That such a state of things tended to inflame the "*amor pugnæ*," the fighting propensities, which, if we may judge from facts, are in all circumstances, strong in human nature, is too obvious to need a remark. But it had other consequences which were not so direct but far more fortunate. It produced refinement of manners. For the weak, unable to defend themselves and finding no protection in innocence, sought it in the strength of the powerful. Hence those arts of respect and deference, by which only the favor of the strong could be gained. If there is any generous feeling in the breast of a man it will be excited by the view of the helpless imploring his interference. In this proud situation the feudal lords and persons distinguished for their spirit and prowess were often placed. They felt honored by the affecting appeals which were often made to their generosity, and soon discovered that to redress the wrongs of the injured and to protect the innocent was the readiest way to increase both their power and reputation. Lofty, generous and humane sentiments would be thus frequently called into exercise. The tone of feeling thus produced was raised still higher by female influence. This, under all circumstances, has no small agency in the formation of the character of man. Each sex seems to be formed by nature to admire those qualities which distinguish the other; the male the softer and more gentle attributes of woman; the female the sterner properties of man. And, in that state of improvement which lies in the middle, between the rudeness of savage life and the refinement of highly cultivated society, there is no form which so readily captivates the female eye as that of the plumed warrior. The northern nations seem always to have treated the female sex with greater tenderness and respect than are usually paid to them by barbarians; but when their taste and manners become more refined; when their females began to gratify that love of ornament which is instinctive in the sex, and to heighten their native charms by the use of those elegant productions which commerce began to minister to the wants of luxury; when the rich furs of the north, the gay silks of the east and the jewels and gold of the south began to illuminate the halls of the feudal chieftain, while the music of the bard added inspiration to the entertainment, woman rose on the tide of enthusiastic feeling to her throne in the imagination and the hearts of assembled heroes. The infusion of gallantry into the composition of martial qualities and lofty sentiments which distinguished the feudal nobility constituted the spirit of chivalry.

It is not easy for us who live in these dull times to understand the nature of that romantic feeling in the midst of which female beauty was enshrined. It was not love, though it sometimes degenerated into that passion. Far less was it the sentiment of platonic friendship. It belonged more to the imagination than the heart, and partook rather of the nature of devotion than of any earthly affection. Its object was always a goddess, and her worship consisted not in offerings of sighs and amatory songs, but of the trophies and valor and laurels plucked from the edge of danger. The religion of Rome was a religion of imagination; her business was war, and the spirit of chivalry was allied to both. The knights of the duke of Burgundy, when devoting themselves to a crusade, connected in their vow the names of God, the virgin mother and the ladies, adding even the peacock and the pheasant, birds which I know not for what reason were esteemed sacred. And we are told that Louis II, duke of Bourbon, when instituting the order of the golden shield, enjoined it upon his knights to honor above all the ladies, and not permit any one to slander them, "because from them, after God, comes all the honor that man can acquire."

The order of knighthood obtained distinguished honor under the feudal system, and was one of the most important institutions which kept alive the spirit of chivalry. The ceremony of receiving arms at the age of manhood is mentioned by Tacitus as a custom among the ancient Germans. It prevailed, indeed, among all the northern nations, and seems to have given rise to the institution of knighthood. It was considered at first purely military, and its honors were confirmed by a stroke of the sword, to intimate that this was the last insult that the person so dubbed could in honor receive. But during the time of the crusades, when ideas of romance, war and religion were so strangely blended in the minds of men, and when the institution was in its utmost vigor, it came to be considered as partaking more of a sacred than of a martial character. It was conferred by a priest, and the candidate for its honors, previous to investiture, passed whole nights in prayer in a church, received the sacrament, bathed, was clad in a white robe, his sword was consecrated and blessed and ever after at mass, when the gospel was read, the knight held his sword drawn, to signify his readiness to fight for the honor of his religion and in support of the gospel.

Tilts and tournaments were the occasions when the knight was in his glory, and the spirit of chivalry was raised to its highest pitch. Imagine a space to be enclosed and a brilliant circle of nobility and beauty collected around as spectators. Clad in steel and bearing shields emblazoned with the insignia of their respective mistresses, the combatants, mounted on their steeds, rush to the conflict of honor. There is a breathless suspense while the combat hangs doubtful. At length the thundering shout, "Honor to the brave!" proclaims the conqueror, who is led amidst the din of martial music to receive the prize from the fair hand of the delighted and envied object of his devotion. The moment was one of ecstacy, and the honor it conferred would be maintained by the successful champion at the sacrifice of an hundred lives were they in his power. Full of military ardor, elated by a high sense of personal dignity and urged by a romantic spirit of devotion and gallantry, he was ready for any bold adventure in which new honors might be gained. These sentiments characterized in some degree all the feudal nobility, but they were the life and soul of knighthood. A true knight was loyal, valiant, courteous and munificent, faithful to all his engagements, tacit or express, to friend or foe, ceremonious in his deportment, tenacious in the extreme of the point of honor, generous to a fault to a conquered enemy, profuse in his liberality, especially to minstrels, pilgrims and the poorer members of his own order, possessed of a lively sense of justice, but without much discrimination, and ardently indignant against wrong. But with these great and splendid virtues he was also, generally speaking, dissolute and profligate, haughty and overbearing, rash, vindictive and supremely devoted to the false glory of war. In short, his good and bad qualities may be seen at once, as portrayed in the character of Achilles and preserved in Homer's immortal verse. They have been condensed by the great master of the Roman lyre into two lines with more spirit than justice, for the darkness of the picture is not relieved by the slightest illumination of any good quality

> "" Impiger, iracundus, inexorabilis, acer,
> "Jura neget sibi nata, nihil non arroget armis."
> "Intrepid, fierce, of unforgiving rage,
> " Like Homer's Hero, let him spurn all laws,
> " And by the sword alone, assert his cause."

The spirit of chivalry is so exactly exhibited in an incident reported by Joinville that I shall close this sketch by repeating it. A poor knight asked, on his knees, of Henry the Liberal, count of Champagne, as much money as would serve to marry his two daughters. One Arthault de Nogent, a rich burgess, who was standing by, said to the petitioner, "My lord has already given away so much that he has nothing left." "Sir Villein!" said Henry, "you do not speak the truth, saying I have nothing left, when I have yourself. Here. sir knight, I give you this man and warrant you possession of him." The knight seized the burgess by the collar and did not allow him his liberty till he had paid him his ransom, five hundred pounds.

The influence of the love of war and a misguided zeal in religion, the two principal ingredients in the spirit of chivalry, display themselves in a series of extravagant undertakings, which began near the close of the eleventh century and continued to be prosecuted through the space of two centuries, and which, after the sacrifice, as has been computed of not less than six millions of human lives on the part of the Europeans alone, ended in nothing. I refer to the crusades.

An opinion, the origin of which though exceedingly curious and instructive it is not necessary on this occasion to trace, had taken possession of the public mind that the church of Rome possessed a fund of merit, constituted out of a surplusage of good and pious deeds on the part of her numerous saints and martyrs, which might be dispensed to such as, conscious of the defect of their own goodness, felt their need of supplementary aid. The redundancy on the one hand might supply the deficiency on the other. Penance was the appointed channel through which the communication was to be made. But as this was painful to the sufferer and useful to nobody, it was suggested that the payment of money or the performance of pilgrimage might answer the purpose. Under the influence of these strange and ridiculous opinions thousands were in the habit of visiting the holy sepulchre at Jerusalem. Early in the eleventh century this holy place fell into the possession of the Turks, a fierce people, who hated and despised the Christians and treated the pilgrims with every species of imposition and insult. The report of such indignities, spread abroad by these fanatics on their return home, kindled a flame of indignation and revenge all over Europe. About the same time the belief that the end of the world was at hand generally prevailed, and the Savior and Judge of the World, it was expected, would make his second appearance at Jerusalem. It would be a disgrace to His professed followers that on such an occasion the very place should be found in the possession of unbelieving Turks. Alexius Comnenus, emperor of Constantinople, implored at the same time the aid of the pope against the Turks, who threatened his capital. These causes combined their influence and excited the public mind to the highest pitch of enthusiasm. Peter the Hermit, his feet and head bare, his meager body wrapped in a coarse garment, mounted on an ass, passed from province to province rousing the people by his impassioned eloquence to the holy war. Miracles were wrought and prophecies uttered in abundance. The banner of the cross was unfurled, and whoever resorted to it was assured of fame, riches and power in the present world and eternal rewards in the next. The vicar of Christ called a council at Clermont. Forty thousand attended. "It is the will of God" was the universal shout. Barons, counts, knights, monks, priests, all orders, even women and children, prepared to march for the holy land. The 15th of August, 1096, had been fixed upon in the council for the departure of the crusaders. But the impatient multitude set out early in the spring. Peter the Hermit, and Gualtier *sans avoir*, or Walter the Pennyless, commanded. The promiscuous rabble took their course guided by a goose and a goat, which were thought to be inspired, along the banks of the Danube. Multitudes perished in the forests of Hungary; and the residue, to the number of 300,000, were overwhelmed by the Turkish arrows and their bones piled into a pyramid on the plains of Nice. These, however, afforded no fair specimen of the armies that followed, which were composed of the chivalry of the age and commanded by the most gallant and skillful leaders. In their first campaign a considerable part of lesser Asia and all Syria and Palestine submitted to their victorious arms.

But these countries were remote; an active and warlike enemy was on their borders. The Greeks, who first implored the assistance of their western brethren, became jealous of their success and turned against them. The crusaders themselves, drawn from so many different states, were not always united in their measures, and the conquests they had gained could not be held but at a vast expense of life and money. Yet such was the enthusiastic pertinacity with which the people of Europe adhered to their object that it was not abandoned till after five successive crusades, made at intervals through the course of two hundred years.

A comparison between the different institutions which we have just been in a very cursory manner reviewing, could we pursue it into details, would afford abundant matter of amusing and instructive speculation. Though so exceedingly different and even opposite in their external features, they were pervaded by the same spirit and sprung from the same original cast of character. The virtues and vices of the monk and of the knight, however differently modified by circumstances, were shoots of the same stock. Simon the Stylite seems, at first view, a very different sort of being from the lion-hearted Richard; and he would probably be thought extremely fanciful who should attempt to have a resemblance between the flagellants and the followers of Godfrey of Bouillon. Yet there is a resemblance. The same persevering temper which under the influence of superstition, directed in a particular way, would enable a man to remain for upwards of thirty years, night and day, summer and winter, on the top of a pillar till he stiffened into a skeleton, or that, if prompted by the sympathetic action of enthusiasm upon a multitude, would lead them to whip each other to death, by way of penance, would, under the guidance of martial feelings, induce them to march half round the globe to find an enemy with whom they might fight for tombs and relics. The shield and spear of the knight and the altars of the monastery afforded protection to the suppliant on the same principle. The devotion which paid homage to the Virgin Mary was substantially the same with that which adored those earthly goddesses who were to be found in every village. If monachism had its legends, chivalry had its romances, and the same state of mind which could see a meritorious efficacy in penance and pilgrimage could recognize the judgment of God in the issue of a single combat. Whether the enthusiasm of chivalry or the superstition of monachism was the least corrupting to public morals it would be difficult to determine. The radical vice of the latter was fraud, of the former lawless force. The one filled the church with legends, relics and indulgences; the other deposited in the very foundations of the state the principles of a military aristocracy. The reformation of Luther and his coadjutors has not yet delivered religion from the corruptions of superstition, and notwithstanding the repeated struggles of patriotism, aided by the progressive influence of science and civilization, the liberties of Europe still continue to languish under the hateful relics of feudal oppression. The connection of chivalry with religion, or the mutual penetration, rather, of each system by the other completed the corruption of both. Chivalry employed the force of the sword, the only logic with which it was acquainted, to evince the truth of religion, and religion baptized the votaries of chivalry in the blood of heretics. And unhappily for the interests of truth, the voice of modern history, instead of making an impartial distribution of blame between the two, has heaped it all on the head of religion, whereas the massacres which have been charged to her account were owing to that native thirst for blood which characterized from the first the barbarians of the north, and which was afterwards ennobled by the institutions of chivalry and sanctioned by a gloomy superstition which had nothing of Christianity but the name. It is happy for us that a wide ocean and the revolution of '76 have in a great degree separated us from the influence of feudal rights and superstitious institutions, and it would be happier still were the separation more complete. The absurd practice of duelling and the prevailing taste for intoxicating liquors proclaim at once our shame and our descent, and although the relics of saints and pilgrimages to the holy land never had any value among us, yet there are other things deemed pious which must be supplantd by knowledge and moral virtue before we can truly boast of a complete deliverance from the lingering traces of superstition. On the other hand, it is but just to observe that while we have separated ourselves from the mass of those evils in church and state which grew out of the feudal system and a corrupt hierarchy in the old world, it is exceedingly unfair that the odium which is justly due to them should be transferred to things of a directly opposite nature among us, though some, to serve their purpose, should choose to call them by the same name. Why should Protestants, for instance, be censured for what belongs to the church of Rome? Why should the detestation which is due to a system of worldly domination, under the name of an established religion, be inflicted upon religion itself without an establishment? Why should the spirit of the reformation, to which we are indebted for our civil as well as our religious liberties, be branded with the odious name of that tyranny which it abhors? Why should that charity which gives the bible to the poor be confounded with its antagonist principle that would lock up the sacred volume from all but the clergy? Why involve in indiscriminate condemnation that devotion which springs from light, loves the light and seeks to diffuse the light with that which boasts of ignorance as its mother? Why should the name of priests, which has been rendered odious by the practice of infidels ministering at the altars of a secularized hierarchy, be affixed to those who have protested against that hierarchy and abjured all its abominations? The evils of a feudal aristocracy have been purged from our civil polity, and we have wisely left the prejudices which they produced along with them. Why then should we listen to alarmists in religion who have imported prejudices from Europe, or who love to inflame them when imported by others, which, though not unfounded in that part of the world, have no object—no, not the shadow of the shade of an object here?

INDIANA HISTORICAL SOCIETY PUBLICATIONS

VOLUME I NUMBER IV

THE NATIONAL DECLINE
OF THE
MIAMI INDIANS

BY

JOHN B. DILLON

(Delivered before the Society May 23, 1848)

INDIANAPOLIS
THE BOWEN-MERRILL COMPANY
1897

THE NATIONAL DECLINE OF THE MIAMI INDIANS.

In the northern part of the state of Indiana on the 28th of November, 1840, the chiefs and the head men of the Miami nation were holding a council with two commissioners of the government of the United States. The council ground was at the forks of the river Wabash. A treaty—it was the thirteenth treaty between the Miamies and the United States—was, with the usual formality, laid before the red men. The first article of that treaty, which was cautiously explained in the presence of the Indians by skillful interpreters, was in these words:

"The Miami tribe of Indians do hereby cede to the United States all that tract of land on the south side of the Wabash river not heretofore ceded, and commonly known as the 'residue of the Big Reserve'—*being all of their remaining lands in Indiana.*"

For different reasons, and with various emotions, twenty chiefs and headmen, some willingly, but others reluctantly, signed the treaty; and thus the last remnant of the National Domain of the Miamies passed from them forever.

If we look backward, through a period of more than one hundred and fifty years, to the dawning of civilization in the west, at every point where a ray of light illumines the condition of the Miami Indians, we shall behold mournful evidences of the downward progress of a great aboriginal nation, and we shall learn, too, something of the slow and sad means by which a vast and beautiful region has been reclaimed from a state of barbarism.

According to the best traditional authorities, the dominion of the Miami confederacy extended, for a long period of time, over that part of the state of Ohio which lies west of the Scioto river—over the whole of Indiana—over the southern part of Michigan—and over that part of the state of Illinois which lies southeast of the Fox river and the river Illinois. The Miamies proper, whose old national name was Twightwess, formed the eastern and most powerful branch of this confederacy. They have preserved no tradition of their migration as a tribe, from one country to another. The great extent of the territory which was once claimed by them is some evidence of the degree of national importance which they formerly maintained among the Indian tribes of North America, but neither the names nor the numbers of the several kindred tribes of the ancient Miami confederacy can now be stated with accuracy. Within the boundaries of their territory the arms of hostile nations have clashed on many a battle field—barbarism opposed the advance of civilization—truth struggled against error—creed rose in hostility against creed—race fought against race—and over the field of conflict, for more than a hundred years, the proud banners of monarchy floated until at last they were struck down by the strong arms of free men. In thirty hostile expeditions, warriors of the white race have carried their desolating arms into the territory which was claimed by the Miamies. Twenty battle fields, and the ashes of fifty Indian towns are among the memorials of the triumphs of civilized man in this region.

In the early part of the eighteenth century, and perhaps for a long period before that time, the Miamies had villages at various suitable places within the boundaries of their large territory. Some of these villages were found on the banks of the Scioto—a few were situated in the country about the head waters of the Great Miami—some stood on the banks of the river Maumee—others on the St. Joseph of Lake Michigan—and many were founded on the borders of the Wabash and on some of the principal tributaries of that river. The villages which stood on the banks of the St. Joseph of Lake Michigan, those which lay about the head waters of the Maumee, and those which stood on the borders of the river Wabash, were visited by Catholic missionaries and French fur traders before the middle of the eighteenth century, but the several periods at which the French *founded settlements* at or near the principal Miami villages can not now be told with any degree of certainty. Neither the occasional presence of missionaries nor the periodical visits of fur traders, nor the building of rude temporary trading posts, can be regarded as the founding of permanent civilized settlements.

In 1672 the Indians who resided in the country about the southern shores of Lake Michigan were visited by the missionaries Allouez and Dablon, who opened the way for several subsequent but almost fruitless attempts to establish missions within the territory of the Miamies. Among the missionaries who visited this territory between the years 1672 and 1712 were Ribourde, Mambre, Hennepin, Marquette, Pinet, Bineteau, Joliet, Rasles, Periet, Bergier, Mermet, Marest, Gravier, DeVille and Chardon. The history of the missionary labors of these men is a record of perseverance, disappointment and suffering. The efforts of Christian missionaries have been often embarrassed and sometimes wholly paralyzed by obstacles which were based upon the adverse religious tenets and the political stratagems of rival Christian nations. For a period of one hundred and fifty years, Protestant England and Catholic France were rivals in the great works of acquiring territory, planting colonies and establishing trade among the Indian tribes of North America.

Of the missionaries of these two nations few were free from the influence of the hostile rivalry which was brought into action and maintained by their respective governments.

In the year 1687 Governor Dongan, an officer of the English government, met the Five Nations in council at Albany, and made to them a speech in which he said: "My opinion is, that the [Indian] brethren should send messengers to the Utawawas, Twightwees [or Miamies], and the farther Indians, and to send back, likewise, some of the prisoners of these nations, if you have any left, to bury the hatchet, and to make a covenant chain, *that they may put away all the French that are among them*, and that you will open a path for them this way * * * that, by that means, they may come hither freely, where they may have everything cheaper than among the French. * * * There was no advice or proposition that I made to the [Indian] brethren all the time that the priest lived at Onondaga, but what he wrote to Canada, as I found by one of his letters which he gave to an Indian to carry to Canada, but which was brought hither; therefore, I desire the brethren not to receive him or any *French* priest any more, having sent for *English* priests with whom you may be supplied to your content."

Among a number of reasons which were assigned for the planting of British colonies in New England there was one which declared that it would "be a service unto the church of great consequence to carry the gospel into those parts of the world and raise a bulwark against the kingdom of anti-Christ, which the Jesuits labor to rear up in all parts of the world."

The Reverend Cotton Mather, in his Ecclesiastical History of New England, says that in the year 1696 an Indian chief informed a Christian minister of Boston that the French, while instructing the Indians in the Christian religion, told them that the Savior was of the French nation; "that they were the English who had murdered him, and that, whereas he rose from the dead and went up to the heavens, all that would recommend themselves unto his favor must revenge his quarrel upon the English.''

Thus, in North America, throughout a long period, between the early colonists of England and the early colonists of France there was no friendly intercourse; there was no long season of peace. Ever eager to advance the interests of their respective governments, small and weak branches of Christian nations, with antagonistic creeds, hot animosities, bitter revilings and deadly warfare, were agitating and destroying one another. The Indians heard and saw and felt these things, and listened doubtingly to the instructions of the few pious men who told them that the truths of the Christian religion were revealed to the world by the son of the only true God, to establish on earth "peace and good-will towards men.''

By means of the persevering efforts of missionaries, and by the enterprise of a few adventurous traders, pacific relations and a small traffic were established between the Miamies and the French colonists of Canada before the close of the seventeenth century. The governor-general of Canada laid before the English colonial authorities at Albany in 1684 a remonstrance, in which it was stated that the Five Nations (between whom and the English a league then existed) were interfering with the rights and property of French traders among the remote western Indian tribes. The Five Nations, when they were informed of this charge, replied by saying that their enemies were furnished with arms and ammunition by French traders. Soon afterwards the governor-general of Canada held a council with a large number of Indians of the Five Nations. He told them that they, the Senecas, Cayugas, Onondagas, Oneidas and Mohawks, had abused and robbed French traders who were passing to the west. Grangula, an Onondaga chief, in replying to the charge said:

"We plundered none of the French but those that carried guns, powder and balls to the Twightwees [Miamies] and the Chictaghicks, because those arms might have cost us our lives. * * * We knock the Twightwees and the Chictaghicks on the head because they had cut down the trees of peace, which were the limits of our country. They have hunted beaver on our lands. They have acted contrary to the custom of all Indians, for they left none of the beavers alive; they killed both male and female. * * * We have done less than either the English or the French, that have usurped the lands of so many Indian nations and chased them from their own country."

After the discovery by La Salle of the mouth of the river Mississippi, the government of France began to encourage a project of establishing a line of trading posts and missionary stations, in the country lying west of the Allegheny mountains, from Canada to the Gulf of Mexico; and this project was supported by France with considerable perseverance, but with only partial success, for a period of about seventy-five years. During a longer period the zealous labors of French missionaries among the Indian tribes of the west were continued, amid many obstacles, without producing much general and permanent improvement of the condition of the aborigines.

The missionary Hennepin visited some of the tribes of the Miami confederacy in 1680:

"There are," says Hennepin, "many obstacles that hinder the conversion of the savages, but in general the difficulty proceeds from the indifferency they have to everything. When one speaks to them of the creation of the world and of the mysteries of the Christian religion they say we have reason, and they applaud in general all that we say on the great affair of our salvation. They would think themselves guilty of a great incivility if they should show the least suspicion or incredulity in respect of what is proposed. But, after having approved all the discourses upon these matters, they pretend likewise on their side that we ought to pay all possible deference to the relations and reasonings that they may make on their part, and when we make answer that what they tell us is false, they reply that they have acquiesced to all that we said, and that it is a want of judgment to interrupt a man that speaks and to tell him that he advances a false proposition; all that you have taught touching those of your country is as you say—but it is not the same to us, who are of another nation, and inhabit the lands which are on this side the great lake. The second obstacle which hinders their conversion proceeds from their great superstition."

The third obstacle, says the same missionary, "consists in this, that they are not fixed to a place," and "the traders who deal commonly with the savages with a design to gain by their traffic are likewise another obstacle. * * * They think of nothing but cheating and lying to become rich in a short time. They use all manner of stratagems to get the furs of the savages cheap. They make use of lies and cheats to gain double if they can. This, without doubt, causes an aversion against a religion which they see accompanied, by the professors of it, with so many lies and cheats."

"The Illinois," says Hennepin, "will readily suffer us to baptize their children, and would not refuse it themselves but they are incapable of any previous instruction concerning the truths of the gospel, and the efficacy of the sacraments. Would I follow the example of some other missionaries I could have boasted of many conversions, for I might easily have baptized all those nations, and then say (as I am afraid they do without any ground), that I had converted them.

* * * Our ancient missionaries of Canada, and those that succeeded them in that work, have always given it for

their opinion, as I now own it is mine, that the way to succeed in converting the barbarians is to endeavor to make them men before we go about to make them Christians. * * * America is no place to go out of a desire to suffer martyrdom, taking the word in a theological sense. The savages never put any Christian to death on the score of his religion. They leave everybody at liberty in belief. They like the outward ceremonies of our church; but no more. * * * They do not kill people but in particular quarrels, or when they are brutish, or drunk, or in revenge, or infatuated with a dream, or some extravagant vision. They are incapable of taking away any person's life out of hatred to his religion."

The Miamies, or Twightwees, were visited by missionaries before the year 1670, and Allouez, it is said, founded the principal mission to these Indians on the banks of St. Joseph of Lake Michigan. An account of the religious exercises which were observed by the early missionaries among the Illinois Indians is related in a letter written by P. Gabriel Marest, at Kaskaskia, on the 9th of November, 1712. That missionary said: "The following is the order we observe each day in our missions. Early in the morning we assemble the catechumens at the church, where they have prayers; they receive instructions and chant some canticles. When they have retired mass is said, at which all the Christians assist, the men placed at one side and the women at the other; then they have prayers, which are followed by giving them a homily, after which each one goes to his labor. We then spend our time in visiting the sick to give them necessary remedies, to instruct them and to console those who are laboring under any affliction. After noon the catechising is held, at which all are present, Christians and catechumens, men and children, young and old; and where each, without distinction of rank or age, answers the questions put by the missionary. As these people have no books and are naturally indolent, they would shortly forget the principles of religion if the remembrance of them was not recalled by these almost continual instructions. In the evening all assemble again at the church to listen to the instructions which are given, to have prayers, and to sing some hymns. * * * These hymns are their best instructions, which they retain the more easily, since the words are set to airs with which they are acquainted and which please them."

The river St. Joseph of Lake Michigan was called the river of the Miamies in 1679, in which year La Salle built a fort or trading post on its banks and near the shore of the lake. The principal station in the mission of St. Joseph, which was founded for the instruction of the Pottawattamies and Miamies, was established on the banks of this river; and, from the foundation of this mission, the river bore the name of the St. Joseph of Lake Michigan.

The missionary Hennepin gives the following account of the building of the first French post within the country of the Miamies: "Just at the mouth of the river Miamies there was an eminence with a kind of a platform naturally fortified; it was pretty high and steep, of a triangular form, defended on two sides by the river, and on the third by a deep ditch which the fall of the waters had made. We felled the trees that were on the top of that hill and cleared the same from bushes for about two musket-shot; we then began to build a redoubt forty foot by eighty, with great square pieces of timber laid one upon another, and prepared a great number of stakes of about twenty-five feet long, to drive into the ground to make our fort the more inaccessible on the river sides. We employed the whole month of November [1679] about the work, which was very hard, though we had no other food but the bears' flesh our savage killed. These beasts are very common in that place because of the great quantity of grapes they find there, but their flesh being too fat and luscious our men began to weary of it, and desired leave to go a hunting to kill some wild goats [or deer]. M. La Salle denied that liberty, which caused some murmurs among them, and it was but unwillingly that they continued their work. This, together with the approach of the winter, and the apprehension M. La Salle had that his ship was lost, made him very melancholy, though he concealed it as much as he could. We had made a cabin wherein we performed divine service every Sunday, and Father Gabriel and I, who preached alternately, took care to take such texts as were suitable to our present circumstances and fit to inspire us with courage, concord and brotherly love. Our exhortations produced a very good effect and hindered the men from deserting, as they designed. We sounded in the meantime the mouth of the river, and having found a sand on which our ship might strike, we fixed two great posts therein, to which we fastened bears' skins, as so many buoys to direct the course of our ship through the channel she ought to pass; and, for a greater precaution, two men were sent back to Missilimakinak, to wait there till the return of our ship and serve as pilots. * * * The fort was at last perfected and called Fort Miamis."

In 1711, the missionary Chardon, who was "full of zeal and who had a rare talent for acquiring languages," had his station on the river St. Joseph, among the Pottawattamie and Miami Indians.

In 1721, about fifty years after the time that Allouez and Dablon traversed the country lying on the southern shores of Lake Michigan, Charlevoix visited a trading post on the river St. Joseph, where there was a missionary station. In a letter dated "River St. Joseph, August 16, 1721," Charlevoix says—"It was eight days yesterday since I arrived at this post, where we have a mission, and where there is a com-

mandant with a small garrison. The commandant's house, which is but a sorry one, is called the fort, from its being surrounded with an indifferent pallisado, which is pretty near the case in all the rest. * * * We have here two villages of Indians, one of the Miamies and the other of the Pottawattamies, both of them mostly Christians; but as they have been for a long time without any pastors, the missionary who has lately been sent them will have no small difficulty in bringing them back to the exercise of their religion. *
* * Several Indians of the two nations settled upon this river are just returned from the English colonies, whither they had been to sell their furs, and from whence they have brought back in return a great quantity of spirituous liquors. The distribution of it is made in the *usual manner;* that is to say, a certain number of persons have daily delivered to each of them *a quantity sufficient to get drunk with*, so that the whole has been drank up in eight days. They began to drink in both villages as soon as the sun was down, and every night the fields echoed with the most hideous howlings. One would have thought that a gang of devils had broke loose from hell, or that the two towns had been cutting one another's throats."

More than one hundred years have passed away after Charlevoix wrote this letter, yet spirituous liquors and riotous drunkenness, maintaining their power among the passing generations of the aboriginal race of North America, were still opposing and baffling the labors of Protestant and Catholic missionaries, not only at Indian towns on the banks of the St. Joseph, but at every Indian village throughout the northwestern territory of the United States.

Sebastian Rasles, a missionary, in a letter which is dated "12th October, 1723," says—"It is a blessing to the Illinois that they are so far distant from Quebec, because it renders it impossible to transport to them the 'fire water' as it is carried to others. This drink among the Indians is the greatest obstacle to Christianity, and the source of an infinite number of their most shocking crimes. We know that they never purchase it but to plunge into the most furious intoxication; and the riots and sad deaths of which we were each day the witnesses ought to outweigh the gain which can be made by the trade in a liquor so fatal."

Another missionary, Vivier, in a letter dated "at Illinois, the 17th of November, 1750," says—"We have three stations in this part of the world, one of Indians, one of French, and a third composed partly of French and partly of Indians. The first contains more than six hundred Illinois, all baptized, with the exception of five or six, but the 'fire water' which is sold to them by the French, and especially by the soldiers, in spite of the reiterated prohibitions on the part of the king, and that which is sometimes distributed to them under pretext of maintaining them in our interest, has ruined that mission and caused the greater part of its converts to abandon our holy religion. The Indians, and especially the Illinois, who at other times are the gentlest and most tractable of men, become, when intoxicated, frantic and brutally ferocious. Then they attack each other with their knives, inflicting terrible wounds. Some have lost their ears, and others a part of the nose in these tragical scenes."

The Miamies were visited in 1751 by Christopher Gist, who was an agent of the Ohio company. In his journal of that visit he says: "The Twightwees (Miamies) are a very numerous people, consisting of many different tribes under the same form of government. Each tribe has a particular chief or king, one of whom is chosen indifferently out of any tribe to rule the whole nation, and is vested with greater authority than any of the others. They are accounted the most powerful nation to the westward of the English settlements, and much superior to the Six Nations, with whom they are now in

amity. They formerly lived on the farther side of the Wa
bash, and were in the French interests. They have now re
volted from them and have left their former habitations fo
the sake of trading with the English." The "revolted" Mi
amics, however, renewed their friendship and intercourse wit
the French in 1753.

In 1754, George Croghan, a British officer in the India
department, visited some of the western tribes. The follow
ing passages are taken from his journal: "On the 14th c
January we set off to Logstown, where we found the *Indian
all drunk.*" "January 16th the *Indians were all drunk.*"
"From the 16th to the 26th we could do nothing, the *Indian
being all drunk.*" In 1765, the Miami nation or confederac
was composed of four tribes whose total number of warrior
was estimated at one thousand and fifty men. Of this num
ber there were two hundred and fifty Twightwees, three hun
dred Weas or Ouiatenons, three hundred Piankeshaws and tw
hundred Shockeys. The principal villages of the Twightwee
were situated on the head waters of the Maumee river, at o
near the site of the town of Ft. Wayne. The larger We
villages were found near the banks of the Wabash, in th
vicinity of Ouiatenon, and the Shockeys and Piankeshaw
lived on the banks of the Vermillion river, and on the rive
Wabash between Vincennes and Ouiatenon. At differen
periods branches of Pottawattamies, Shawnees, Delaware
and Kickapoos were permitted to enter and reside at variou
places within the boundary of the large territory which wa
claimed by the Miamies. On the 15th of April, 1784
Thomas J. Dalton held a council with the Piankeshaws tribe
of the Miamies at Vincennes. At the close of the counci
the principal Piankeshaw chief said: "This being the day o
Joy to the Wabash Indians we beg a little drop of your milk
(meaning rum) to let our warriors see it came from your owr
breast. We were born and raised in the woods. We neve

could learn to make rum. God has made the white flesh masters of the world. They make everything, and we all love rum."

In a letter which was written at Vincennes on the 16th of June, 1793, and addressed to Winthrop Sargent, secretary of the territory of the United States northwest of the river Ohio the writer said:

"There are parties of Indians continually coming to and going from this place, where they are furnished with liquor for their skins in such quantities as they are able to pay for— which disturbs much the good order and peace of the village. They remain here eight or ten days, which is one continual round of drunkenness and disorder. * * * The laws are worse executed at this place than at any other in the territory. There are but few of the inhabitants of this village that do not violate that part of the law which prohibits the sale of spirituous liquors to Indians."

In the summer of 1796 a distinguished traveler and author, Constantine Francis Volney, went to Vincennes, partly to observe at his leisure the Indian tribes in that quarter. In one of his works this traveler says: "My stay at Vincennes afforded me some knowledge of the Indians who were assembled to barter away the produce of their red hunt. There were four or five hundred of them, men, women and children of various tribes, as the Weas, Peorias, Sawkies, Piankeshaws and Miamies. * * * The men and women roamed all day about the town merely to get rum, for which they eagerly exchanged their peltry, their toys, their clothes, and at length, when they had parted with their all, they offered their prayers and entreaties, never ceasing to drink until they had lost their senses. Hence arise ridiculous scenes. They will hold the cup with both hands like monkeys, burst into unmeaning laughter and gargle their beloved cup, to enjoy the taste of it the longer. They will hand about the liquor with clamorous invitations, bawl aloud to each other though close together, seize their wives and pour the liquor down their throats, and, in short, display all the freaks of vulgar drunkenness. Sometimes tragical scenes ensue. They become mad or stupid and fall in the dust or mud to lie a senseless log till the next day. We found them in the streets by dozens in the morning, wallowing in the filth with the pigs. * * * I at first conceived the design of spending a few months among them, as I had done among the Bedouins, but I was satisfied with this sample."

On the 5th of November, 1805, Governor Harrison, of the Indiana territory, addressed to Governor Tiffin, of Ohio, a letter from which the following passage is copied: "Conformably to the request of the legislature of this territory, I have the honor to enclose herewith a law passed at the late session, entitled 'An act to prohibit the giving or selling of intoxicating liquor to Indians.' Your excellency will observe that the law is not to take effect until a similar one is passed by the states of Kentucky and Ohio and the territories of Louisiana and Michigan. The necessity of this provision arose from the great inconvenience which the citizens who reside on the frontiers of this territory would suffer if the prohibition to sell liquor to Indians did not extend to their neighbors as well as to themselves. With regard to the propriety of the prohibition it is I presume unnecessary that I should make a single remark. The dreadful effects which have been produced among our Indian neighbors, *by the immense quantities of ardent spirits which have been poured in upon them by our citizens*, have long been known and lamented by every friend of humanity."

In the message addressed to the Indiana territorial legislature in 1806, Governor Harrison said: "It is true that the general government has passed laws for fulfilling not only the stipulations contained in our treaties (with the Indians) but also those sublimer duties which a just sense of our prosperity and their wretchedness seemed to impose. The laws of the territory provide also the same punishment for offenses committed against Indians as against white men. *Experience, however, shows that there is a wide difference in the execution of those laws. The Indian always suffers and the white man never.* This partiality has not escaped their penetration and has afforded them an opportunity of making the proudest comparisons between their observance of treaties and that of their boasted superiors."

A letter dated "May 3d, 1814," written by an officer of the general government to a gentleman who held a high official station, contains the following remarkable passages: "The idea of a treaty will fix the attention of the Indian and will keep them quiet for the present. I have (caused) the information of the treaty (with this view) to be spread far and wide in the Indian country; in order to insure a general attendance of the remote tribes, two months notice will be requisite. I have such channels of intelligence established through the Indians that nothing of importance can be going forward without my knowledge. They are so much distracted and divided now that no scheme of hostility against us could be carried into effect. With the view of increasing their wants and distresses and thereby rendering them more harmless, I have permitted all the traders to sell as much liquor as they thought proper. This in a political point of view, at this time, is of more effect than many would suppose."

The treaty referred to in this extract was concluded at Greenville, in July, 1814. The Miamies, who were present, expressed with great earnestness a wish to remain neutral in the war which was then going on between the United States and Great Britain, but one of the commissioners of the United States government said to them: "You have now come forward to take us by the hand; we are equally anxious and willing to take you by the hand, but you must take up the tomahawk and with us strike our enemies. Then your great father, the President, will forgive the past."

I will read two short extracts from the official journal of the commissioners at this treaty: "July 16th, 1814—The council adjourned after giving instructions to the agent to furnish the Indians with whisky to whet their hatchets, etc." "July 18th, 1814—The Indians having received a quantity of whisky in order to sharpen their hatchets, as they expected, were unfit for any business this day."

The national character and the condition of the Miamies in 1817 were faithfully described in a letter written by Benjamin F. Stickney, an Indian agent who resided among them. This agent, writing at Fort Wayne on the 27th of August, 1817, said: "The civilization of the Indian is not a new subject to me. I have been between five and six years in the habit of daily and hourly intercourse with the Indians northwest of the Ohio, and the great question of the practicability of civilizing them ever before me. * * * That I might have an opportunity of casting in my mite to the bettering the condition of these uncultivated human beings and the pleasure of observing the change that might be produced upon them was the principal inducement to my surrendering the comforts of civilized society. Upon my entering upon my duties I soon found that my speculative opinions were not reducible to practice. What I had viewed at a distance as flying clouds, proved on my nearer approach to be impassable mountains. * * * It will be proper for me to be more particular and give you something of my ideas of the nature and extent of the obstacles to be met.

"First. The great, and I fear, insurmountable obstacle, is the insatiable thirst for intoxicating liquors that appears to be born with all the yellow skin inhabitants of America. And *the thirst for gain* of the citizens of the United States appears to be capable of eluding all the vigilance of government to stop the distribution of liquor among them. * * * If the whites can not be restrained from furnishing them with spirituous liquors nor they from the use of them, I fear all other efforts to extend to them the benefits of civilization will prove fruitless. The knowledge of letters serves as the means of entering into secret arrangements with the whites to supply the means of their own destruction; and within the limits of my intercourse, *the principal use of the knowledge of letters or civilized language has been to obtain liquor for themselves and others.* This has made it proverbial among them that the knowledge of white people makes very bad Indians.

"Secondly. The general aversion to the habits, manners, customs and dress of civilized people; and in many cases an Indian is an object of jealousy for being acquainted with the civilized language, and it is made use of as a subject of reproach against him.

"Thirdly. General indolence, connected with the firm conviction that the life of the civilized man is that of slavery—and that savage life is manhood, ease and independence—from which proceeds the opinion among them that to say a white man is equal to an Indian is the highest compliment that can be paid him.

"Fourthly. The unfavorable light in which they view the citizens of the United States—believing that their minds are so much occupied in trade and speculation that they never act from any other motive—and that they universally lie to and cheat them. Their opinion of the government of the United States is in some degrees more favorable, but secretly they view all white people as their enemies and are extremely suspicious of anything coming from them, and if they had the power they would extirpate, or at least drive them all from the continent.

"Fifthly. Their extreme fondness for their children, and fear of their being absent from their sight You request to be informed in relation to their numbers and manner of living, and whether they have had any schools or missionaries among them. All the Miamies and Eel River Miamies are under my charge and about one thousand four hundred in number, and there are something more than two thousand Pottawattamies come within my agency. The proportion of children can not be ascertained, but it is much less than among the white inhabitants of the United States. They have had no schools among them nor missionaries since the time of the French Jesuits. They have places that are commonly called villages, but perhaps not correctly, as they have no uniform place of residence. During the fall, winter and part of the spring, they are scattered in the woods hunting. The respective bands assemble together in the spring at their several ordinary places of resort, where some have rude cabins made of small logs covered with bark, but more commonly, some poles stuck in the ground and tied together with pliant stripes of bark, and covered with large sheets of bark or a kind of mat made of flags. Near those places of resort they plant some corn. There are eleven of those places of resort called villages within my agency. The Miamies and Eel River Miamies reside principally on the Wabash, Mississinewa and Eel rivers and the head of the White river. The Pottawattamies reside on the Tippecanoe, Kankakee, Iroquois, Yellow river, St. Joseph and Iroquois of Lake Michigan, the Elkhart, Miami of the Lake, the St. Joseph emptying into it and the St. Mary's river.

"Inasmuch as you contemplate the introduction of the Christian religion through the medium of letters you will wish to know something of their present religion. They all believe in a God as Creator and Governor, but have no idea of His will being communicated to man except as it appears in the creation, or as it appears occasionally from His providential government. Some of them have been told of the communications having been made to the white people a long time since—and that it is written and printed—but they have neither conception or belief in relation to it. Their belief in relation to a future existence is a kind of transubstantiation—a removal from this existence to one more happy, with similar appetites and enjoyments. They talk of a Bad Spirit, but never express any apprehension of his troubling them in their future existence. They pay respect to the religious opinions of others and appear to conceive that the same is due theirs in return. There is no people who appear to be more firmly fixed in their theological faith. The Jesuits made some impression on a few of them with the external form of their religion but taught them no science."

Now, by the aid of various authentic documents, I have traced faintly the outlines of the history of the Miami Indians backwards from the present time through a period of one hundred and fifty years. Yet even these faint outlines form a long and mournful picture of ignorance, superstition, war, barbarity and the most debasing intemperance. There are some sincere and good men, who, successfully entering the field of missionary labor, endeavored to establish among these Indians the foundation of civilization and the doctrine of Christianity. But these philanthropists were few in number—with an imperfect knowledge of the language of the Miamies—without schools, without homes, often placing their lives in peril, and in some instances falling the victims of savage violence. They were, in the west, the pioneers in the conflict between barbarism and civilization. At the present day a few small, mixed and miserable bands constitute the remnant of the once powerful Miami nation. Their ignorance, their errors, their misfortune and devices which they learned from the white race still cling to them with unabated power to degrade and destroy. Thus shrouded in darkness, with the lights of civilization and religion beaming around them, the last fragments of one of the most powerful aboriginal nations of North America are passing away from the earth forever. The arms of the Miamies are now powerless. Their last lingering bands are slowly tottering towards the grave of their nation. Sometimes they pause on their way and turn their faces to the east, to cast their latest reproaches upon their conquerors. Listen! Do they not say to us: ' Men of the white race, you are faithless. You drive us onward towards the setting sun. We shall go down in the west like him. He will rise again, but we shall be seen no more upon the earth. Our nation is dying and it received its death wounds from you. You came to our land in weakness many years ago when we were strong. You promised to enlighten our minds. You promised to make us acquainted with the arts of civilized life. You promised to establish schools among us. You promised to teach us a pure and holy religion. When you became strong you told us that we were your children. And you taught us to call you our father. You spoke of peace on earth and good-will to men, but you made war on one another. How could we believe your words? We gave you leave to establish trading posts in our country. And you brought your fire-water to your posts, and with that fire-water you made those places the scenes of drunkenness, lying, theft, profanity, debauchery and murder. You did those things for the love of gold. You promised us blessings—they never came to us, but you taught us vices and crimes of which we were ignorant until you became our instructors. You have used your superior knowledge to deceive and debase our nation. You have poured your fire-water over our whole land. You have used your superior strength to destroy us. You have violated the treaties which you have made with us. You entered our country by force; you took possession of our lands; you told your warriors to strike us hard; you drove us from our homes; you killed our men and women; you destroyed our scanty crops of corn that we might starve; you gave our villages to the flames that we might be homeless. You have encouraged jealousies, divisions and enmities between our different tribes that we might be powerless. You told us that you were our protectors. Our protectors! When or where did your strong arm ever strike a white oppressor of the Indian race? Behold us now! Where are the lands of our nation? Where is our nation? Where are our homes? Where is the civilization that you promised to bring to us, to enlighten our benighted minds? Where are the arts you promised to teach us? Where are the schools that you promised to establish among us? Where is that holy religion of which you told us? Oh! You are a strong, false, false race." Have civilized nations nothing to say in reply to such reproachful language? Yes. The philanthropist of the white race might say to the departing red man: "We found you in a state of ignorance and barbarism. We sent good men among you to enlighten your minds and to teach you the purifying doctrines of the Christian religion. You disregarded their instruction. We warned you constantly of the evils which your love of the fire-water would bring upon your nation. You neglected our warning and you madly continued to indulge your appetite for the liquid poison. We tried to establish agriculture and other useful arts among you, but you turned away from the plow and the school and the missionary station to roam in the forests, or to revel in drunkenness, or to seek the war path. We carried many of your race to our colleges and universities where they were educated in the knowledge of the white people, but, with few exceptions, they returned to the wilderness and relapsed into the customs of their tribe. We have tried many expedients to save your nation from ruin. We gave you warning after warning of the fate which awaited you if you continued to neglect our advice. We tried to treat you with forbearance, moderation and humanity even when your tomahawks and scalping knives were red with the blood of our murdered men, women and children. From generation to generation, with unyielding and unreasonable obstinacy, you stood in the way of advancing civilization and Christianity, and when neither our kindness, nor our entreaties, nor our threats were sufficiently powerful to induce you to move, we were compelled in sorrow to force you from your position by the might of a strong arm. The land which you once claimed was not made to remain forever a wilderness, to be used only as a vast hunting ground for the race of red men."

INDIANA HISTORICAL SOCIETY PUBLICATIONS

VOLUME I NUMBER V

EARLY HISTORY OF INDIANAPOLIS AND CENTRAL INDIANA

BY

NATHANIEL BOLTON

INDIANAPOLIS
THE BOWEN-MERRILL COMPANY
1897

A LECTURE

DELIVERED BEFORE THE

INDIANA HISTORICAL SOCIETY

ON THE

EARLY HISTORY OF INDIANAPOLIS

AND

CENTRAL INDIANA

AT THE HALL OF THE HOUSE OF REPRESENTATIVES ON MONDAY EVENING
THE 31ST OF JANUARY, 1853

BY NATHANIEL BOLTON
STATE LIBRARIAN

INDIANAPOLIS
AUSTIN H. BROWN, PRINTER
1853

PREFACE.

The Indiana legislature having granted the use of the hall of the house of representatives to the Indiana Historical Society for the delivery of a lecture on the Early History of Indianapolis and Central Indiana, for the first ten years after their settlement by the whites, from 1820 to 1830, by N. Bolton, Esq. state librarian, the Hon. Isaac Blackford, by request, took his seat as president of the society. The large hall was filled to overflowing with ladies and gentlemen. At the conclusion of the lecture, on motion of William J. Brown, Esq., a resolution was unanimously adopted by those present requesting a copy for publication, which, having been procured, will be found in the succeeding pages. It was intended by Mr. Bolton as an introduction to a festival of the old settlers of Indianapolis and central Indiana, which is to take place at an early period during the present year and to make arrangements for which a committee has been appointed.

As there are quite a number of poetical extracts introduced into the lecture, it is but justice to add that they are from the pen of Mrs. Sarah T. Bolton.

LECTURE.

Assembled in this beautiful capital of the fourth state in the Union, who is not startled by the recollection that the rains of scarce thirty winters have obliterated the tracks of the Indian from the spot on which it stands? Who can realize that little more than thirty years ago the red man built his bark lodge and kindled his council fires in the dense wilderness that then covered the site of this fair and flourishing city? Yet this is true, and there are men living in our midst, men still in the full vigor and strength of manhood, who witnessed it all—aye more, the delegate, who once represented what now constitutes the states of Indiana, Illinois and Wisconsin in the congress of the United States, is still living. Surely, when he looks on these three mighty states, now sending six senators and twenty-three representatives to our national councils, he must feel that he is in a new existence; or, like Rip Van Winkle, he has taken a long sleep, so great is the change. But still greater must be the surprise of those yet living, who were on the stage of action in 1799, when General William Henry Harrison was elected the first delegate to congress from the territory northwest of the Ohio river, whose boundaries were Pennsylvania, the Ohio and Mississippi rivers and Canada. The country west of the Mississippi then belonged to another power, and was acquired by Mr. Jefferson from France in 1803. Arthur St. Clair had been governor of the territory for several years previous to 1799, under a territorial government of the first grade—having no delegate in congress.

In 1800 the northwestern territory was divided into the

Ohio and Indiana territories—the Indiana territory retainin within her limits the greater part of Michigan, the whole of Illinois and Wisconsin and what now constitutes the state of Indiana. In 1801 General Harrison was appointed governor In 1805 Michigan was made a separate territory and the same year the first territorial legislature for the Indiana territory assembled at Vincennes. In 1807 the population, within the present limits of Indiana, was only about twelve thousand. In 1809 the territory was again divided, and the territory of Illinois established, General Harrison still continuing the governor of the Indiana territory.

The first delegate from the Indiana territory was Benjamin Parke; the second, Jesse B. Thomas, before alluded to, who is still living; and after the separation from Illinois, from 1810 to 1816 the Hon. Jonathan Jennings.

In the fall of 1812, Governor Harrison having been appointed to the command of the northwestern army in the war then in existence between the United States and Great Britain, Thomas Posey, an officer of the Revolution, was appointed governor. In 1813 the seat of government was removed to Corydon. Governor Posey resided at Jeffersonville, and the building in which he lived is still standing.

In 1816 Indiana was admitted into the Union as a state, and her population was estimated at 65,000 inhabitants. Jonathan Jennings was her first governor; Waller Taylor of Vincennes, and James Noble of Brookville, were elected senators to congress and William Hendricks her first representative in the popular branch of the national legislature.

In 1818 Governor Jennings, in connection with Lewis Cass and Benjamin Parke, as commissioners, on the part of the United States, succeeded in purchasing from the Indians, with the exception of the Miami, Thorntown, and a few other reserves, all their lands in central Indiana, embracing the very spot on which this building is erected, south of the Wabash river. General Cass was subsequently a commissioner, in connection with Governor Ray and General Tipton, in purchasing the extensive Pottawattamie possessions, north of the Wabash, where, at the instance of Governor Ray, the valuable grant was obtained for Indiana of a section of land for every mile of a road from Lake Michigan to the Ohio river. Of these commissioners General Cass is the sole survivor. He is now the patriarch of the United States Senate, and having occupied so conspicuous a part in the early history of the state, we instinctively turn to him as to a friend. Like his great compatriots Calhoun, Clay and Webster, he had his eye fixed on the highest office in the nation. Like them he was unsuccessful. But who will forget the burning eloquence of Clay, the brilliant qualities of Calhoun, or the giant strength of Webster, because they failed to reach the goal of their ambition? The last great effort of Henry Clay was for his country, and Webster and Cass were his associates.

In 1820 the lands in central Indiana, acquired in 1818, having been surveyed, commissioners were appointed, under the act admitting Indiana into the Union, to make a selection of four sections, or 2,560 acres for a permanent seat of government. George Hunt, John Conner, Stephen Ludlow, Joseph Bartholomew, John Tipton, John Gilleland, Thomas Emerson, Frederick Rapp and Jesse B. Durham constituted this board, who, according to the proclamation of Governor Jennings, met at the house of William Conner, on the west fork of White river, elected Benjamin I. Blythe their clerk, and proceeded to the discharge of their duties. They had the whole of the then recent purchase from which to make a selection; but the Bluffs of White river and the site where Indianapolis now stands, were the rival points—the latter only gaining the location, I am told, by a majority of one vote.

The commissioners in their report to the legislature in 1820 state: "The undersigned have endeavored to connect with an eligible site the advantages of a navigable stream and fertility of soil, while they have not been unmindful of the geographical situation of the various portions of the state; to its political center as it regards both the present and future population, as well as the present and future interest of the citizens.''

I will here give, as an item of interest and curiosity, the following extracts from the private journal of Gen. John Tipton, one of the commissioners, now in the possession of John B. Dillon, Esq. He says, in the commencement:

"On Wednesday the 17th of May, 1820, I set out from Corydon, in company with Governor Jennings. I had been appointed by the last legislature one of the commissioners to select and locate a site for the permanent seat of government of the state of Indiana. We took with us Bill, a black boy, and having laid in a plentiful supply of bread and coffee, and provided a tent, we stopped at P. Bell's two hours, then set out and at seven o'clock came to Mr. Wineman's, on Blue river, and stopped for the night.''

The general continues his journal, giving the same interesting and detailed account of events from day to day until Wednesday, the 7th of June, 1820. Under that date is the following account:

"A fine clear morning. We met at McCormick's, and, on my motion, the commissioners came to a resolution to select and locate sections numbered 1 and 12, and east and west fractional section numbered 2, and east fractional section 11, and so much of the east side of west fractional section number 3, to be divided by a north and south line, running parallel to the west boundary of said section, as will equal in amount four entire sections, in township 15, n. of range 3, east. We left our clerk making out his minutes and our report, and went to camp to dine. Returned after dinner. Our papers not being ready B., D. and myself returned to camp. At four o'clock they went to sleep and I to writing. At five we decamped and went over to McCormick's [who then lived on the bank of White river in a cabin, near where the White river bridge now stands]. Our clerk having his writing ready, the commissioners met and signed their report, and certified the services of the clerk at $45.06. The first boat landed that ever was seen at the seat of government It was a small ferry flat, with a canoe tied alongside, both loaded with the household goods of two families, moving to the mouth of Fall creek. They came in a keel boat as far as they could get it up the river, then unloaded the boat and brought up their goods in the flat and canoe. I paid for some corn and w. [whisky, I suppose], 62½."

In 1821 the lots were laid out by Alexander Ralston, as engineer, under the direction of Christopher Harrison as acting commissioner, and in October of the same year the first sale of lots took place.

Soon after the choice of the four sections at this point in 1821, attracted by the selection of a permanent seat of government for the young and growing state of Indiana, a company of some two hundred persons immediately emigrated to the place. With the exception of a few unimportant improvements made by the traders and Indians, the whole country to the south, east and west, for more than forty miles in each direction, was an unbroken wilderness. To the north the purchase extended some forty miles and beyond that the lands were still in the possession of the natives of the forest. The aggregate amount at which the lots were bid off, at the first sale, was $35,596.25. The first inhabitants principally settled immediately on the bank of White river and the lower or western part of the city. Many of their log cabins were erected before the town was laid off, and when the survey was made their residences presented a singular appearance as to location. Some were in the center of the lots, others in the streets, and all without the least regard to the streets or alleys. Immediately in front of where the state-house now stands, near the center of Washington street, was the residence of Dr. Mitchell, an early physician, and known as one of the best of men. He was associated for a time in business with Dr. Livingston Dunlap, who was one of the very first physicians who came to the place.

I can enumerate but a few of those who first settled in Indianapolis and the surrounding country. Amongst others the names of Pogue, Harding, Johnson, of several families, O'Neal, Duncan, Fletcher, McCormick, Basye, Norwood, McDougall, Reagan, Rooker, Dunning, Vanblaricum, Wilson, McIlvaine, Coe, Henderson, Gregg, Smith, Foote, Currey, Wilkins, Blake, Ray, Morris, Yandes, Reed, Bates, Wick, Duvall, Wood, Caleb and Dr. Scudder, Nowland, Given, Walpole, Osborn, Morrow, Stephens, Brenton, Russell, Hawkins, Dunlap, Cox, McGeorge, Landis, Collins, McClung, Luse, Lake, etc., etc., were most conspicuous.

The year 1821, over a great part of Indiana, as well as other portions of the west was very sickly, and the early emigrants suffered much, removed as they were from many of the comforts of life to which they had been accustomed. But the pioneer settlers of this portion of Indiana were men, and women, too, of noble impulses and generous hearts, and friendships were then formed that no circumstances have ever been able to sever.

In January, 1822, in connection with a relative, I commenced the publication of the *Indianapolis Gazette*, under the firm name of Smith & Bolton, and in 1823 Messrs. Gregg & Maguire established another paper called the *Western Censor and Emigrants' Guide*. The author of Chamberlain's *Gazetcer*, in 1848, in paying a compliment to the survivors of these firms, in which he gives their standing in their respective parties—for editors of rival papers always will differ—

states: "N. Bolton, of the one firm, is now register of the land office, and D. Maguire is the auditor of public accounts." The honors of both, however, were of short duration. Although one was a Whig and the other a Democrat, each belonged to the wrong party to be continued in office. But Mac had the advantage. The Democrats, who obtained the ascendancy in the state, were compelled to let him serve out his term before they supplanted him. My head was cut off, with those of many good Democrats, by the cabinet of General Taylor as soon as my successor could be chosen from the numerous applicants that applied for the office. Pardon this egotism, for Mac's sake, and I will promise to say less of myself hereafter. I was only giving a chapter from the political experience of two of the first editors of Indianapolis.

The history of the *Indianapolis Gazette* for a short time after it came into existence is rather interesting to printers. It was established in a buckeye log cabin of but one room, part of which was occupied for a family residence. It was printed on new type, but on the first pattern of a Ramage press. The ink was put on with balls made of dressed deerskin, stuffed with wool. The balls, when out of use, were kept soft by the application of raccoon oil. There was no postoffice nearer than Connersville, a distance of sixty miles; but a private mail was established and a person employed to go to Connersville every four weeks to bring the letters and newspapers. In the month of February, the President's message, which had been delivered in December, came to hand and was published in the two or three succeeding numbers of the *Gazette*. Mr. Monroe was then President and made but short messages.

During the year 1822 a United States mail was established, and in a short time we had a mail from the east every two weeks, unless detained by high waters.

The men who first came to Indianapolis, as a body, unlike those who usually settle new countries, were persons of superior intelligence. For a considerable time the nearest magistrate was sixty miles distant, yet so honorable was the bearing of all that but little inconvenience was experienced.

The year 1822 ushered in the election of county officers. James M. Ray was elected clerk, Joseph Reed recorder, and James McIlvaine and William McCartney (the latter then residing at the falls of Fall creek) associate judges, and something like the establishment of civil government ensued. The Hon. William W. Wick was the first circuit judge and Hervey Bates the first sheriff for Marion county; and during the year Judge Wick commenced holding his courts. I attended several of these, including the counties of Shelby, Decatur and Johnson. A number of lawyers from the surrounding settlements attended to witness the first introduction of civil government amongst the settlers of the "New Purchase"—a term given to the whole country then recently acquired from the Delaware Indians. In some instances the grand jury, attended by a bailiff, selected some large fallen tree, where they held their inquisitions, and sometimes the courts were also held in the open air. But at night was the great scene of merriment amongst the members of the bar. There were no court-houses in those days, and the courts were usually held in the largest cabin of the neighborhood. The fireplace was generally eight or ten feet wide, and in the fall season of the year beds were spread upon the floor, before the huge log fire, where some thirty or more attorneys and others would take up their lodgings for the night. Notwithstanding many a sleepy soul was greatly disturbed by the anecdotes of the party, it was impossible to enter the dream land until two or three o'clock in the morning. As the trials before the courts were generally of an unimportant character, consisting of appeal cases from justices' dockets, or for petit misdemeanors on indictments by the grand juries, they were generally conducted in such a manner as to afford the most amusement, yet still with the greatest possible respect for the court. The attorneys, being all anxious to distinguish themselves before the multitude who attended, would generally volunteer, so as to have at least two or three lawyers on each side of almost every question. I shall never forget the first court held in Decatur county, where the far-famed Jim Brown then resided, and where he was employed in all the suits on the docket, especially in two appeal cases, where there were cross suits. An old gentleman had a blooming daughter, to whom a young man of the neighborhood had been paying his addresses. After a short courtship he was unsuccessful. The young man sued the father for chopping wood, making fires, and other labor while pressing his suit. The old gentleman sued the unsuccessful swain for the nice things the daughter had prepared for her lover, such as pumpkin pies and other dainties, including a splendid bowl of eggnog. Brown was the advocate for the old gentleman, and it is only those acquainted with the man who can imagine the nature of his arguments. There were three or four lawyers on each side and a day was consumed in these important trials.

In preparing these remarks I was reminded of a circumstance which transpired in Johnson county, which I must relate, notwithstanding my promise not to introduce myself very conspicuously in this lecture. I attended the first organization of the circuit court in that county, which took place at Smiley's Mills, some six or seven miles southeast, I believe, of the present seat of justice. In company with Judge Wick, Calvin Fletcher, Esq., and others, I started from Indianapolis to attend this court. We stopped for the night at Mr. King's, adjoining where Franklin now stands. Next morning we traveled four miles for breakfast and stopped at the house of a widow of an early settler, whose residence has been known for several years since that time as a general stopping-place for most travelers journeying to the Ohio river in that direction. The arrival of the judge of the circuit court and so distinguished an attorney as my friend Fletcher, not to say anything of the young editor of the only newspaper at the seat of government, rather disconcerted the hostess, who was an intelligent Kentucky lady, with all the high notions of hospitality peculiar to the citizens of that state. She prepared for us a most excellent breakfast; but, with many apologies, insisted that we should call again, when she would honor the judge and his distinguished companions with an entertainment worthy of the high stations they occupied. We accepted the invitation and promised to return the next evening. The court was held at Smiley's Mill, in the open air, with the usual circumstances attending the organization of courts in the New Purchase. But when the time arrived for us to comply with the invitation of our hospitable landlady, the judge had fallen in with a company that insisted he should go with them the direct route to Columbus, and Mr. Fletcher had been employed by a client who insisted that he should accompany him home, that he might be placed in possession of the facts of his case. Mr. Fletcher felt bound to accept the invitation, for a lawyer could not, at that day, neglect the wishes of his clients, as they were like angels' visits, few and far between; particularly those that brought much money to the purse. I was left alone to go to the widow's and make an apology. This was a difficult job for a modest young man like myself. But I screwed my courage up to the sticking point, and, solitary and alone, I returned to partake of one of the best prepared entertainments I ever enjoyed in my life. The landlady had an accomplished daughter, and with the rest of the family, we partook of the repast; and I spent a happy evening, after I had convinced the ladies that nothing but the direst necessity prevented my friends from partaking of their hospitality, and how mortified they would feel when I related the pains that had been taken to entertain them. I nearly lost my heart in the adventure. Certain I am that their kindness will never be forgotten.

Before I dismiss the judiciary I must notice the justices' courts in Indianapolis, where, amongst others, a Fletcher, a Breckinridge and a Currey were sometimes the heroes. The eccentric Obed Foote, a man of great goodness of heart, a profound lawyer and a ripe scholar, was one of the first magistrates. He was a bachelor, and kept bachelor's hall. His eccentric disposition was no doubt partly the cause of his residence in Indianapolis. He was an economist, and possessed a stout, muscular frame. He labored constantly in his gardens when not engaged in professional business, and the virgin soil of Indianapolis yielded him an incredible quantity of potatoes and other vegetables. These he was always ready to divide with his neighbors. He enjoyed remarkably good health, but was always the first to visit the sick couch of the stranger and minister to his wants. These traits of character made him very popular with the settlers. When he opened his magistrate's office the attorneys, having but little other business, were sometimes employed in his court. He was very fond of potatoes, and when a trial was coming on generally had a fire full to serve up, when the pleadings commenced. After examining the witnesses very carefully he would uncover his potatoes, and having placed them on the table, would remark, turning his back to the lawyers—"Now Messieurs Pettifoggers, you can proceed with your arguments while I eat my potatoes."

The beautiful eminence in the center of Indianapolis called the governor's circle in 1821, and for some years afterwards, was covered with a delightful grove of sugar trees. Here seats were prepared, and here the first public services were performed in honor of our holy religion. The Rev. Mr. McClung, a man of but little pretensions but of great piety, was the preacher. No one inquired to what creed or profession he belonged—the whole population was necessary to make a respectable audience—but the pure and simple doctrines of Christianity were here inculcated, with a force and power perhaps never equaled. The divisions of the Christian church were here unknown, but the glorious gospel, which brings life and immortality to light, shone forth with all its brilliancy.

On a beautiful Sabbath morning in the spring of 1822, I first took my seat in this church of nature, dedicated to the living God; and it was here, like our fathers on Plymouth rock, that the blessings of heaven were invoked on the embryo city. God grant that the prayers then offered up may continue to be answered as we feel they have been, to the latest generations, and may civil and religious liberty, as then enjoyed, ever be the portion of the metropolis of Indiana.

In the course of a year or two, as population increased. Methodist, Baptist and Presbyterian churches were established. Dr. Coe, Caleb Scudder and one or two others organized a Presbyterian church early in 1823 and procured the services of the Rev. David Proctor for their preacher. By this time Mr. Scudder had built a frame cabinet shop, some thirty feet in length, on the state-house square, nearly in front of where the capitol now stands. This building was cleaned out for Sundays, and afforded a very comfortable place for public worship. It was here, in April, 1823, that the first Sabbath school was organized, consisting of some twenty or thirty scholars and eight or ten teachers. It was founded on the union principle, and embraced all denominations for several years. Doctor Isaac Coe was the most active in its organization, but Caleb Scudder, James Blake, Douglass Maguire, James M. Ray, Henry Bradley, B. F. Morris, Dr. Dunlap, and others, were of the early male teachers, and the Misses Coe, Mrs. Morris, Miss McDougall, and Mrs. Scudder and Mrs. Paxton were amongst the early female teachers. The Sabbath school had the good wishes of all the inhabitants, and scarcely a child of the proper age, in a very short time, failed to attend. The teachers took great interest in their classes, and no scholars ever advanced in their studies with greater rapidity. Moral and religious principles were here instilled, which have been gratefully acknowledged by scholars scattered over many of the states of the Union. The founders have been greatly benefited by their labors, and have blessed the day that led them to engage in so glorious a work. The history of Sabbath schools in Indianapolis must be the work of another. It is too wide a field for me on the present occasion; but here was the commencement of a work which has extended until at this time the number of children that now weekly attend the Sabbath schools in Indianapolis, by a recent report, is 2,127.

It has been truly remarked that in the settlement of the west the cabin of the pioneer is scarcely covered before the Methodist preacher makes his appearance. So it was here. Old Father Cravens, noted for his eccentricities, was amongst the first, but John Strange, a man of devoted piety and self-sacrificing spirit, was early in the field. The latter was one of nature's orators, drawing inspiration from the scenes around him, and being a man of deep feeling he carried his audience with him, when the fountains of his heart were broken up with love to God and love to man. He had a small and slender frame and from appearance seemed but little calculated to carry away the minds of his hearers from the scenes of earth. But the man was soon forgotten when in an imagery drawn from the clouds, the stars, the elements and heaven, he depicted the joys and sorrows of the Christian soldier.

His lot on earth was one of poverty and self-denial, but h; was always rich—yes, rich in the hopes of a blessed immor- tality beyond the grave. He lies quietly now in our city graveyard. James Scott and Edwin Ray were also early Methodist preachers; the latter a young man of great prom- ise, who afterwards became distinguished in the ministry, but has been many years dead. He preached here every three or four weeks, for a considerable time, to large audiences, and was the man who pushed forward to completion the first brick meeting house in this city, where Wesley Chapel now stands. He had many revivals under his ministry.

The first fourth of July was celebrated at a large spring, two and a half miles above the town on White river, near the residence of Mr. Anderson, by a few individuals in 1821. In 1822 the whole population for many miles around turned out to celebrate the anniversary of our nation's independence. I had the pleasure of attending this celebration. A public dinner was provided, and amongst other things a large deer was barbecued whole and placed upon the festive board as emblematical of the recent settlement of the country. Toasts were drank and speeches delivered amidst the cheers of the multitude. A splendid ball succeeded in the evening, for we had beautiful women and gallant men who tripped it gaily on the light fantastic toe. As an editor I was there, of course, to note the proceedings.

A common amusement amongst our young and old men, and which was turned to a good account, was fire-hunting. This was arranged by placing a light in the front part of a canoe which was suffered to float down the river without noise. The deer would be found drinking, or eating the grass that grew in the water near the shore. The glare of light that burst upon him would so bewilder and blind his eyes that he would generally stand still until the deadly aim of the rifle would lay him low in death. I have frequently witnessed at the landing, in the morning, a canoe laden with from six to eight deer as the trophies of one night.

The inhabitants learned from the Indians their method of preparing their venison. It being a common article of food, the large chimney of every log cabin was well supplied with dried venison or jerk, as it was familiarly called. Every settler was in the habit of carrying with him a large pocket-knife, and the first ceremony, on entering a neighbor's cabin, was generally to take down a slice of venison and commence eating while the conversation progressed. We also had many wild turkeys and other game in abundance. White river abounded with fish of a fine quality, and the corn-fields afforded corn for hominy, and vegetables were produced in abundance, which were denominated Indiana fruit.

Time passed on and a regiment of the militia was organized in Marion and two or three of the surrounding counties. The election of colonels, majors and captains was truly exciting; these stations being considered, at that time, in Indiana, as the stepping stones to civil office.

It was about this time that a young man arrived in Indianapolis, of about twenty years of age. He was a native of Pennsylvania, but, with his widowed mother, had resided in Tennessee for several years. He was of dignified bearing, and possessed an intelligence not usual with young men of his years. He was without money, and being a printer, sought employment in the printing offices. He found a temporary situation for a short time of two or three days' work in each week. The balance of the time, having a good education, he was constantly engaged in storing his mind with useful information, and he became very much attached to this new and rising country. The printing offices, however, being unable to afford him longer employment, it seemed his destiny to leave the place. He was sitting one day on Washington street, in rather a melancholy mood, at the prospect before him, when some countrymen passing by, he heard one of them remark that he would be glad to find a schoolmaster. The young man started upon his feet in a moment and declared at once that he was ready to engage in this calling. On further conversation the countryman agreed that he should go home with him, when the neighbors would determine whether they would employ him or not; so, without further ceremony he got into a wagon and started to a neighborhood nine or ten miles to the northwest of Indianapolis. Here he commenced a school of a few scholars, and in a short time became a great favorite with the settlers. Having studied surveying, they procured for him a compass, etc., and he run out the lines of their lands. When the election for the first captain of a military company in the neighborhood came on, there appeared to be but one man, of a suitable age, who had any military pretensions, and he, with some of the inhabitants, was unpopular. An old gentleman, who had served in the American army in the war with England, and who was a good tactician, took it into his head that the schoolmaster was the man to be elected. The schoolmaster, however, although as a printer boy he had handled American Canon, peculiar to the craft, yet he had no military knowledge whatever, and had never set a squadron in the field. The old soldier determined not to be foiled in his wishes, so he instructed his favorite, who was an apt scholar, of evenings, with grains of corn, in military maneuvers. A house raising, where the whole population attended, took place but a short time before the election. The candidate with military pretensions was there; and, confident of success, challenged the crowd to a trial of military skill. The schoolmaster, at the urgent entreaties of his military tutor, consented to enter the lists. They each were to form the company into line and perform several military evolutions. The result was a triumph in favor of the schoolmaster; who, fresh from the military school of the old soldier, had learned everything he undertook to the greatest perfection. The young schoolmaster was elected captain, as a matter of course. This paved the way to his election to the legislature, over one of the most popular men of the county, and afterwards auditor of state, and to the command of a regiment. After this he was twice elected to congress; but during his second term, on his journey to Washington, near Cincinnati, by one of those unfortunate steamboat accidents which have sometimes played such havoc with human life on our western waters, he was sent from time to eternity, in the very bloom of early youth, with all the hopes and expectations of the successful American statesman clustering around him. Had he lived he might this day have been occupying a seat in the United States Senate. While at Washington he had contracted a matrimonial engagement with the daughter of one of the first men in the nation, and was hastening to Philadelphia, on his route to Washington, to lead his bride to the altar, when he met with his melancholy fate. Few in this community will fail to recognize in the portrait I have drawn, the name of the lamented George L. Kinnard. I give this extended history of a dear friend as a commentary on our free institutions, and as an encouragement to the young men of our country to industry, perseverance and upright conduct, however lowly their condition may be.

At an early period in the history of Indianapolis, the citizens were astonished by the announcement that a theatrical company had arrived and would perform in the dining-room of the principal hotel. This company consisted of a Mr. and Mrs. Smith, late from the New York theater. Mr. Smith was some fifty-five years of age and Mrs. Smith about sixty. A musical society had just been established, of which I was a member, which was invited to be present. Mrs. Smith was to sing the "Star Spangled Banner," and dance a hornpipe blindfolded, amongst eggs, with other entertainments of a theatrical character, in which both the members of the company were to participate. Mrs. Smith, when arrayed in her theatrical robes, looked astonishingly well for a woman of her years, and sang and danced to the admiration of the audience. The landlord was a church member of long standing, who had scarcely ever heard of a theater in his life, and who determined that there should be no undue levity manifested by the audience, so he endeavored to restrict the musicians to the performance of slow and solemn music. This restriction, considering the nature of the performances and the character of the players, was so extremely ludicrous that the audience was convulsed with laughter during the whole evening. This was the commencement of the drama in Indianapolis.

Our early merchants were James & John Given, Luke Walpole and afterwards Nicholas McCarty, Esq. Mr. Walpole, together with his whole family of sons and daughters, came up White river in two large keel boats, bringing with them a large assortment of merchandise of almost every description, iron, castings, etc. Their journey from Zanesville, Ohio, was a tedious one, occupying several months. A record of this trip would be very interesting. This arrival, in 1822, was a great event in the early history of Indianapolis, and the whole population turned out to witness the landing of the boats. This family was a great accession to the social circle. The eldest daughter, now no more, and afterwards the wife of Obed Foote, Esq., was a lady of the highest social and literary accomplishments.

The stores of Given and Walpole, however, would sometimes run short of the articles essential to the comfort of the citizens. Then it was that John Hagar, Esq., afterwards, for a number of years, clerk of Hancock county, became famous as the ox-driver of central Indiana. His trips to Cincinnati and back would frequently occupy a full month—there being nothing but the winding roads and traces of the emigrants over which to travel. His arrival, with a fresh supply of groceries frequently elicited more attention than does now the landing of half a dozen steamers at New York.

Mr. McCarty, as an early merchant, displayed great energy of character. On several occasions, when his stocks would get low, he would rig up a wagon and proceed to the different settlements, and sometimes as far as Illinois, until his goods were completely sold out. These traits of character laid the foundation he afterwards acquired of the leading merchant in Indiana. General Joseph Orr, now of La Porte county, was also early in the field as a merchant in central Indiana. He laid the foundation at Indianapolis and other points, as an itinerant trader, as early as 1822, of his present fortune.

In 1823, James Gregory, of Shelby county, was elected the first senator from the counties of Hamilton, Marion, Madison, Henry, Shelby, Decatur, Rush and Johnson, which constituted a senatorial district, and James Paxton was elected a representative from the counties of Marion, Madison, Hamilton and Johnson, who attended the session of the legislature for 1823–'24 at Corydon. That winter a law was passed providing for the meeting of the next session of the legislature at this place, on the 10th of January, 1825. In anticipation of this event, the young men of Indianapolis met at the land office one evening and determined to form themselves into a legislative body. Benjamin I. Blythe, who had been a member of the Indiana legislature, from Dearborn county, being present, was chosen the first speaker. Several of the older members of the community afterwards joined in and we soon had the late Governor Noble, Judge Wick, General Hanna, Hiram Brown, Morris Morris and many others, as regular members. Of the young men who were the first to participate as members, William Quarles, K. A. Scudder, Austin W. Morris, John Frazee, Israel Griffith, Alexander W. Russell, William New, Joseph K. Looney, Douglas Maguire, John Cain, Joseph M. Moore, Thomas H. Sharpe, Thomas A. Morris, William P. Bryant, Newton S. Heylin, Andrew W. Ingram, Hugh O'Neal, George W. Kimberly, Benjamin S. Noble, Fabius M. Finch, Simon Yandes, and many others, were amongst the number.

The Indianapolis court house was finished about this time, from the proceeds of the sales of lots, with the understanding that the Indiana legislature should occupy it for a place of meeting if desired, until the year 1860. It was then considered one of the finest public buildings in the state, and the Indianapolis legislature held its meetings in the senate chamber. Every variety of subjects were here discussed, and its meetings, which were on every Saturday evening, were largely attended by the members of the Indiana legislature during the sessions of that body. It was a great resort for the ladies of the place, which greatly added to the interest of the discussions. It continued in session, without intermission, in summer and winter, once a week, for four or five years. No wonder that those of us still living look back to these scenes of our youth with the fondest recollection, and cherish the memories of our companions in the greenest spot on memory's waste.

Those acquainted with the names I have mentioned will perceive that death has made fearful inroads upon our number. Dr. Scudder was an early victim. Our legislative hall was clad in the habiliments of mourning at his death. He was an early pioneer, had been recently married, and a bright career in his profession seemed to lie before him. Israel Griffith was a young man of much promise, and had just been admitted to the bar when the fell destroyer took him hence. John Frazee was a universal favorite, and for many years was known as a merchant in this city. Within the last few months three of our most prominent members—the associates of my youth—have passed to the land of silence and of death. William Quarles, Austin W. Morris, and Alexander W. Russell are no more. How often has the old senate chamber resounded with the eloquence of a Quarles, or been greeted with the pleasant smile and ever joyous countenance of a Morris—and Russell, how shall I speak of him—for many years not only the life of our society in the city, but throughout the whole country. He was, for several years, the general attendant of most of the bridegrooms in the neighborhood, and young men for miles around thought it the greatest honor for him to be present at their weddings. This gave him an unbounded popularity. I have been present with him on many such occasions, and know how dearly he was beloved. The following stanzas, written on the death of the lamented Quarles, will better express my feelings than anything I can say on the subject:

> "Mournfully, mournfully, toll for the dead—
> They passed from our side, in their manhood's pride,
> Ere the glow of their rainbow-hopes had fled;
> When their sky was bright with meridian light,
> Death bore them away, to a dreamless night—
> Mournfully toll for the dead.
>
> "Tenderly, tenderly bid them adieu—
> The garland that love with their life-chords wove
> Lies withered and pale on their breasts so true.
> The beautiful chain Death rended in twain
> Can never be joined on the earth again—
> Tenderly bid them adieu.
>
> "Silently, silently let them sleep on—
> From the hurry and strife of the battle of life,
> Victors, away to their home they've gone.
> Gone, gone from the tears, from the sorrows and fears,
> That come to the heart, on the tide of years—
> Silently let them sleep on."

After the removal of the seat of government to Indianapolis, the social intercourse of the people seemed to partake more or less of a legislative character, particularly amongst the young of both sexes At a wedding party, a society was instituted, consisting of young ladies and gentlemen, on the legislative principle; yet not quite so democratic in one of its departments as that of our state government. The aristocratic branch consisted of four young ladies, who constituted a council or board of directors, having a strong veto power on all matters brought before the society. The other branch was purely democratic, and consisted of ladies and gentlemen. The subjects brought before the society were generally such as tended to matrimony. There was a marshal or sergeant-at-arms appointed whose special business it was to carry out the decrees of the council or board of directors. James Blake, the Indianapolis marshal of thirty years' standing, was first elected. Moonlight excursions, in a large ferry boat, on the river were projected; and the society on fine evenings, under the direction of the marshal, would proceed to the boat, where by the light of the soft silver moon, as our bark floated over the waters to the sound of sweet music, many a tale of love was told. A grave charge was made against several of the first directory of ladies, who, instead of attending to the interests of the society at large, were the first to form matrimonial alliances for themselves. When their wedding parties came on, these charges were a source of much amusement.

In 1823, having received a contract from the postmaster-general, I proceeded with the first United States mail north of Indianapolis, to the then recently deserted Indian village of Andersontown. A post-office, on the route, was established at the house of William Conner, four miles south of Noblesville. He had been an Indian trader and had resided on this spot for about twenty years, and had just erected a handsome brick residence. Never shall I forget his kindness and hospitality. In the course of the year I spent many delightful evenings at his mansion. A young gentleman was there, by the name of Rosseau, from Detroit under the direction, I believe, of General Cass, or the war department, collecting Indian traditions from the natives who were still, in considerable numbers, trading with Mr. Conner; and there I gathered much of Indian character that was highly interesting. He was a good musician, and with Josiah F. Polk, from Washington City, who was also an inmate, and frequently Indian chiefs and other natives, we spent many happy evenings. Mr. Conner's new house was on the second bank of White river, which formed something like a horse shoe around three hundred acres of rich prairie that had been selected as a donation under the treaty, immediately in front of his dwelling, which was located on a considerable eminence. This prairie was enclosed by a good fence, and was all under cultivation by the early settlers. I never beheld a more delightful scene than when I looked down from the second story of Mr. Conner's dwelling, on a field of three hundred acres of waving corn, some two feet high, with fifteen or twenty merry plowmen scattered over it at work. It was doubly interesting, coming, as I did, out of nature's forest, only broken by the occasional cabins and small patches of cleared land of the early settlers.

There was another post-office at Strawtown, a prairie of considerable magnitude, where many remains of the Indian village that had been there located were still standing. It was at Andersontown, however, that all my kindly feelings were enlisted for the race of men who had just deserted the graves of their fathers. They had left this beautiful country to take up their residence in the far west, soon to follow the setting sun as he sinks from our vision; but never, like him, to arise again to gladden the earth with their presence. Andersontown had been the seat of government of the Delaware nation, and it is said, at one time, to have contained a thousand inhabitants. More than fifty of the Indian dwellings were still standing in a dilapidated condition. The residence of Anderson, their last chief, was in good repair, and was occupied by my old friend, Captain John Berry, a pioneer of the right stamp. I had the melancholy pleasure, on several occasions, of sleeping in one of the rooms where Anderson and his family had lodged.

It has been stated, by Mr. Johnson, long an Indian agent of Ohio, that when the treaty was signed by the chiefs of the Delawares, at St. Mary's, in 1818, for the relinquishment of this country, they were melted into tears. Inevitable destiny stared them in the face and they were forced to submit.

It was in the month of June when I first visited Andersontown. The blue grass was growing luxuriantly around the ruins of the Indian's dwelling. The ripe rich strawberries were hanging in delicious clusters on their vines, and all nature, under the influence of the God of Day, seemed joyous and happy. But the poor Indian, where was he? Stranger hands were to reap the benefits of his earthly paradise. My heart was overpowered, for the realities of life had not then chilled the warm feelings of youth. Generous tears came to my relief, and a prayer was offered up for the red man and his fate.

Time admonishes me that I must refrain from the relation of a thousand incidents in the early history of Indianapolis that crowd up from the memories of the past. But I must not forget that excellent man and able teacher, Ebenezer Sharpe, who, with his son and daughter, gave an impulse to the cause of education that will never be forgotten by those who attended their school.

Events, in early history, apparently of the most unimportant character at the time, are frequently links in the great chain of human progress, and they should be treasured up in the common store-house of knowledge, as a foundation upon which the future historian may build his more stately edifice The contemplated festival of the early settlers, I have no doubt, will rescue many of these from oblivion.

The progress of the west is truly wonderful. I am only forty-eight years of age, but I passed over the ground where Columbus, the capital of our sister Ohio, is located, when there was but a solitary log cabin upon the banks of the Scioto at that place. Here a proud city now stands forth in all the grandeur of the metropolis of the third, and soon to be the second, state in the Union. I have beheld, more recently, the site of this beautiful city covered with a dense forest, now the capital of the fourth state in our glorious confederacy. The future, with all its mysteries, is yet unknown. I would not lift the curtain, for God, in his providence, for wise purposes, withholds the scenes that lie before us from mortal vision. But the immortal mind can not be chained, and with something of that inspiration which guided the prophets of old, we may soar in imagination through the ranges of coming generations. Indiana is a central state, and it is supposed by the best judges, from the quality of her soil, that with her 36,500 square miles or 23,300,000 acres, she is susceptible of as dense a population as any country of equal extent in the known world, there being but few acres of land that can not be cultivated. Her metropolis is now radiated by railroads and telegraph lines in every direction. If we wish to visit Canada, the northern lakes, the copper and iron regions of Lake Superior, the beauties of Minnesota, or the Indian's hunting grounds, still farther to the northwest, a direct railroad communication to them all is nearly completed via Lafayette and Michigan City. If we wish to visit St. Louis, the gap in Illinois, under the superintendence of a Brough, will soon be filled up, leading to Benton's great route to the Pacific. Our communication with Evansville, on the Ohio river, will soon be completed, which will give easy access to a railroad now in progress to the extreme south. With New Albany, Louisville and Jeffersonville, we have already daily communication, and five or six hours takes us to either of these points, there uniting with the great Nashville road which will soon be completed. Our railroad communication with Madison is of some four or five years' standing, and is looked upon as an old road, the mother of all the rest in our state. With Lawrenceburg and Cincinnati our connection will be complete in the next twelve months, all the arrangements being made and the work in rapid progress. The great Central road via Centreville, Richmond, Dayton and Columbus, Ohio, will also be in full operation next season. The connection on the Bellefontaine road is now complete with Cincinnati, and a new route of communication is opened up, over which I traveled, in part, but twenty-eight years ago, by an Indian trace. The Peru road, now completed beyond Noblesville, will be extended, the coming year, both to Peru and Logansport, and eventually to Goshen and to the Southern Michigan road. Having boxed the compass, I will desist from a further detail of railroads radiating from this city when I notice one just started, under favorable auspices, which will form a direct communication, through Rockville and Montezuma with Springfield, Illinois, and another through Rushville on the most direct route to Cincinnati. To-morrow, I have just been informed, the railroad connection between both Lafayette and Terre Haute and Cincinnati will be complete; and to-morrow morning the traveler can start from the Wabash river, at either Terre Haute or Lafayette, come to Indianapolis and remain two hours for dinner, and be in Cincinnati via the Bellefontaine road the same evening. Where now is Hagar and his ox team? The old gentleman is still alive, but his team is entirely too slow for the progress of the age! For

They have given the iron horse the rein,
And he flies away o'er the sunny plain—
'Shrieking and clanking the bolts and bars
That fetter his strength to the rumbling cars.
Away, through the valley and mountain-pass,
O'er the dark ravine, and the dank morass;
By the lonely forests and fertile fields,
Shaking the earth with his iron heels,
And flashing the sparks from his fiery eyes,
Like a hunted fiend, he shrieks and flies!
On, on through the tunnel so dark and drear—
On, over the bridges that quake with fear—
By the stagnant fens and the limpid rills—
Through the clefted hearts of the ancient hills,
Where the startling echoes faint and die,
In their vain attempts to repeat his cry,
Now faster away, as if terrible need
Were adding a spur to his fearful speed—
Hushed is the voice of the rushing river;
The winds are low, but the old trees shiver;
The sun, like a drunkard, reels around;
The wild beasts start from the haunted ground,
And the bending sky seems rent apart,
With the dreadful throbs of his mighty heart!
Hurrah! he is mocking the wandering wind,
And leaving the laggard far, far behind.
City, and hamlet, and river, and plain,
Like pictures of chaos, confuse the brain,
As they loom in sight and vanish away,
Like the shifting scenes in a giant play.
And thus the horse with the iron heart,
Bearing his burden from mart to mart—
Panting and puffing his clarion peals;
Shaking the earth with his clanging heels—
Flashing the sparks from his fiery eyes,
Like a hunted demon shrieks and flies.

The state of Indiana has many battle-fields, where a heroism has been dislayed, by Americans, in border warfare with the Indian tribes, that has scarcely a parallel in the annals of history. I have only time to glance at these.

The capture of the British governor, Hamilton, and Vin-cennes, by George Rogers Clark, as early as 1779, was a mo[st] brilliant victory. It is stated that Hamilton had made a:-rangement to enlist the southern and western Indians for th[e] next spring's campaign; and, if Mr. Stone be correct in h[is] suppositions, Brant and his Iroquois were to act in concer: with him. Had Clark, therefore, failed to conquer the gov-ernor, there is too much reason to fear that the west wou:[d] have been, indeed, swept from the Mississippi to the mount-ains, and the great blow struck which had been contemplated from the outset by Britain.

The defense of Fort Harrison, near Terre Haute, is worthy of a prominent place in our country's history. It was there, perhaps, more than anywhere else, that General Zachary Taylor, then but a mere stripling, as a captain of this frontier post, exhibited a presence of mind, a military skill and noble daring hardly equaled by his most brilliant exploits in Mex-ico. His fort was attacked late in the night of the 4th of September, 1812, by a large party of Indians. The engage-ment continued for seven hours. One of the block-houses which formed a part of the fort, was set on fire, which baffled every effort to extinguish it. General Taylor, in his graphic account to his commanding officer, after the battle, remarks:

"As that block-house adjoined the barracks that make part of the fortifications, most of the men immediately gave them-selves up for lost, and I had the greatest difficulty in getting my orders executed—and, sir, what from the raging of the fire—the yelling and howling of several hundred Indians—the cries of nine women and children (a part soldiers' and a part citizens' wives, who had taken shelter in the fort), and the despondency of so many of the men, which was worse than all—I can assure you that my feelings were unpleasant—an[d] indeed there were not more than ten or fifteen men able to do a great deal, the others being sick or convalescent. *But my presence of mind did not, for a moment, forsake me."*

This last trait in Zachary Taylor's character, no doubt, saved the fort, and this brilliant defense was accomplished by the loss of but two men killed and two wounded.

The battle of Tippecanoe, which took place near the Wabash river, seven miles above where the city of Lafayette now stands, on the 7th of November, 1811, is so well known that it is unnecessary to give any particulars. The nine acres of ground where the Americans were encamped, and where the battle was principally fought, now belong to the state of Indiana as a donation from General John Tipton—who was an officer in the engagement—and arrangements are about to be made by the state to enclose it, I hope with a good and substantial cast iron fence. The New Albany and Lake Michigan railroad passes immediately by the battle ground, and the Masonic fraternity of Indiana and Kentucky have made arrangements to erect a monument on this beautiful eminence to the memory of the heroic Daviess and others, who gallantly fell fighting in that sanguinary contest. It will present a grand appearance from the cars, as they pass along, and will be witnessed by the thousands that will travel on that road.

The following description is the result of a visit to the spot, by a member of my own family, in October, 1845:

> My heart was still within me, for I stood,
>   In trembling awe, on consecrated ground—
> Upon the soil made sacred by the blood
>   Of western chivalry; and though I found
> No storied marble there to proudly sound
>   The names of those who fell, or bear a trace
> Of gratitude, the old trees stood around,
>   Like giant sentinels, to guard the place,
>   Wearing the bullet-scars Time could not all efface.

Oh! there are times when the unfettered mind
  Goes out from its clay tenement, and strays,
In dreams all fanciful and undefined,
  Amidst the moldering records of old days.
Dim forms start up before us as we raise,
  In fancy's light, the dark mysterious seal
Of buried years; shadows are there; we gaze
  Upon the terrible; hear, see and feel
Things that no sign, no word hath power to reveal.

Thus was I spell-bound there, and fancy wrought
  A thrilling scene before me. It was night
Within a green old forest, and I thought
  A line of watch-fires, burning strangely bright,
Sent up phantastic streams of fitful light
  Amidst the autumn leaves. Then tents arose,
And war-like weapons gleamed upon my sight,
  And men, unconscious of approaching foes,
Wrapt in that sweet oblivion, toil-earned repose.

Many a one, forgetting every care,
  Had wandered far away, and in his trance,
Was sitting in his quiet home, and there
  Recounting his strange perils, and perchance,
He smiles to see how dangers past enhance
  The joys around him. Sleeping soldier, pour
The wealth of thine affection in that glance
  At thy heart's idols, for thy days are o'er;
Thou'lt never see thy home, thy bright-eyed children more.

A death-shot rang upon the midnight air.
  Hark! hark! Oh God, that wild unearthly yell,
Told but too truly that the foe was there,
  And froze the very life-blood where it fell.
Then from prairie, thicket, stream, and dell,
  Arose the sound of the unequal strife,
And ere the half-awakened men could tell
  From whence the death-blows came, the ground was rife,
With many a ghastly corse and crimson stream of life.

Secure within the tall prairie grass
  That grew in wild luxuriance round the scene,
The painted warriors firmly kept the pass,
  And still behind this slight but fitting screen

Took fatal aim, themselves the while unseen.
Oh! God, there is no scene so full of dread,
As such a battle in the night I ween;
The rallying cry, the shrieks, the groans, the tread
Of marching squadrons o'er the dying and the dead.

The sharp, shrill fife-note and the clashing steel;
The lightning flashes, smoke, and streaming gore,
As ranks advance, make ready, charge, and wheel,
Many of whom, perchance, will charge no more.
The loud command, the deep incessant roar,
As volley after volley loudly tells
Its tale of blood, repeated o'er and o'er
Along the deep ravines and secret cells;
Amidst the craggy rocks where babbling echo dwells.

Long, long they fought and bravely, but the foe
Had the advantage; where the watch-fires threw
Along the broken ranks a ruddy glow,
Like winged lightning-shafts the bullets flew,
With the unerring aim, so strangely true,
Of savage marksmen; not a single eye,
Quailed as the dreadful contest deeper grew;
They counted it a little thing to die;
A wound, a pang, a groan, a struggle, and a sigh.

At length a streak of light, all cold and gray,
Slowly along the deep horizon spread;
Then the dark battle-cloud rolled up and lay
Like a strange pall above the unshrouded dead.
No dirge was sung, no word of prayer was said,
As weeping comrades took their mute farewell,
Ere they departed hence, with stealing tread,
Leaving the hastily made graves to tell,
Where many a gallant soldier nobly fought and fell.

My dream departed; the blue sky above
Was bending down as beautiful and fair,
As if the spirit of Almighty love
And God's omnipotence were resting there.
The forest leaves waved in the morning air
Caressingly, and there was not one stain
On the bright pebbles or green sward to bear
The record of the battle-strife, the pain,
The groans, the agony, the death-wounds of the slain.

The scene was strangely changed since that sad night;
   Then soil, grass, bramble-brush and stream, were red.
Now, all were fresh, green, beautiful, and bright;
   The flower-embroidered carpet Nature spread,
Was fair enough to grace an angel's tread.
   The dew-drops trembled in the passing breeze
And fell in fairy showers upon my head;
   The wild birds carolled in the leafy trees
As though they strove with strange variety to please.

The memory of that lovely spot doth seem
   To tremble o'er my heart-strings with a thrill,
Like some bright fragment of a broken dream.
   A gentle stream, now narrowed to a rill,
Winds, like a line of sunbeams, round the hill,
   And ripples o'er the shining stones that pave
Its narrow channel, with a soft low trill
   Of music to the flowers that stoop to lave
Their petals in the spray, or kiss the laughing wave

I have one token of the dreamy hour
   I spent beside the ashes of the brave;
It is a little faded purple flower
   That grew, alone, upon the common grave.
I love it, for it saw the old trees wave
   Their giant-arms above it in mid-air,
That stood there on the battle-night and gave
   Protection to the men, and bore a share
Of bullet-wounds with those who nobly perished there.

Fair Indiana, thou wilt not forget
   It was for thee they poured life's crimson tide;
It was for thee, my own bright home, they met;
   'Twas on thy bosom that they battled, died.
And it will be thy glory and thy pride
   To bid the monumental marble rise,
Where now their ashes slumber side by side,
   Beneath the flowers that lift their dewy eyes
Toward the stars that burn and sparkle o'er thy skies.

I do not belong to those who by unjust means would wrest from neighboring countries any of their dominions, but I believe the framers of the American constitution laid the foundations of this government deep in the everlasting principles of nature herself. The general government represents the sun, and the states the planets. Each has its peculiar sphere, in which it moves. Astronomers, from time to time, as science has been developed, have discovered new worlds, some of them far in the distance of unlimited space—all harmoniously moving in their proper orbits, but illumined by the great central light. Such has been the progress of our free institutions. New stars have been added to our glorious constellation; and so long as we follow the landmarks of our fathers and confine the general and the state governments to their proper limits, there will be no danger. It is enough for me to say that I believe the day is not far distant when the whole western continent of America, and the adjacent islands, will be found looking to the stars and stripes as their national ensign.

> "Far, far beyond the deep blue sea,
> This starry ensign of the free,
> Shines lovelier than the purest gem,
> In Europe's proudest diadem.
> For ever honored be the band,
> That wrested from the tyrant's hand
> The charter of the glorious land,
> That fears no haughty despot's rod,
> And pays no homage, save to God.
> Her giant mountains, hoar and high;
> Her balmy air, and sunny sky;
> Her towering forests, dim and old;
> Her inland seas, her mines of gold;
> Her mighty streams, her old blue hills;
> Her starry flowers, her laughing rills—
> Make her as fair as fancy deems,
> The Eden of the poet's dreams.
> As freely trills the voice of mirth,
> Around the poorest cottage hearth,
> As where the sparkling wine is poured,
> By wealth around the proudest board,

> For loving hearts and sunny eyes,
> Have made an earthly paradise,
> As well within her lowest homes
> As in her grandest marble domes."

Indiana, as one of the stars, has progressed with unexampled rapidity. In 1765 her whole population consisted of about one hundred families, principally located at Vincennes. In 1778, thirteen years afterwards, according to General Clark's memoir, the militia in the vicinity of Vincennes was about four hundred; but there was but little accession to the population of other portions of the country within our limits. In 1807 a census of the territory was taken, and the entire population was found to be about 12,000. In 1816, the year Indiana was admitted into the Union, the number was estimated at 65,000. In 1820, according to the United States census, the population was 147,178. In 1830, 343,031. In 1840, 685,866. In 1850, 990,258.

From 1840 to 1845 there was but little increase in our population, owing to the general disarrangement in the monetary affairs of the whole country, and the misfortunes growing out of the failure of our internal improvement system; but from 1845 to 1850 improvement and population progressed with their usual rapidity. In 1846 our state debt arrangement was made with our foreign creditors, which was the crowning act of Governor Whitcomb's administration, and since that period we have faithfully complied with all our engagements, and our bonds have recently been sold, in the New York market, at a premium over their par value. From 1840 to 1846 there was a general gloom and despondency hanging over many of our citizens. But there were not lacking men, who, in the halls of our state legislature, boldly proclaimed that Indiana intended, at every hazard, faithfully to comply with all her engagements. It was during the pendency of the state debt bill that the gallant General Joseph Lane, in the state senate, proclaimed, in the strong language of the backwoodsman, that he would cut cord wood to pay his proportion of the public debt, rather than see Indiana dishonored. Further back than this, however, in 1842, Indiana's gifted orator, on the floor of this hall, uttered the true sentiments of the people, in a strain of burning eloquence, almost unequaled. It was at a time when, according to the public prints, the bonds of our state were selling in the New York market at but seventeen cents on the dollar. In a speech of great power, of which but an imperfect report has been given, he concluded as follows:

"I tremble as the words come upon my lips—repudiation of every dollar of our public debt. I do not go as far as the gentleman from St. Joseph, as to the moral obligation resting upon us to pay for bonds procured through fraud, and for which we have received no consideration. But, so far as the rest are concerned, I would sooner part with my last coat, and divide my last crust of bread, than sully the honor and fame of Indiana, or sanction a principle so abhorrent to all my ideas of justice, and so dishonorable, whether practiced by men or by nations. Unless something be done, and that speedily too, repudiation, as I said before, will be our only alternative. Then will follow loss of fame, of honor and of credit, of all that is valuable in reputation to states and individuals. When Indiana refuses to pay her just debts the judgments of God will be upon her and upon her children From that day the name of Hoosier will become a by-word of reproach, as well among the nations as throughout the limits of our sister confederacies. On that day anarchy must reign in our midst; the sound of the church-going bell will no longer break upon the slumbers of the virtuous and happy; law and justice will be dethroned, and this edifice, intended to perpetuate the glory of Indiana, will be yielded up to the dominion of fiends and robbers. When that day arrives, the columns which support the structure of this hall will be defiled by the slime of serpents, and, as they exhibit their poisonous fangs, will hiss us into scorn for having resorted to a subterfuge so base to evade the solemn obligations that rest upon us."

I shall never forget the occasion or the speaker. Many of you can imagine the eloquence of a Hannegan, in his brighter and happier days, from this imperfect specimen.

The increase of population in Indiana, during the past three years, has been almost without a parallel; and by the commencement of the year 1855 we may safely estimate the number of inhabitants at very little short of one million five hundred thousand.

From the latest estimates, 760 miles of railroad are now completed in the state—979 miles more in course of construction, of which 400 will be completed in the course of the next six months.

We are just entering upon a new common school system, from which there is much to hope, under the guardianship of our indefatigable state superintendent of public instruction. Our benevolent institutions, for the education of the deaf and dumb, and blind, and for curing or ameliorating the condition of the insane, brought into existence during the darkest period of our state's history, are our pride and glory.

The law reports of Judge Blackford have given us a legal reputation not surpassed by any of the states, and our universities and colleges are shedding light amongst the people, in the higher branches of science and literature.

We have also a state agricultural society, recently established, of which the governor is the president, and which is composed of delegates from all parts of the state. We have had one state fair, at which about thirty thousand of our citizens were present, and where specimens of agricultural products, of science, of the mechanic arts, and of other branches of home industry, were exhibited, but little behind those of the oldest states in the Union.

With these advantages, our course must be onward.

In conclusion, and in this connection, we should not forget the early friends of education and literature in our state, The following sentiments, found in the message of our first governor, Jennings, delivered at the commencement of the second session of the Indiana legislature, in 1817, are his proudest monument:

"The commencement of a state library forms a subject of too much interest not to meet your attention. I recommend to your consideration, the propriety of requiring, by law, a per centum on the proceeds of the sale of town lots, to be paid for the support of schools and the establishment of libraries therein. The establishment of a system of common schools throughout the inhabited portion of our state, will meet that consideration which its importance dictates. The operation of such a system, so arranged as to afford the means to every description of our citizens, to educate their children, will secure the morals of the rising generation; the better prepare them for the discharge of their several and respective duties, and to estimate the value of our free institutions—the surest guaranties of that love of country, so essential to the permanence of our form of government."

INDIANA HISTORICAL SOCIETY PUBLICATIONS

VOLUME I   NUMBER VI

JOSEPH G. MARSHALL

BY

PROF. JOHN L. CAMPBELL

(Delivered before the Society November 26, 1873)

INDIANAPOLIS
THE BOWEN-MERRILL COMPANY
1897

JOSEPH G. MARSHALL.

Joseph G. Marshall was born in Fayette county, Ky., January 18, 1800. His early life was spent on the farm in the usual work incident to farm life. He was taught chiefly by his father, the Rev. Robert Marshall, of county Downs, Ireland, who was in the habit of teaching school a part of each year, mainly for the purpose of training his own children. Joseph continued with his father until he was prepared for the Junior class in college. He graduated at Transylvania University, Lexington, Ky., in 1823, at the time presided over by the distinguished Horace Holley, D. D., LL. D.

Of his college life I have a single pleasant incident, related to me by my friend the Hon. Henry S. Lane. One of the exercises assigned by Dr. Blythe, professor of rhetoric in the university, was a dissertation or sermon on some topic selected from Scripture. In the fulfillment of this duty Joseph and Samuel Marshall (afterward Rev. Sam Marshall, of Louisville), took texts and prepared their sermons. When presented to the instructor, Joseph was commended for his exposition and the faithfulness with which he adhered to his subject, but to Samuel the professor replied: "Very well, very well, Sammy, but any other text would have answered your purpose quite as well." He received his second degree, M.A., in 1826. In 1828 Mr. Marshall removed from Kentucky to Madison, in our state, and entered on the practice of his profession. The days of waiting for clients were few. His career seems to have been successful from the beginning, and prosperity attended his earliest ministrations in the temple of justice. During his entire professional life in Madison, his practice was in all the state and federal courts in Indiana. The by no means partial testimony on personal grounds by Oliver H. Smith in his sketches is that Marshall "stood among the very first in the state. His great forte as an advocate was in the power with which he handled the facts before the jury. He seemed to forget himself in his subject, and at times I have thought him unsurpassed by any man I ever heard in impassioned eloquence. He had a large practice of heavy cases requiring all his forensic powers."

In personal appearance Mr. Marshall was large and fleshy, his hair of auburn color, his eyes hazel and penetrating. In any company of distinguished men he would be selected as one of the most prominent. When fully aroused his influence with a jury was unbounded. A single case related to me by Senator Lane will illustrate this. A tradesman on the Ohio started south with two flat boats of produce; one of these boats was lost on the falls at Louisville and the other fell into the hands of the city sharks. Meanwhile, during his absence, since misfortunes seldom come single, his wife and two children died, and the poor penniless trader returned to his home to find it desolate.

For a part of his produce the trader had executed his promissory notes and at maturity the owners brought suit to recover. Judge Dewey—the greatest intellect in Indiana—prosecuted the case and Marshall defended. The action being on a plain promissory note, Judge Dewey submitted the case without argument, but Marshall, with not a vestige of proof, so worked up the feelings of the jury and drew so touching a picture of the troubles of his client, that they passed for the defendant. Among all the exciting trials in the court history of Indiana, the Freeman case—1853—

stands most prominent. In the days when that infamous code of barbarity, the fugitive slave law, was in force, a free negro of Indianapolis, a respected citizen, whose only crime was his color, was arrested on the application of his alleged masters and was about to be forced into slavery. Never was the honest indignation of the people of Indianapolis so thoroughly aroused. The court room was crowded to excess. The able attorneys for the defense were the Hon. John Coburn, Lucien Barbour, and John Ketcham. The case progressed towards judgment and the court was summing up against the prisoner. In the crowded audience there was a lion apparently asleep. From the court came the utterance —"the presumption of slavery exists against the prisoner because of his color"—when with one bound and roar the aroused lion sent a shaking tremor to the marrow of the pale and trembling judge. Leaping forward regardless of the proprieties of courts and attorneys, Marshall demanded to be heard. "In what capacity do you appear in this case, not being an employed attorney?" "As a free American citizen, sir, to say to you that under the glorious constitution which we have sworn to support, there can be neither presumption nor fact of slavery." Then with a wild outburst of eloquence, never perhaps equaled in the practice in the state, he proceeded to plead the cause of the oppressed against the oppressors. Following this speech was a scene of the wildest confusion— rescue was hinted at and mob violence for a time threatened court and prosecutors, but milder counsels finally prevailed, and after months of delay and expense the victim was released from his prosecutors, but not until after the identical slave for whom Freeman was taken had been visited in Canada by the Hon. John Coburn and an attorney for the prosecution. The proper field for his political powers was national, and it was a great disgrace to the Whig party of Indiana that he was not sent to the United States Senate. For this high nomination he received the caucus nomination of the party, but by the wily tricks of pretended friends, he was compelled to give place to the less gifted and more unscrupulous. Had he condescended to barter for the place, he could have secured it, but with the loss of self-respect to Marshall the so-called honor would have been empty indeed. He was the Whig candidate for governor in 1843, but failed of election, the state giving a Democratic majority that year in the choice of the Hon. James Whitcomb. He served a number of years in our state legislature, and was always recognized unquestioned as the leader of the party, shaping mostly its plans and directing its purposes. He exerted always the most decided influence in the Whig party, whether in or out of the office. In the brilliant campaign of 1840, Mr. Marshall was elected at large on the Whig ticket. He was then in the full prime of his life, with a physical frame of splendid proportions, in perfect health. The echoing tones of his profound and convincing eloquence yet linger in the memories of the Whigs of 1840. At Crawfordsville, Mr. Marshall met in a joint political discussion the silver-tongued Hannegan, but the beautiful periods and graceful gestures of the latter failed before the impetuous power displayed by Marshall, as he dwelt on the exploit of the hero of Tippecanoe. The older citizens of Madison retain a vivid recollection of the reception in their city of Daniel Webster, and the elegant welcome in their behalf by their own most honored citizen, and of the same expression of regard and respect made by Mr. Webster of the reputation and ability of Mr. Marshall. Mr. Marshall died at Louisville, Ky., April 8, 1855, in the residence of R. K. White. He had been afflicted with bronchitis for about five years, and the disease assumed the form of consumption a few months previous to his death. He left his home in Madison in March for the South, hoping that a more genial climate would be of benefit to his health, but his strength was sufficient only to permit the trip down the Ohio to Louisville. Too ill to go farther, he remained there to die. The following are extracts from the Louisville papers at the time:

(Editorial in *Daily Democrat*, Louisville, Monday, April 9, 1855.)

Died, at the residence of Col. White in this city, yesterday morning, the Hon. Joseph G. Marshall, of Indiana. He was a native of Kentucky, the son of a distinguished Presbyterian clergyman, who will be remembered, perhaps, by many of our readers. Joseph G. Marshall was born in January, 1800, and has been cut off early in life's afternoon. His disease was consumption, but his demise, so sudden, was unexpected. He appeared better on Saturday morning, but a change for the worse soon terminated his life. The deceased chose our neighboring state of Indiana as his home and the law as his profession; and has left behind him few, if any, equals at the bar of his adopted state. He appeared but seldom in public life outside his profession, but that was not for lack of ability, or an exalted reputation. He was first in the school of politics to which he was honestly attached, and enjoyed the universal respect of his opponents. He was, in fact, a great man, and his character only shone with less luster from his unobtrusiveness and, perhaps, fastidious self-respect. His death will be felt as a public calamity by a large circle of acquaintances. Personally few stood higher or had more warm and devoted friends or fewer enemies. He was an ornament to his profession and in his employment never forgot his character as a man or citizen. He had a heart of warm and generous sympathies. A poor and friendless client found in him an advocate that would overlook a fee in the interests of his cause. He cherished a political faith different from our own, but we sincerely regret his loss, for the world has not many of such to lose. He died in the faith of a Christian, surrounded by his afflicted and bereaved family.

Death of a Great Man.
(Article in *Louisville Journal*, Monday, April 9, 1855.)

We deeply regret to announce the death of the Hon. Joseph G. Marshall, of Madison, Ind. He died at the house of Mr. R. K. White, on Broadway between Third and Fourth, whence his remains are to be taken to Madison at 10 o'clock this morning. He has been afflicted with bronchitis for abou' five years, and the disease, being much aggravated by a long speech which he made before the supreme court in February last, became consumption. He left home two or three weeks ago on his way to the South in the hope that his health might be benefited by a genial climate; but on his arrival in Louisville, he found himself too ill to go further and remained here to die.

In the death of Mr. Marshall, Indiana and the west have sustained a most serious loss. He was a good man and a great man. The purity of his heart was ever unstained, he discharged his duties in all the relations of life with fidelity and zeal, and the power of his intellect and vigor, and effectiveness of his eloquence as a lawyer and a statesman won the unbounded admiration of all who listened to him. The hearts of a whole people will throb with grief for the death of such a man.

Death of Joseph G. Marshall.
(Editorial in *Louisville Weekly Courier*, April 14, 1855.)

We announce this morning, with unfeigned regret, the decease of the Hon. Joseph G. Marshall, of Indiana. This distinguished gentleman died yesterday morning at the residence of Col. Robert K. White in this city, having arrived here on his way to the south, where he proposed spending some time for the benefit of his health. Mr. Marshall was a native of this state, having been born in Fayette county. He removed when young to Indiana and made Madison his place of residence, where he practiced his profession with great success. As a lawyer he was one of the most powerful advocates in the west; his abilities being very superior, both when addressed to the discussion of the most abstruse legal points, and in appealing to the sympathies of jurors. As a politician Mr. Marshall obtained no great degree of eminence, his unswerving devotion to Whig principles in a Democratic state having hindered his attaining those positions to which his eminent talent entitled him. He however occupied several stations of honor, and during last winter was a prominent candidate for United States senator.

The cause of Mr. Marshall's death was consumption, with which he had been suffering for some time. Its ravages had been stayed by Mr. Marshall having refrained of late from any active participation in the active duties of his profession. Recently he made a most powerful argument before the supreme court at Indianapolis, the excitement attending which completely prostrated his strength. Leaving home he reached Louisville en route for the south, and here at the home of an attentive friend died.

The remains of Mr. Marshall will be taken to Madison on the mail boat, from the residence of Col. Robert K. White, on Broadway near Third.

TESTIMONIAL TO THE HON. JOSEPH G. MARSHALL.

(*Louisville Courier*, April 14, 1855.)

At a meeting of the Louisville bar held at the chancery court room, April 9th, 1855, the Hon. Henry Pirtle was called to the chair and P. B. Muir was appointed secretary. On motion of Henry C. Wood, Esq., a committee of five was appointed to prepare and present resolutions expressive of the sense of the Louisville bar at the death of the Hon. J. G. Marshall. The chairman appointed on said committee H. C Wood, Esq., Hon. W. P. Thompson, Hon. W. S. Bodley, Nathaniel Wolfe, Esq , and D. W. Wilson, Esq. The committee reported the following resolutions, which were unanimously adopted:

"WHEREAS, Death has come into our midst and removed from the scene of his labors the Hon. Joseph G. Marshall, an eminent citizen and member of the bar of the state of Indiana. He died in this city on the morning of April 8, 1855, in the fifty-sixth year of his age. The deceased was a native of Kentucky and was justly entitled to rank among the great men of the Union. He was a man of the largest capacity, of high professional attainments, and of wonderful powers as an orator. There was a force in his logic, and an energy and earnestness in his manner which, graced by his delightful voice, made him one of the most powerful and successful advocates of which the American bar could boast. He was, too, a distinguished politician, and in all walks of life beloved for the purity and uprightness of his character, the frankness and generosity of his nature. The members of the bar of the city of Louisville are desirous to testify the respect in which they hold his views, his talents, and his fame. Therefore,

"*Resolved*, That we have received the intelligence of the death of Joseph G. Marshall with emotions of deep sensibility, and we unite with our brethren in the profession in the state of Indiana in deploring his loss.

"*Resolved*, That the members of the bar of Louisville tender to the widow and family of the deceased their sympathy and condolence, and that, with the permission of the family, they will join as a body in the ceremonies of the funeral.

"*Resolved*, That we request the publication of the proceedings of this meeting in the papers of this city and the city of Madison."

On motion of Bland Ballard, Esq., the foregoing resolutions were directed to be entered on the record of the various courts of Louisville.

On motion the meeting adjourned.

H. PIRTLE, *Chairman*.

P. B. MUIR, *Secretary*.

In the district court of the United States, Messrs. Oliver H. Smith, Samuel C. Wilson, Simon Yandes, Joseph A. Wright and James Raridan, all the worthy compeers of Marshall—and, whether living or dead, names most prominent and honored in our state history—were appointed by Justice McLean a committee on resolutions to express the esteem held by the bar of the character and ability of this one of their own number. In the appointment of the committee Justice McLean remarked: "At any bar in the Union Mr. Marshall's ability would have been marked and he would have been considered an antagonist to require the highest efforts." In the supreme court of Indiana the committee on resolutions appointed by Judge Perkins consisted of David McDonald, Thomas Nelson, R. W. Thompson, Jeremiah Sullivan, George Dunn, William T Otto and Randall Crawford. The resolutions adopted contain the following tribute:

"We deem it due to the high character of Mr. Marshall as a man, and to the elevated distinction he had won by his great ability and eloquence as a member of the bar of Indiana, that we, who have been so long associated with him in private and professional life, should express the distinguished estimation in which we held him before his death, and our sincere regret that his brilliant career has been so soon terminated; therefore,

"*Resolved*, That as we recognized him in life as occupying a place in the front rank of our bar—as possessed of an intellect of the highest order, and of powers of oratory rarely excelled, so we regard his death as a serious and irreparable loss to us his professional associates, and to the state which he so long and faithfully served."

These resolutions were, by order of the court, placed upon its records and the presiding officer, Judge Perkins, in language touching and beautiful, testified to the high intellectual character of the deceased.

INDIANA HISTORICAL SOCIETY PUBLICATIONS

VOLUME I   NUMBER VII

JUDGE JOHN LAW

BY

CHARLES DENBY

(Presented to the Society November 26, 1873)

INDIANAPOLIS
THE BOWEN-MERRILL COMPANY
1897

JOHN LAW.

The writer approaches the task of sketching the life and delineating the character of the late John Law with great misgivings. He brings to this duty (for such it is) some of the qualities necessary to do it justice, and these are, affection for the man, respect for his character, admiration for his abilities. But time is wanting—amid the pressure of the most exacting of all occupations, the law, to whose practice the subject of this sketch also devoted his life—to write such biography as is due to the memory of a distinguished man, and the writer has not the requisite literary skill for the task. The author of the history of English literature holds it to be true that the biographer "should love his subject, but should not flatter any one." No one who knew Judge Law will fail in the first requisite. He leaves "troops of friends," but no enemy behind him. The elements were so gently mixed in his disposition, his manners were so pleasing and gracious, his temperament was so even and kindly, that no one could know him and fail to love him. An accomplished gentleman, a brilliant *raconteur* in his best days, the witchery of his manner won all hearts.

Judge Law came of a distinguished family. He traced back his lineage through a long line of ancestors who won honor in the profession of the law, which was regularly transmitted from father to son. They filled positions of distinction in the public employment and were honorable, high-minded men. They do not seem to have devoted themselves to mere money-getting, but were men of comfortable means, whose moral and intellectual worth gave them an influence and weight which money can not buy. It happens to but few families—the Adamses are the only one I can now recall—that a scion of theirs in three succeeding generations has occupied a seat in congress. The parallel is more striking from the fact that three generations of the Adamses were represented in congress successively at the same time that those of the Laws held their seats. The grandfather of Judge Law, Richard Law, sat with John Adams; the father of Judge Law sat with John Quincy Adams, and Judge Law himself with Charles Francis Adams.

John Law was born in New London, Connecticut, on the 28th day of October, 1796; he died at Evansville, Indiana, on the 7th day of October, 1873. His grandfather, Richard Law, was a member of the continental congress. He was elected in 1776, and was therefore a member of the congress which adopted the "Declaration of Independence." The great honor of signing that memorable instrument would have been his, but at the time that congress sat, Richard Law, and several members of his family were afflicted with the smallpox, and he did not take his seat until 1777. He served as a member of the continental congress until the close of the war, and at the expiration of his term he was appointed by President Washington United States judge for the district of Connecticut, and discharged the important duties of that office with honor and ability until his death, which occurred in 1806. He is remembered as a gentleman of the "old school," possessing all the grace and dignity which belonged to a style of men who have passed away. Western manners and life on the frontier among the French and Indians, in the rough and tumble practice of the law on circuit, tended to modify in John Law a stateliness which he fairly inherited, and to infuse into his character more humor, wit and brilliancy than his ancestors probably possessed; but it is safe to say that to the last he was a worthy descendant of the "gentlemen of the old school," clothe them with what solid good qualities, fact or imagination may.

Lyman Law, the son of Richard and father of John Law, was born in New London, Connecticut, in the year 1770. He graduated at the old New England school, Yale college, in 1791. Naturally he became a lawyer, studying in his father's office. Public stations in those days, and in that land of austere purity of public men, were more honorable than in these later times. Lyman became a member of the state legislature and speaker of the house. In the year 1811 he was elected to a seat in congress, and remained a member of that body by successive elections until 1817. He died in New London in February, 1842. Coming of such ancestry, what course naturally opened itself to John Law, the bright, sparkling, brilliant inheritor of a distinguished name, brought up with tender care, endowed with an acute and flashing intellect, schooled in his family, and by teachers as few young men are taught, honest and honorable as the parent stock, but ambitious of distinction, and feeling within him the praiseworthy desire to add lustre to an honored race?

Of course John Law was sent to Yale. What New England man regards his destiny as performed unless he starts his active life with the indorsement of that grand and dear *Alma Mater?* Of course he went there young. It is plain to us who knew him here that he was always precocious, always intellectually brilliant, and always revelling in the glowing pages of literature. He graduated in 1814 at Yale college, being then eighteen years old. Think of it, boys of the present generation! While yet you are but beginning the elements of the classics, and the rudimentary treatises on mathematics, this young man, or boy, had finished the college curriculum. To a mind like his, classic literature possessed a wonderful charm. I do not fancy him as poring over Euclid, Bourdon or La Place with any great fervor. But the pictured pages of Livy, the flowing numbers of Virgil, the rounded periods of Cicero and the heroic verses of Homer were no doubt his delight and his inspiration.

In after life, and in common conversation, there flashed from him apt quotation, beautiful illustration, the poetic phrase garnered in school-boy memory, and lingering there always. How he relished the distich culled from Horace or Terence! He was a great reader of English, but the college nature, engrafted by years of study, predominated, and in later years, before his faculties weakened and waned, there flashed from him the *jeu d'esprit* that has come down to us flavored with Falernian from the masters of antiquity. This classic course of study raises always a mooted question of advantage, and the practical and the mathematical enter the lists against it. I do not propose to attempt its solution here.

In the family of the Laws, money was never the main object. Professional distinction, once won, as it only can be won by real merit, brought public recognition in its train, and these secured, competence was all they asked, accompanied as it was by high social standing and universal respect of their fellow-men. To minds like John Law's, a harder, rougher, more scientific and practical course of study might produce a more practical, energetic and labor-seeking after-life, but where would have been the charm of that vivacity which was fed by the springs flowing perennially from antiquity, where the brilliancy which peculiarly made his reputation as a lawyer, and the graceful oratory, which, in his younger days, made him the favorite of audiences? "*Non omnes possumus omnia,*" while the inventor, the engineer, the mathematician have their appropriate places in niches of fame, let graceful scholarship, the mere accomplishments of learning, the intellectuality which charms rather than benefits mankind, receive appropriate praise.

Who that well knew another noted man in this community, the late John J. Chandler, will not in this connection recall the charm that he, in his happiest moods, wove around his hearers, drawing ideas and phrases from "the pure springs of English undefiled," whose waters were so sweet to him?

Graduating in 1814, John Law in turn read law with his father, as his own son subsequently did with him. In the hurry of our rapid western life, when the past seems forgotten, when the goal of yesterday is the starting point of the morrow, this old family-history, where each son takes up the early position of the father and steps in his footsteps, finds no parallel. But young Law had caught the enthusiasm of young America, which the war of 1812 fanned into flame. This grand western country, the Eldorado of intellect at the bar, was wooing the talent of the East to its fresh and glowing embraces. Here lay a region where all men might start on even terms; here were fresh fields to be held by the brain and tongue of the occupant; here were forums where new questions were to be raised and settled, not by ancient precedent, but by the keen encounter of rival debate. Here, unembarrassed by social surroundings, devoid of family ties, the lists were opened to all comers, but the ground was to be held by skill and courage only. The young lawyer encountered no hoary-headed reputation here to overawe judge and the jury by its gray locks; no circle of kinsmen would pour briefs into his bag; no social or churchly standing would give him prominence. The attorneys, the bench, the people were young. All started in public life together and merit was the only test. It is conceded that such circumstances in all new states produce more legal ability than belongs to older bars, and so it was in Indiana. We still look up to Dewey and Blackford as the brightest lights of our profession, and we draw our highest learning from their opinions preserved in Blackford's Reports.

In the year 1817 Judge Law was admitted by the supreme court of Connecticut to the practice of his profession. He left Connecticut in the month of October, 1817, and arrived in Indiana in the following month. He found Indiana a wilderness. Hiring a horse he proceeded to Corydon, in Harrison county, which was then the seat of government. The supreme court, consisting of three judges, Scott, Holman, and Blackford, was then in session. On the fourth day of December, 1817, he was examined by the judges, in open court, for admission to the bar. He was then just twenty-one years and a few weeks of age. His examination was brilliant and excited the commendation of the judges. He was young, in fact, and seemed in appearance younger than he really was. He was full of life, vivacity, and good humor, and became then, and always remained, a favorite of the bench. Of the members and attorneys of that court none are left. Judge Law was the last survivor. Judge Jeremiah Sullivan was admitted to practice at the same time. He located at Madison, then the rising town of the state. Judge Sullivan became a judge of the supreme court and filled the position with great distinction for several years and preceded Judge Law to the grave but a short time. When the supreme court adjourned young Law left in company with Charles Dewey, who afterwards became a judge of the supreme court and filled the position well. Dewey settled at Paoli, and Law at Vincennes. He arrived at Vincennes on the 15th day of December, 1817, and immediately commenced the practice of his profession. He afterwards became the historian of Vincennes, and has recorded the condition of the town at the time he saw it, in a sketch which has been much admired. The inhabitants were mostly French, and the gayety and vivacity of their national character were exemplified in their easy, enjoyable mode of life. There were numberless balls and horse races. There was mass on Sunday in the morning, and pony races on the prairies after dinner. This population has mostly died out, but the old settlers will never cease to remember, with kindly feeling, the good nature, the warm hearts and the gentle manners of these loving children of France. To them and to the brave and pious fathers who were pioneers with them, and advised them in things temporal and pointed their simple devotions to the "Cross," this country owes a debt of gratitude and admiration which has been poorly paid. Progress, with its handmaidens, science and art, has left this gay and nonchalant race no part to play in the grand diorama through which this state has marched to the tap of the stirring drum from a wilderness to an empire in one's life duration, but there was a time when the black robe of the Jesuit father symbolized nearly all the civilization, the civil liberty and the christianity that existed in the country of the northwest.

At that time, in the beginning of the year 1818, there were three judicial circuits in Indiana. This circuit was composed of the counties of Knox, Gibson, Posey and Vanderburgh. Afterwards the county of Warrick was attached to this circuit. The county seat of Warrick was Darlington, at the mouth of Cypress creek. The ancient cities of the world have not more completely disappeared from view than has Darlington. It lives only in tradition. The first county seat in Posey was Springfield. Advancing time has left only a memory of Springfield. The first county seat of Vanderburgh was Evansville. From her small beginning, she alone of the three has grown and prospered. The second city in the state to-day, she seems just entering on her career of greatness, and if the energy of her people shall not falter and they remain true to themselves, he that shall write the biography of one of her present youthful citizens after his death will be able to repeat the story of a progress as remarkable as that which was witnessed by the subject of this sketch, Judge William Prince was the judge of the first circuit at that time. He was soon appointed to an Indian agency and resigned his judgeship. David Hart was appointed to succeed him. In February, 1818, the circuit court convened at Evansville. Judge Hart appointed John Law prosecuting attorney for his circuit. For some reason Judge Hart did not attend the session, and court was held by the associate judges, Waggoner and McCreary. Judge Law acted as prosecuting attorney. There were no civil cases and but four criminal cases. Two were for assault and battery and two for adultery. The court adjourned the second day. It was held in a tobacco warehouse on Main street, situated on a lot adjoining the location of the Evansville National Bank. The lawyers present were Charles Dewey, Jacob Call, who afterwards represented the district in congress, Richard Daniel, who was afterwards judge of the circuit, and William Prince.

In 1825, Brown Ray, governor of the state, appointed John Law prosecuting attorney for the first judicial circuit. In 1826 he was reappointed for the term of two years. In 1824-5 he was elected a member of the house of representatives, which met at Corydon. In 1826 the seat of government was transferred to Indianapolis. In 1830 he was elected by the legislature judge of the seventh judicial circuit. The counties in his circuit were Knox, Sullivan, Monroe, Owen, Vigo, Martin, Putnam, Clay, and Daviess. The population was very sparse, and the judge and lawyers had a hard time to get to the county seats. They rode on horseback and often bivouacked in the woods for the night. They were men of talent, and afterwards filled important and honorable positions in the public service.

There are few more distinguished names in Indiana than those of Whitcomb, Hannegan White and others of the bar of the seventh circuit. They became governors, senators and ministers abroad. In 1844 Judge Law was elected judge of the same circuit for the term of seven years. That year he was appointed receiver of public moneys at Vincennes, and thereupon resigned his judgeship. He moved to Evansville in 1851. In connection with his brother William, James B. McCall and Lucius H Scott, he purchased seven hundred acres of land adjoining Evansville, for the purpose of laying out a town. There was some trouble in giving the new place a name. The difficulty was removed by combining parts of the names of the "proprietors" which resulted in "Lamasco." The investment so made proved very profitable. Large numbers of lots were immediately sold, and in a few years a thriving town sprang up. In 1857 it was added to Evansville, and is now as large, or larger, and perhaps more valuable than what was formerly Evansville. Judge Law purchased a residence in Lamasco and resided there continuously until his death.

In 1855 he was appointed by President Pierce judge of the court of land claims, to be held at Vincennes. He was engaged in holding court during the years 1855 and 1856, and settled a great many land titles to the satisfaction of the people concerned.

In 1860 he was nominated and elected a representative in congress from the first congressional district, and again in 1862.

In early life Judge Law was a Whig. For the last twenty-five years he was a consistent Democrat, abiding by the usages of the party and upholding its organization. Twice he was elected to congress by his party by a handsome majority. Neither in politics nor in aught else was there anything bitter in his nature. He was tolerant of all opinions on all subjects, but very firm in his own. The kindly nature of the man was well shown by his introduction of a bill into congress to give to the surviving soldiers of the Revolution—being only twelve in number—a pension of one hundred dollars per annum. This bill passed unanimously. During his congressional service, he acted with his party on all political questions. Personally he was on the best terms with all the members.

And now I have gone over the most prominent incidents in the life of Judge Law, but how little do they go towards making up the real life of the man! Of his home life, of time passed among his flowers and fruits, of that ardent love for nature that comes to old age—so sweetly touched by Shakespeare when he makes Falstaff, on his death bed, "babble of green fields," of his old time hospitality, of his affection for his family—these are subjects not to be dwelt on.

Since Judge Law left congress, in 1864, that which should accompany old age, as honor, "love, obedience, troops of friends, he has had." A gentler, more unassuming, kindlier life has not been passed in our midst. I doubt whether a serener, evener, purer life has been lived in this generation Engaged in political life in stormy times, he walked amid the fiery flames untouched by slander. Did anyone ever accuse him of a meanness, or attach a shade of dishonor to his name? Engaged largely in real estate transactions, was he ever accused of grasping or oppression? Holding offices of trust, did he ever soil his palm with unearned public money? How well he illustrated in that serene old age the blessings of an early education! Books, magazines, papers were his world, in which to the last moment he reveled with unbounded pleasure. From them to his garden, where trees and flowers and fruits were his familiars. How pure his private life! He could look back upon a lifetime passed in the public eye, as lawyer, judge, legislator, and find nothing that, dying, he could wish to blot. His early years were laborious. Few men traveled so much on professional business, or labored harder. Yet he remembered them with pleasure always. At the bar, in the prime of his manhood, he was acute, industrious and eloquent. As an advocate he had few equals. In his later years his real estate investments had made him wealthy. His disposition was far removed from being avaricious. And so he settled into the quiet, unpretending home life we know so well, and calmly waited for his last summons. It had no terrors for him. The broad, majestic river flowing gently to the sea dreads not the moment when its waters shall mingle with the ocean, less than he dreaded his absorption into eternity. To that calm, placid and honorable nature, death could bring no terrors, for it could bring no remorse. Life to him was no fitful fever, and death no sudden shock. His life resembled these bright autumnal days that are on us now, and his death was but the gradual sinking of the sun. Indiana may have lost more noted men, but in all the state, no one name will awaken more kindly recollections, and no death wider regret than the name and death of John Law.

INDIANA HISTORICAL SOCIETY PUBLICATIONS

VOLUME I   NUMBER VIII

ARCHÆOLOGY

BY

PROF. E. T. COX

(Delivered before the Society, February 14, 1877)

INDIANAPOLIS
THE BOWEN-MERRILL COMPANY
1897

ARCHÆOLOGY.

Gentlemen of the State Historical Society of Indiana:

No department of natural history is, at this time, receiving more attention from the votaries of science and thoughtful readers than that which pertains to man and his antiquities. Indeed, so familiar are its students with the present status of anthropology that it will be difficult for me to present novel facts in research or new channels of thought worthy of the attention of a body of such able co-laborers. I crave your indulgence, therefore, if some parts of my address should prove to be devoid of special interest.

Matter and life are universal. The solar system, as well as all other heavenly bodies, is the result of simple substances aggregated into compound substances. These complex bodies forming the universe are produced by the affinity or affection which certain elementary and compound substances have for each other, and the process of evolution in the mineral kingdom, as well as in the organic world, is in constant operation.

Organized matter, or life, results from the combination of the fewest number of simple substances, namely: Carbon, hydrogen, oxygen and nitrogen. These four elements constitute the chief part of all organized tissues. Woody fiber, sugar, starch, gum, fat, oils and many organic acids contain only three—carbon, hydrogen and oxygen—yet I must not omit to mention that in organized matter a small per cent. of other elements is found, such as phosphorus, sulphur, calcium, potassium, sodium, magnesium, silicon, and some others, but the chief mass of plants and animals are formed of the four elements first mentioned. The fourteen or fifteen elements which constitute the principal mass of the mineral world are almost the same which occur in organized matter, the difference being chiefly this: That in inorganic nature the predominant elements, nearly in the order of their abundance, are oxygen, hydrogen, nitrogen, silicon, chlorine, sodium, aluminum, carbon and iron, after which follow potassium, calcium, magnesium, sulphur, phosphorus, iodine and fluorine, while in the organic departments the order is nearly as follows—carbon, hydrogen, nitrogen, potassium, calcium, phosphorus, silicon, sulphur, sodium, magnesium, chlorine, iron, iodine and fluorine.

From this it will be apparent that no essential distinction can be made between inorganic and organic bodies founded on the nature of the elements concerned in their production.

Since spectrum analysis has revealed the presence of these elementary substances, common to organized bodies, in the stars, sun and all of its dependent planets, how can we doubt the existence of life in some form throughout the universe. The heavenly bodies which come to us in the shape of meteorites are in many instances found to contain graphite, a form of carbon most likely due to the destruction of organized matter in some form or other.

The law of change pervades all nature, and there appears to be no such thing as stability. The solid crust of our globe and the life evolved upon it when passed in review before the eye of the earnest student of nature presents an ever-changing panorama from old to new forms of life, and though we are not able to assign specific dates in the history of progress from the lowest forms to the earliest traces of man, geology has pointed out the way by which relative records may be established.

If we dig down into the earth beneath our feet, we find that it is composed of layers of many kinds of stone, resting upon unstratified crystalline rocks—the so-called archean rocks, which form, as it were, the backbone of the earth. The superstructure of stratified rocks were formed by the destruction of older rocks, and once lay at the bottom of the ocean in the condition of mud or ooze. The sedimentary rocks, so formed, are of very great thickness, since we are able to deduce not less than ten miles by measuring from the top of mountain peaks to the bottom of deep sea soundings, while the aggregate thickness of the earth's crust within the reach of the geologist may be set down as twice this amount.

A close study of this crust, composed of stratum upon stratum that enfold the earth like so many successive rings of growth, reveals a most wonderful history, for they are largely made up of the petrified skeletons of the denizens of an ancient ocean. The bottom layers were necessarily formed first, and are therefore the oldest in time; they likewise contain old forms of life, most of which have long since been lost to the world—so that, step by step, as we ascend in the series, new types of life are met with, and by successive epochs we finally pass through eozoic or dawn of life, palæozoic or ancient life, mesozoic or middle life, to cenozoic or recent life. These are simply great divisions of the earth's stony crust, like dividing a column into lower, middle and upper parts, and will serve our present purposes of pointing out the vast time required for the accumulation of such a mass of sedimentary matter, and the long endurance of life, in one form or another, on the globe.

Lyell, in his Principles of Geology, has undertaken to furnish datum for ascertaining, approximately, the length of time required to form a given amount of strata, by measuring the quantity of sediment annually brought down by the Mississippi river and deposited in the area of 12,300 square miles comprising the delta. "Borings near New Orleans have gone to the depth of 600 feet in these fluviatile deposits, and the average depth was assumed to be 528 feet, or the tenth of a mile. The quantity of solid matter brought down annually by the river is given at 3,702,758,400 cubic feet, and the accumulations of the whole deposit must have taken 67,000 years." Yet this deposit made by the Mississippi river represents but a mere fraction of geological history, and belongs to the Quaternary or modern epoch. It will serve, however, to prepare your minds for the reception of a chronology which, though we can not fix the exact date of the beginning, is absolutely demanded at the very threshold of the earth's history.

In tracing the history of mankind, back or down the stream of time, various systems of classification have been proposed, having for their object the division of the subject into distinct periods.

Sir John Lubbock recommends a division of prehistoric archæology into four great epochs:

1. Palæolithic (ancient stone period), that of the Drift, when man shared the possession of Europe with the cave bear, the woolly haired rhinoceros and other extinct animals.

2. Neolithic (polished stone age), a period characterized by beautiful weapons and instruments made of flint and other kinds of stone, but without a trace of any knowledge of metals except gold, which appears to have been used sometimes for ornaments.

3. Bronze Age, in which bronze was made for arms and cutting instruments of all kinds.

4. Iron Age, in which that metal had superseded bronze for arms, axes, knives, etc.; bronze, however, still being in

common use for ornaments and frequently for the handles of swords and other arms, though never for blades.*

These divisions are more strictly applicable to European archæology than to that of America, for during pre-columbian times man on this continent had not advanced beyond the second or neolithic age.

There can be no doubt that primitive man was a cannibal, scarcely more elevated, in a moral sense, than the beasts which surrounded him, and he was long devoid of a knowledge of all but the simplest forms of art, and was taught by necessity to clutch a stick or unwrought stone as implements of defense or offense, or with which to crush roots or crack nuts for food.

Indeed, this was the condition of the inhabitants of Australia when that continent was first discovered by Europeans. While, therefore, we may justly regard these four ages as natural steps through and by which mankind have progressed from the simplest to the present grand achievements of art, yet the fact can not be overlooked that this progress was not uniform over the entire globe, and that from the present civilization of Europe and the United States we may point to vast regions of country peopled by native races in the lowest state of savagery, "people who have not conceived the art of fashioning a stone or shaping a bow."

In digging up the bottoms of many of the caves which abound in France, Belgium and Spain, the remains of man, associated with the bones of extinct animals, flint flakes, arrow points and stone knives, have from time to time been found. In some instances these remains were found buried beneath a solid floor of stalagmite of very great thickness, and covered up by many feet of cave-earth (red-ferruginous

---

* "Prehistoric Times." Sir John Lubbock.

clay), which is again overlaid by another stalagmitic floor and cave-earth.

Dr. Charles C. Abbott, of Trenton, New Jersey, has, for some years past, been finding large numbers of palæolithic implements in the glacial drift which forms the lower terrace of the valley on the north side of the Delaware river. The deposit is twenty to thirty feet above the freshets of the river, and extends beneath the bed of the stream. It is composed of large boulders, pebbles and sand, many of which are from archean beds which lie beyond the borders of the state. Though unable to find here any traces of glacial striation on the boulders or pebbles, Dr. Abbott considers the deposit similar to the drift seen in other parts of the state, where striation and grooves are prevalent, and clearly point to glacial origin. The implements are, from their form, called " turtle-back " celts.

Prof. F. W. Putnam also visited the locality where these implements are found, and informed me that he saw numbers of the "turtle-back" celts sticking out of the drift, where they are exposed by cutting away several feet from the face of the cliff, going to prove that they were not brought from near the surface by the sliding of the bank.

Prof. N. S. Shaler, state geologist of Kentucky, subsequently visited the locality, and while corroborating the testimony of Dr. Abbott and Prof. Putnam that the implements were in place, could not satisfy his mind that the rounded pebbles and boulders belonged to the glacial epoch. This very important discovery of human implements in the drift deposits of New Jersey, by Dr. Abbott, tends to strengthen the evidence in regard to finding a human skull in the glacial deposits of California.

Though there are highly probable accounts of finding the remains of man in the Pliocene deposits of America and Europe, the evidence is not clearly such as will satisfy the strictest demands of science. We may, therefore, look upon the cave-dwellers, who were contemporaries of the extinct elephant, woolly-haired rhinoceros, hippopotamus, cave-bear, etc., as the most ancient man, and they antedate the dog and other domestic animals.

The cave-dwellers were probably followed by the mound-builders and the constructors of earth and stone circles; and if, at any period, universal man exhibited but one status, it might justly be claimed for the mound builders' age—tumuli, or mounds, being in Egypt, Turkey, Arabia, India, China, Germany, England; indeed, in all countries of Europe, North and South America. Stone circles are reported even in Australia, where the lowest type of man is found, and they are also seen in Japan.

Mr. Shuze Isawa, a native of Japan, who read a paper on the origin of the Japanese people at the Nashville meeting of the A. A. A. S., informed me that the Japanese always built a mound when an emperor died. Mr. Isawa stated in his paper that the Japanese people came from India, and found the island inhabited by a race of savages. These savages were driven to the north part of the island, where a remnant of the race are still to be found.

Notwithstanding this universality of tumuli and stone and earth circles, I think we may justly claim North America as preëminently the home of the mound-builder. Here his works are seen in greatest numbers, and culminated in the (so to speak) perfection of his humble but laborious style of architecture, when we consider the simple tools with which the work was accomplished. The step of progress in art, from the cave men to the mound-builders, prevailed only with a branch or offshoot from the primitive stock of men. So it is with regard to all other races who show a decided progress in civilization and arts up to the present time. They are the results of so many developed branches, while the primitive races are still in the lower stages of savagery and barbarism with brains as incapable of ratiocination as their congeners of remote ages. In this stage they will continue until exterminated by the spread of civilization, with which they are unable to cope. In the white race we find the perfection of anatomical and physiological development, and a brain that exceeds that of all other races of men in its size and weight, and immeasurably superior to them in its refined powers of thought. By whatever means we may strive to elevate the Turanian races, and however apt they may be in accumulating ideas and expressing thought, a limit is soon reached, and no amount of training will suffice to surmount the barriers to progress interposed by physiological inabilities. Each race in its respective sphere may continue to achieve triumphs in progressive arts, and grow more and more perfect in knowledge, yet each has its limit, and that limit is determined by organization.

In the prosecution of our investigations of the antiquities of pre-historic man, it is not inappropriate to take a look at the condition and differences which are apparent in his living representatives of to-day.

Ethnologists and naturalists divide mankind into a number of distinct races. Cuvier makes but three, Pritchard seven, Agassiz eight, Pickering has as many as eleven, but the most commonly received classification is that of Blumenbach, who makes five. First is the Caucasian, or white race, including the greater part of the European nations and western Asia; Mongolian, or yellow race, occupying Tartary, China, Japan and India; Ethiopian, or negro race, occupying all Africa south of the Sahara; American, or red race, embracing the Indians of North and South America; Malayan, or brown race, inhabiting the islands of the Indian archipelago and Australia.

There is such a blending of characteristics in some of the

lower races that it is by no means easy to establish a boundary line between them, and hence the diversity of opinion in the classification.

Prof. Huxley, with that clearness of thought and profound research that characterizes all his labors, in a paper read before the International Congress of Pre-historic Archæology, which assembled in England in 1868, divides the human family into four races, and I take the liberty of reproducing entire what refers to this point. He says: "By races I mean simply the great distinguishable groups of mankind—such groups as a naturalist would form if all mankind were put before him to be sorted according to their physical likenesses and unlikenesses. And by distinct races I mean those which do not grade into one another, except under such circumstances as make it certain, or at any rate highly probable, that inter-breeding has taken place. The number of races in this sense appears to me to be small; indeed, I do not see my way to the recognition of more than four, which I shall call Australioid, Negroid, Mongoloid and Xanthochroic races.

"The characteristics of the Australioid are: A dark complexion, ranging through various shades of light and dark chocolate color; dark or black eyes; the hair of the scalp black, neither coarse and lank, nor crisp and woolly, but soft, silky and wavy; the skull always belonging to the dolichocephalic group, or having a cephalic index of less than 0.8.

"Under the head of Negroid race are included those people who have dark skins ranging from yellowish brown to what is usually called black; dark or black eyes; dark or black hair, which is crisp, or what is usually called woolly in texture; with very rare exceptions these people are dolichocephalic.

"In the Mongolian race the complexion ranges from brownish yellow to olive; the eyes are dark, usually black; the hair of the scalp black, long, coarse and straight; that of the body remarkably scanty; the proportions of the skull, so constant in the two preceding races, vary in this from extreme dolichocephalic to extreme brachycephalic.

"Finally, in the Xanthochroic race the complexion is very fair; the eyes are blue or gray; the hair yellow or yellowish-brown. In this race again the skull ranges through the whole scale of its varieties of proportion from extreme breadth to extreme length."

All other forms of mankind he considers lie between some two of these primary stocks.

"The Australioids include only the inhabitants of Australia, and are not found in any of the neighboring islands. But, in the Dekkan, which is bounded on the north by the valley of the Ganges, Indus and Himalaya mountains, and on the east and west by the sea, there is a people—the coolies of East India—which, though they have undergone considerable change by intermixture with an invading arianised population, are, he thinks, clearly referable to the Australioids. While the inhabitants of Moluccas and the Andaman islands are not considered sufficiently distinct to form a separate race from the true negro who inhabits Africa south of the Sahara, he has applied to them the name of Negritos.

"The Mongolians have their most prominent home in central Asia, and extend from thence to Lapland and the Arctic Circle on the northwest and north; to North Hindostan on the south to the Malay archipelago on the east; on the east to China and thence over the whole of the Pacific islands (except those occupied by Negritos), in the extreme northeast to America, and then through its whole length and breadth.

"The Xanthochroi inhabit a much smaller area of the earth's surface than the Mongoloids. Their center being in central Europe, whence they extend into Scandinavia and the British islands on the northwest. They extended their wanderings over the great plains of northern Asia to the frontier of China, and are traceable southward into Syria, and in a fragmentary fashion through northern Africa to the islands of the western coast, while eastward they occur as far as northern Hindostan."*

The manner in which these races dispersed themselves from specific centers to their present habitats, is a matter of very great interest. It is generally believed that the Mongoloid, or Indians of America, came from Asia by way of the Aleutian islands, but it is far more difficult to understand how the Australioid people found their way to the Dekkan, and the negroes to the islands of Polynesia, that are separated by "broad and stormy seas, when their only known means of navigation was a rude raft."

Mr. A. R. Wallace, president of the biological section of the British association, in his address at the Glasgow meeting in September, 1877, among other points of interest bearing on the subject before us, says that "while all modern writers admit the great antiquity of man, most of them maintain the very recent development of his intellect, and will hardly contemplate the possibility of men equal in mental capacity to ourselves having existed in pre-historic times." The weakness of this argument, he says, has been shown by Mr. Albert Mott, in his "very original but little known presidential address to the Literary and Philosophical Society of Liverpool, in 1873," in which he maintains that "our most distant glimpses of the past are still of a world peopled as now with men both civilized and savage," and "that we have often entirely missed the past by supposing that the outward signs of civilization must always be the same, and must be such as are found among ourselves." In support of these views Mr. Mott, as quoted by Mr. Wallace, calls attention to the exist-

---

*Report International Congress Pre-historic Archæology, 1808.

ence of gigantic stone images, now mostly in ruins, often thirty or forty feet high, and formed of stone, some of which must weigh over one hundred tons. The Easter islands, he says on which these images are seen, are more than two thousand miles from South America and two thousand miles from Marquesas and more than one thousand from the Gambier islands. It has only an area of thirty square miles. The existence of such works, Mr. Mott says, "implies a large population, abundance of food and an established government," and to maintain all of which, he thinks, necessarily implies the power of regular communication with larger islands or continents, the arts of navigation, and a civilization much higher than now exists in any part of the Pacific." Very similar remains in other islands scattered widely over the Pacific, Wallace says, adds weight to this argument.

While there is little room to doubt, as I have already stated, the existence of various stages of civilization in pre-historic times, yet we must admit that if the Pacific islanders ever possessed the art of navigating broad seas and carrying on commerce from island to island, or with the continents, they must have lost it before losing the art of fashioning the soft coral rock into images, since Capt. Cook mentions that on some of the islands these images were being constructed at the time of his visit, and the canoe constituted their only means of ocean trade. But it may be well to state here, that it is very singular, in his special mention of Mr. Mott's lecture, Mr. Wallace overlooked the fact that Mr. J. H. Lampry read a paper, in 1868, before the British meeting of the Pre-historic Congress of Archæology, in which he calls attention to the antiquities in the Easter and other South Sea islands as a proof that "in ancient times these seas may have been traversed in all directions by a race of men of high intelligence, great physical endurance, capable of patient toil in the accomplishment of great works, whose scant remains, simple as they are in form, are not destitute of that mystic rhythm in arrangement which at once entitles them to a place in the records of pre-historic times."

In answer to Mr. Wallace, I desire simply to call your attention to the fact that ethnological authorities seem now disposed to agree that the aborigines of America belong to the Mongoloid race without admixture of other races. Admitting, then, that the latter conclusion is perfectly tenable, how does it happen that the builders of stone images, upon stone terraces, in the Polynesian islands, by a people who are of the Negrito type, if possessed of a superior knowledge of arts and skill in navigation, failed to leave the impress of their race upon the American continent? It is a little singular, also, that while Terra del Fuego and Patagonia are inhabited by man, the large islands of the Falkland group, off their coast, were uninhabited; so with the Galapagos, under the equator, while numbers of inhabited islands in the Pacific are less favorable for man's support. I do not believe that man has been degraded from a higher knowledge of art to a lower, nor do I believe that his dispersion over the Pacific Islands and the American continent can be explained by a passage from Asia to America by the aid of the Aleutian chain of islands alone, but by a much broader and more extended area of land which in pre-historic times connected the two continents. For the existence of such a connection we need not, from a geological point of view, go farther back than the glacial epoch, when, in order to spread over North America a glacial sheet of ice reaching as far south as 37° of latitude required an elevation of the region to the north that would lay bare vast areas of land now covered by the waters of the Pacific ocean. And it is to geological changes in the physical geography of the earth that we must mainly look, as a cause, for the distribution of pre-historic men. The time required to swell the population of America from a few pairs of voluntary or involuntary voyagers to its aboriginal magnitude could scarcely be less than that required by the intervention of geographical changes.

In evidence of the slow rate of increase among savage tribes I may cite the accounts furnished by the Jesuit fathers who settled among the Indians of the Pacific coast soon after its discovery by the whites, for the purpose of converting them to Christianity and instructing them in agriculture and other industrial pursuits. They state that debauchery, tribal wars and exposure of infants, through neglect of the mothers, are fast decimating the race.*

In regard to the character of the works left by pre-historic man, whether in Europe or America, after a careful study of what has been written on the subject, and making due allowance for the inaccuracies of detail woven into many of the accounts from hearsay traditions of the savages, I have failed to see in the antiquities any evidence of a higher order of intellect or mechanical skill than is to be found in the tribes now living. The massive structures, of which the ruins are now only to be seen in New Mexico, Arizona, and other portions of the Rocky Mountain region, Mexico, Central America and Peru, while impressive in size and remarkable for the amount of labor required for their completion, do not surpass or equal for comfort and the moral development of the people the present adobe houses to be found in some of the existing Pueblo tribes of North America.

In studying the ancient Pueblos, we must discard as totally worthless the grossly false and mythical histories published of the conquest of Mexico by Cortez, Bernal Diaz, the anonymous conqueror, and other Spanish writers. They were subject to revision by the seven ecclesiastical censors of Spain, and made to glorify the church and to magnify the importance

---

* Smithsonian Contributions to Knowledge.

of the empire vanquished by the basest treachery and cold-blooded massacres; yet these so-called histories have been copied and quoted from by subsequent historians, eminent as scholars, without questioning their inaccuracies.

We are indebted to Robert Anderson Wilson, author of the "Conquest of Mexico," for a complete refutation of these authors, based upon a careful study of the subject and a survey of the field of Cortez's exploits. Instead, therefore, of seeing in the Aztecs a people highly advanced in the art of government and surrounded with luxuries, indicative of refinement, we must look upon them as they really were, naked savages, and in no way differing from the Pueblo, or town Indians, of the present day.

In this state the antiquities we have to deal with are, so far as at present known, earth mounds, stone mounds, earth wall enclosures and stone wall enclosures. These remarkable monuments of an extinct people may be traced from Texas to Florida, scattered along the shores of the Gulf of Mexico, and extending along the Atlantic coast as far north as South Carolina, and from the mouth of the Mississippi river almost to its headwaters, and following up all its tributaries, and their innumerable branches, to the southern shores of the great lakes. Indeed, so abundant are these antiquities that many have been led to believe that the people who constructed them were at one time the most numerous of all the inhabitants of America. Neither history nor trustworthy tradition can furnish any account of these antiquities, and all efforts, therefore, to define the uses to which they were put, beyond the fact substantiated by exploration, that some of the mounds were used as sepulchers for the dead, is, in my opinion, sheer guesswork. From the fact that these antiquities are never found except along the sea shore, water-courses, or by the side of lakes or living springs of water that are not far from a stream, and that the sites which were selected for them have, in many cases, proved the most eligible locations for modern towns and cities, we may reasonably infer that the builders cultivated the alluvial river bottoms and depended mainly on vegetables, fish and mollusks, for their food. The mounds vary in height from three feet and less, to sixty feet and more, and from a few feet in diameter to several hundred feet.

In shape they are circular, oval and square; some are conical, others truncated, and a few are reported to have winding stairways leading to their summits. The great mound at Grave creek, West Virginia, is said to be seventy feet high, and one thousand feet in circumference at the base. At Miamisburg, Ohio, there is a mound, reported by Squier and Davis to be sixty-eight feet high and eight hundred and fifty-two feet in circumference at the base. The Cahokia truncated mound, in Illinois, is, by the same authority, 700 feet long, 500 feet wide and 90 feet high.

The highest mounds yet found in Indiana are in Knox county. Prof. Collett, in his report on this county, says the "Pyramid mound, one mile south of Vincennes, is 47 feet high, greatest diameter 300 feet, lesser diameter 150 feet; the level area on the top is 15 by 50 feet, and is crowded with intrusive burials of a later race." Sugar Loaf mound just east of the city limits, was opened up by a shaft which, he thinks, reached the bottom at forty-two feet after passing through:

	Ft.	In.
Loess sand	10	00
Ashes, charcoal and bones		10
Loess sand	17	00
Ashes, charcoal and bones		10
Loess sand	9	00
Ashes, charcoal and bones	2	00
Red altar-clays, burned	3	00
Total	42	8

The mound E. N. E. of Vincennes court-house is built on

a spur of the hills, and the top is sixty-seven feet above the plain. Mr. Collett calls it a "terraced mound," which has a winding roadway to the top. Archæologists have, as I think, without due consideration, classified the mounds into altar and sacrificial mounds, sepulchral or burial mounds, lookout mounds and mounds of habitation.

When we dig into a mound and find that it contains human bones, it may then with propriety be called a sepulchral or a burial mound. But to speak of others as altar mounds or mounds of worship, mounds of habitation or lookout mounds, is assigning to them a purpose which can not be sustained unless fortified by some better proof than the mythical writings of Spanish historians.

It is a common occurrence to find in mounds some ashes and charcoal mixed with human bones, and for this reason the builders have been accused of cremating their dead. So far I have not been able to find any charred human bones, though charred wood and charcoal are of common occurrence. A few fragments of charred bones are reported by Squier and Davis in their so-called sacrificial mounds at Mound City, Ohio. My own opinion is that mounds were simply erected as burial places for the bones of dead chiefs or other persons high in authority. The bones were sprinkled over with ashes and finally with earth. Where ashes and charcoal are found in mounds, but no bones, it is possible that the latter disappeared from decay. Charcoal, as is well known, is the most durable of all known substances. Associated with human bones are sometimes seen flint flakes, arrow and spear points, stone axes, knives, pipes, pottery, etc. The practice of burying with the dead, flints, gravel and ashes, prevailed in Europe to a comparatively modern time. It is an old usage, hence "ashes to ashes, dust to dust."

Shakespeare alludes to this custom in the play of Hamlet,

in the scene where the priest who had charge of the burial of Ophelia is made to say, in reply to Laertes:

> "Her obsequies have been so far enlarged
> As we have warranty: Her death was doubtful;
> And but that great command o'ersways the order,
> She should in ground unsanctified have lodged
> Till the last trumpet; for charitable prayers,
> Shards, flints and pebbles should be thrown on her,
> Yet here she is allowed her virgin crants,
> Her maiden strewments, and the bringing home
> Of bell and burial."

In Wisconsin there are a large number of mounds built to imitate the shape of various kinds of animals, not omitting man. These mounds contain ashes and the remains of human skeletons, with copper and carved stone trinkets, pottery, etc. In the latter respect they do not differ from the conical, square and truncated mounds of other localities.

The romance which has been thrown around the so-called *Teocalli*, or temple-mounds of Mexico, by the Spanish historians of the conquest, and so inconsiderately adopted by American archæologists, vanishes when put to the crucial test by accurate observations.

Torquamana, who examined the celebrated Mexican temple-mound of Cholula, says: "It still remains without any steps by which to ascend, or any facing of stone. It appears now like a mound covered with grass and shrubs, and possibly it was never anything more."

Mr. Robert A. Wilson also visited this mound before writing his history of the "Conquest of Mexico," and corroborates the statement of Torquamana, and he is further satisfied, from the general appearance, that it is of common origin with similar mounds scattered through the country.

Associated with the mounds we have earth wall and stone wall enclosures—some are perfect circles, some square, some ovoid, and still a larger number that are anomalous in design.

The height of the walls varies from a foot or two to ten feet or more. Most generally they are accompanied by a fosse, or ditch, which is placed on the inside, rarely on the outside of the wall. In area these works include from a few square feet to upwards of one hundred acres. Like the mounds, they are built on river terraces or high table-lands bordering streams.

The uses for which they were designed by the builders are, in most cases, to say the least, beyond the discernment of careful students of antiquities; and opinions on the subject are almost as numerous as the observers themselves. Where the walls are built around the brow of a high point of land with a level area on top, and is not commanded by the surrounding high-lands, as the "stone fort" at the mouth of Fourteen-mile creek, in Clark county, figured and described in the Indiana Geological Report, 1873, we may reasonably infer that the wall was built as a means of security against intruders upon their privacy or as a defense against warlike foes. The small circular enclosures are generally looked upon as being subservient to some religious ceremonies, I should rather say, superstitious weight, in commemoration of human prowess.

One of the most eminent of American archæologists—Dr. Lewis C. Morgan, of Rochester, N. Y.—in the July number of the *North American Review*, 1876, entertains the opinion, in an ably written article, that the earth walls served as the foundation upon which to construct dwellings. The article is accompanied by figures to show the manner of house that might be adapted to the walls, and the facility with which it could be built by inclining poles of wood against the sides and securing them at the top. The house is divided into a number of rooms to suit their communal customs. These rooms are occupied by separate families. A place for the fire is arranged at intervals in a hall which runs the entire length, so as to accommodate the necessities of four compartments. In answer to this very plausible theory of my learned friend—Dr. Morgan—I wish to say that if his views are correct we should be able to find at intervals on the embankments, ashes and charcoal and other refuse kitchen matter, but, so far as I know, this has never been done.*

What is now demanded of the archæologist is a more careful study of these mounds and enclosures; maps should be made of the grounds, and sections given which accurately delineate the order of arrangement of the internal structure of the works, and a careful record given of the position occupied by the relics which they may contain. We should by all means discourage, and turn a deaf ear to the relation of, ingenious traditions gleaned from unworthy sources, or wormed from the aborigines by leading questions, and concluded in too many cases by affixing imaginary answers. I repeat that the problem of the condition of pre-historic man can alone be satisfactorily solved by a study of his remains and the works he has left behind him.

With regard to the cranial differences in the races of men, I wish to call your attention to a paper read by Dr. T. O. Summers, Jr., at the late meeting of the A. A. A. of Sci., in Nashville, wherein he pointed out that there is a constant relation existing between the length of the spheno-parietal suture and the capacity of the brain case, determining the brachycephalic or the dolichocephalic character of the skull. Dr.

---

* Since writing the above I have had an opportunity to visit a Pima Indian village in Arizona. The houses are usually made of bows stuck into the earth and the tops are bent over and tied, giving the dwelling the shape of a bird cage. A wall of earth, one to two feet high, is thrown up around the base on the outside. I saw many of these earth rings where the brush had been taken away, and they have exactly the appearance of the small circular enclosures seen in this and adjoining states, but there was no ditch on the inside. They were simply thrown up to keep out the wind and water.

Summers has had the rare opportunity of examining the large collections of skulls in the various cities of Europe, and has also a large collection of his own, and by the aid of this important discovery unhesitatingly declares that he could at once separate from one another the skulls of white men, negroes and mulattoes.

The ethnologist has long felt the want of more certain rules for the classification of crania than that afforded by a mere measurement of capacity, dolichocephalic and brachycephalic, and I believe that this discovery of Dr. Summers will, if not infallible, prove to be at least of very great assistance in accomplishing so desirable an object, since it is by a study of the osteology of man that we must look for a true classification and a solution of his capabilities.

Archæologists are now fully aware that the neolitic implements and pottery of the mounds are in no way distinguishable from those made by the aborigines from pre-columbian to the present time, and as a means of classification they must totally fail. My distinguished friend, Dr. Lewis H. Morgan, in his recent and very able work called "Ancient America," has given a division and classification of ethnical periods that indicates a thorough acquaintance with the subject, and his book should be in the hands of every student of ethnology. No man in America has done more than Dr. Morgan to systematize and make known the true status of the aborigines, and I take pleasure in thus publicly acknowledging my obligations to him for so valuable a contribution to our knowledge.

In conclusion I desire to call your attention to the care which must be exercised in reaching conclusions on the examination of objects which come under the notice of collectors.

George Rapp, who was at the head of a community of Germans known as "Harmonists," that came to this state in

1815, and settled on the Wabash river, in Posey county, where they built the town of New Harmony, found at St. Louis a large stone slab, eight feet long, five feet wide and eight inches thick, upon which are seen the images of two human feet; in front of these images is an irregularly rounded mark; the feet have the appearance of being the impress made on mud, and the scroll as having been made with a stick in the hands of the owner, and the mud so impressed subsequently hardened into stone.

This foot-print slab was held in high esteem by Rapp, and he played upon the superstitions of his followers by stating that they were left by the angel Gabriel, who alighted on the earth to warn the people of the near destruction of the world. It must be remembered that the Rappites or Harmonists were Second Adventists.

Schoolcraft, in his journey down the Wabash, in 1821, stopped at New Harmony, and gives an account of this footprint slab, accompanied with accurate drawings. In this account he expresses the opinion that the impressions were those made by an Indian who stepped out of his canoe on a mud beach and made the mark in front of the tracks with a stick and then stepped back into his canoe; subsequently the mud hardened into stone, which preserved the fossil imprints.

Mantell, one of the ablest and most fascinating writers on geology, saw this account of the foot-print slab, and transferred it to his "Wonders of Geology," Vol. 1, p. 75, American edition from third London edition, in the following language:

"*Impressions of Human Feet in Sandstone.*—In connection with the occurrence of human bones in limestone, I will here notice a discovery of the highest interest, but which has not as yet excited among scientific observers the attention which its importance demands. I allude to the fact announced in the American Journal of Science, Vol. V., 1822, of impressions of human feet in sandstone, discovered many years ago in a quarry at St. Louis, on the western bank of the Mississippi river. 'The above figure is an exact copy of the original drawing, and exhibits the impressions of the soles of two corresponding human feet placed at a short distance from each other, as of an individual standing upright in an easy position. The prints are described as presenting a perfect impress of the feet and toes, exhibiting the form of the muscles and the flexures of the skin, as if an accurate cast had been taken in a soft substance. They were at first supposed to have been cut in the stone by the native Indians, but a little reflection sufficed to show that they were beyond the efforts of these rude children of nature; since they evinced a skill which even my distinguished friend, Sir Francis Chantry, could not have surpassed. No doubt exists in my mind that they are the actual prints of human feet in soft sand, which was quickly converted into solid rock by the infiltration of calcareous matter in the manner already described. The length of each foot is $10\frac{1}{2}$ inches, the spread of the toes 4 inches, indicating the usual stature; and the nature of the impression shows that the feet were unconfined by shoes or sandals. This phenomenon, unique of its kind, is fraught with so much importance that I have requested Prof. Silliman to ascertain the nature of the sandstone and the period of its formation.'"

My honored preceptor, the late David Dale Owen, soon exposed the fallacy of the hasty conclusions reached by Schoolcraft, and pointed to the fact that the slab was a limestone belonging to the palæozoic age, and was studded with brachiopod shells, characteristic of the sub-carboniferous period, and the tracks, however perfect in form, were carved into the solid rock by human hands. The most zealous advocate of man's antiquity would hardly dream of tracing him back to palæozoic times. Subsequently Dr. Owen collected a large number of stones containing carved human feet, and from a careful study of the subject came to the conclusion that in most cases they were carved in stone, so situated, as to commemorate the highest water-mark of the streams, or to note some other memorable event.

I mention these facts to show how easy it is for one to be led astray, when every possible phase of the subject is not carefully studied. Let us, therefore, attend strictly to detailing facts of observation, and they are sure to lead to a correct solution of all problems within the compass of the human mind.

APPENDIX.

INDIANA HISTORICAL SOCIETY PUBLICATIONS.

VOLUME I   NUMBER IX

THE EARLY SETTLEMENT

OF THE

MIAMI COUNTRY

BY

DR. EZRA FERRIS

INDIANAPOLIS
THE BOWEN-MERRILL COMPANY
1897

PREFACE.

The following letters were not originally written for the Indiana Historical Society, or printed by it, but it is deemed proper to publish them in connection with the earlier work of the Society because the author, Dr. Ezra Ferris, was a charter member of the Society, and the editor, Oliver B. Torbet, who induced him to write them, was also a member. The *Independent Press*, of Lawrenceburg, Ind., was started in the fall of 1850, the first number appearing on October 18, of that year. The proprietors, Henry L. Brown and James E. Goble, attended to the mechanical and business departments, and employed Mr. Torbet to conduct the editorial department. Mr. Torbet was ambitious to make the paper popular, and wisely undertook to secure a series of historical articles from Dr. Ferris, who was acknowledged on all sides to know more of the early history of that region than any other person. As the *Press* was a Whig paper, and Dr. Ferris was a very earnest Whig, the arrangement was speedily made, and the first article was ready for the *Press* on December 12, 1850. The paper was sold to Rev. W. W. Hibben on August 22, 1851, but the letters were continued for some time afterwards, as appears by their dates.

Dr. Ezra Ferris was born at Stanwich, Conn., April 26, 1783. When he was six years old his parents emigrated to the wilderness north of the Ohio river, and his account of the trip and the subsequent life at Columbia forms a part of the following letters. Among the pioneers at that point were a number of others, who afterwards settled in southeastern Indiana, so that his account of the experiences of the pioneers who were cooped up there is doubly a chapter in Indiana history. Dr. Ferris, as a boy, had the benefit of some schooling at Columbia, and it is said that later he attended a school in the East. When quite a young man he was licensed as a preacher at the Duck Creek Baptist Church, and was afterwards ordained as an elder. For several years he taught school at Lebanon, Ohio, and, during his work in other lines, he studied medicine. Later he removed to Lawrenceburg, where he practiced medicine, and also established a drugstore, which has been continued by his descendants to this day. He was elected a member of the constitutional convention when Indiana was admitted as a state, and in that body served as chairman of the committee on the elective franchise and on elections. Later he was elected to the legislature. When the state government was organized, he was elected by the legislature one of the censors for licensing physicians in the third medical district. In politics he was a Whig, so long as the Whig party lasted, and was always an earnest advocate of his political faith.

Much of the time and talent of Dr. Ferris were devoted to religious work. The Baptist churches of southeastern Indiana were poor, and, as a consistent advocate of "a free gospel," he preached, without compensation, throughout his life, to the congregation at Lawrenceburg, as well as at odd times to the one at Salem, and to some others of the vicinity. An incident in the local church history illustrates the peculiar tact and shrewdness of the man. It was at the time when the doctrines of Alexander Campbell were attracting many members of the Baptist church, and many congregations were going over bodily to the new organization. An agent of the Disciples appeared at Lawrenceburg and found several of the Baptists favorably disposed. A meeting was appointed, at

PREFACE.

which the proposition of going over as a congregation was to be submitted. Dr. Ferris was not taken into the confidence of the movers, but he learned what was going on and appeared at the meeting and took charge of it by virtue of his official position as calmly as if it were one of the stated meetings of the church. The members of the other faction were somewhat startled by this, but imagine their feelings when he arose and opened the meeting by reading Charles Wesley's hymn:

> Jesus, great Shepherd of the sheep,
>   To thee for help we fly;
> Thy little flock in safety keep,
>   For Oh! the wolf is nigh.
>
> He comes, of hellish malice full,
>   To scatter, tear and slay;
> He seizes every straggling soul
>   As his own lawful prey.
>
> Us into thy protection take,
>   And gather with thine arm;
> Unless the fold we first forsake,
>   The wolf can never harm.
>
> We laugh to scorn his cruel power,
>   While by our Shepherd's side;
> The sheep he never can devour,
>   Unless he first divide.
>
> O do not suffer him to part
>   The souls that here agree;
> But make us of one mind and heart,
>   And keep us one in thee.
>
> Together let us sweetly live—
>   Together let us die;
> And each a starry crown receive,
>   And reign above the sky.

When this had been sung he delivered a brief but earnest petition for divine protection from discord or dissension, for freedom from temptation to leave the straight and narrow path, for deliverance from any and all evils that might threaten them. Then he announced that the visiting brother would address the meeting. But the visiting brother was unnerved. He talked for a while, but did not introduce the contemplated subject at all. The meeting was dismissed with the benediction, and the Lawrenceburg church remained in the Baptist fold.

With all his earnestness in political and religious matters Dr. Ferris held the universal esteem and respect of his fellow-citizens. He was a useful member of society, always lending a hand to beneficial movements in the community. After middle life he retired from the practice of his profession, but continued his drug store to the time of his death, April 19, 1857.

THE EARLY SETTLEMENT OF THE MIAMI COUNTRY.

LETTER I.

MR. TORBET—In compliance with your request, I send you the following account of my first settlement in the Miami country: A short time before my father started on his journey to the west, and after he had determined to do so, a sermon was preached at his house on the occasion, from Genesis xii: 1: "Now the Lord said unto Abraham, get thee out of thy country and from thy kindred, and from thy father's house, unto a land that I will shew thee." On the 20th of September, 1789, according to previous arrangement, my father, in company with his own and two other families, left his native village (Stanwich, in the state of Connecticut), and separated himself and family from all the associations and endearing ties which had been formed during the life of fifty years, to seek for himself and them a home in the then western wilderness. Though I was a boy of only six years of age, I have a very distinct and vivid recollection of the affecting occasion. The enterprise at that time was so novel and daring it drew together a vast crowd of people to witness the parting scene. When, for the last time, the family left the house, and bid farewell to relatives and neighbors, it was an affecting scene; what added poignancy to their grief was, that their separation would be, probably, while on earth, final. As they took their seats in the wagon, and moved down the road, they were surrounded by a crowd on every side; many of whom were heard to predict the result of so hazardous a journey. Some feared they would fall a sacrifice to savage cruelty, others thought they would all be drowned in descending the western rivers. But nothing could overcome the dauntless courage of this little company; and they passed down the road on the north side of Long Island Sound to the city of New York, whence they passed over into New Jersey—traveled through that state and Pennsylvania over the Alleghany mountains, until they came to the waters of the Youghiogheny, thence down the river to the Monongahela, and down that river to Pittsburg, thence down the Ohio to Ft. Miami, about three-fourths of a mile below the Little Miami, at which place they arrived on the 12th day of December, 1789, just sixty-one years past; having been two months and twenty days on the journey, thankful to kind Providence, who had preserved them in all dangers through which they had passed, and that at last they had reached their intended future home, where they could enjoy the rest they so much needed after the fatigues of the journey of one thousand miles. In approaching the shore they were met by a crowd of smiling faces, to bid them a hearty welcome, and offer them all the assistance circumstances would admit of. An apartment in the fort (of about sixteen feet square) was assigned each family, in which, for the time, they resided. Ft. Miami consisted of four long rows of buildings in the form of an oblong, or, rather, four long buildings, for they were all connected together, but divided into different apartments, with a block-house at each corner, projecting a few feet beyond the range of other buildings, so that no Indian could approach any part in the ring without exposing himself to the fire of the white people from the block-houses. Here were found collected together some thirty or more families living in this fort, without the restraints of civil law, destitute of all kinds of provisions, except what they could obtain from the woods, surrounded by a vast (and to the white man) unexplored forest, filled with numerous tribes of hostile savages, without manufactories, or even the common work-shops of the mechanic, such as the blacksmith or the shoemaker, without houses, barns or fields, save those that were covered over with forest trees, without a physician for the sick or gospel minister to try to comfort them when dying. They soon learned the repose to be indulged in here was but temporary. Much was to be done to provide for coming wants, and that must be done in the face of great danger. Excessive labor must be performed to clear, fence and cultivate the ground, so as to secure a crop of corn, which was their principal object; for as yet no crop had been raised in the country so as to ripen. The difficulties, however, were all overcome, and, by continued train of exertion, the face of the country has been changed from what I then saw it to what it is now. In looking back to the beginning, and tracing the progress of the improvement of the country from that time to the present, I am ready to inquire, who dare to undertake to prescribe bounds to what human industry and enterprise may accomplish?

Lawrenceburg, Ind., Dec. 12, 1850. E. F.

LETTER II.

MR. TORBET — An observing mind, made acquainted with the circumstances surrounding the infant settlement at Fort Miami, as described in my letter of the 12th inst., would naturally be led to inquire, what motives could have prompted the inhabitants of that place to venture so far in advance of other frontier settlements, and expose themselves to such imminent danger. Such an inquiry suggested itself to my mind, and being personally acquainted with nearly every individual comprising the party who made the first landing to remain as permanent residents of the country, I instituted the inquiry of persons who I supposed had the best opportunity of knowing, which resulted in the following statement of facts, which I submitted to the inspection of several of the same party, after they were penned, who pronounced the whole, so far as it went, to be correct:

Major Benjamin Stites, the pioneer of this company, was a native of Scotch Plains, Essex county, New Jersey, but when young emigrated to western Pennsylvania and settled on Ten Mile Creek, within the bounds of what is now Green county. In the spring of the year 1787, he descended the Ohio river in a flat-boat loaded with castings, flour, whisky, etc., to Limestone (now Maysville), Ky., in pursuit of a market; but after staying there a few days, with but little success, he removed a few miles back from the river to Washington, the county seat of Mason county, where there was a prospect of better sales. One night, while at the latter place, the Indians committed hostilities on the inhabitants of the vicinity by stealing and taking off a number of horses. The next morning a number of militia volunteered to pursue after the Indians and try to recapture the horses and punish the aggressors. Major Stites, who possessed extraordinary physical powers and undaunted courage, volunteered to accompany them. Necessary preparations being made, they commenced the pursuit, following the trail of the horses on the Kentucky side down the Ohio river, a short distance below the mouth of the Little Miami river, to a place where the Indians had crossed the Ohio river with the horses, on a raft. Determined to continue the pursuit, the white men adopted the same plan of crossing the river, and pursued the Indians up the valley of the Miami nearly to an Indian village called Old

Chillicothe, near the headwaters of the Little Miami, but without success. On their return, passing down between the two Miamis, they had a good opportunity to examine the country. Major Stites was so well pleased with the face of the country and the fertility of the soil, that he determined, before recrossing the river, to attempt to make a settlement at the mouth of the Little Miami. After his return to Washington, he closed his business there as speedily as possible, and returned to his family to make the necessary arrangements to enable him to accomplish his object. He stayed a short time with them, then crossed the mountains to visit his native state to try to procure means and men to accompany him, so as to be able to prosecute his previous designs. On his arrival at Trenton, N. J., he had an introduction to the late Judge John C. Symmes, to whom he related the discovery he had made, and the object of his visit to New Jersey. From Judge Symmes he learned, for the first time, that the country northwest of the Ohio belonged to the United States, and that a legal title for the land could only be obtained from congress. Judge Symmes proposed to join in the enterprise to which Major Stites consented. It was then agreed that, as congress was about to assemble at Philadelphia, Judge Symmes (who was a member from New Jersey) should make an application for the purchase of the land, and that Stites should prosecute his journey to raise men to accompany him if Symmes should be successful. It was also agreed, if successful, that Stites, for the discovery, should have ten thousand acres of land at the mouth of the Little Miami, to be laid off as nearly in a square as the nature of the case would admit of, and as much more as he could pay for.

Judge Symmes succeeded in purchasing one million acres, to include all the land lying on the Ohio, between the two Miamis, running back for quantity, congress reserving three sections in each township, viz.: One for the support of schools, one for the support of the gospel, and one for future sale, and in like manner one entire township to support a university; the whole to be laid off in townships six miles square, and sections one mile square, each section to be subdivided into four equal parts.

Major Stites also succeeded in raising a number of men to accompany him, and in making arrangements to prosecute the journey to his intended new home. Previous to making any sales of land they published the conditions of settling the Miami country in a very small pamphlet, printed at Trenton; one of which conditions was that each tract of land sold and not settled on by the purchaser within three years should be subject to a forfeiture of one-sixth part. For the benefit of any male person who was not the owner of land in the country, and who would enter upon it, and raise a log cabin, and clear and cultivate three acres of land three years, such persons should be entitled to a deed for the same, thus presenting to emigrants, without other means, the prospect of acquiring land in the new settlement. It was further agreed to assemble their forces on the western waters and descend the Ohio river to Maysville, at as early a period as practicable, preparatory to taking possession of their newly acquired lands, which shall be the subject of my next letter. E. F.

Lawrenceburg, Ind., Dec. 27, 1850.

LETTER III.

MR. TORBET—The parties of which I wrote in my letter of the 26th, having assembled their forces at Maysville and Washington, Ky., preparatory to taking possession of their newly acquired lands, thought it most prudent to raise a company of volunteer militia to go in advance of their families, and make a further examination of the country. This company consisted of about sixty men, who descended the Ohio to the mouth of the Big Miami in the month of August, 1788, and explored the country some distance back from that place and North Bend. While at the latter place one of the company who had gone out with a small hunting party in search of game was killed by the Indians near the place where the town of Cleves now stands. After making the necessary examination, and after Judge Symmes had determined to locate his party at North Bend, they meandered along the Ohio river, measuring the distance along the beach from the Big to the Little Miami, and returned to Maysville. During the absence of this party Major Stites, who stayed behind for that purpose, was employed in preparing to remove with his company to the mouth of the Little Miami. He fixed on a plan for a fort, and that it might be built with as little delay as possible, he and his son, Benjamin Stites, with others in his employ, went to the woods and made a large quantity of clap-boards, which they hauled to the river and put in a boat; they also took with them the heart pieces of the timber, to be used in filling the open spaces between the logs of their cabin, they also made double plank doors with hangings attached so as to be able to prepare for defense as speedily as possible if attacked. In returning from the woods one evening, while engaged in making these preparations, Nehemiah Stites, a youth who had accompanied them, and who was a nephew of Major Stites, was killed by the Indians.

All things being ready, Major Stites, with the families who were to settle with him, left Maysville on the 17th of November, 1788, to descend the river to the mouth of the Little Miami. (Judge Symmes had to tarry behind a few days to await the arrival of some provisions on the way down the river.) This company consisted of Major Benjamin Stites and family, Elijah Stites and family, Groenbright Bayley and family, Abel Cook and family and Jacob Mills and family. They were also accompanied by Hezekiah Stites, John S, Gano, Ephraim Kibbey, Thomas C. Wade, Elijah Mills, Edmond Buxton, Daniel Shoemaker, Mr. Heampsted, Evan Shelby, Allen Woodruff, Joseph Cox and Benjamin Cox, without families, and there were in the family of Major Stites, Benjamin Stites, Jr., and Jonathan Stites, and in the family of Mr. Bayley, James F. Bayley and Reason Bayley, who were young men, making in all twenty-two male persons able to perform the labor and act the part in defense of men. To take advantage of the cover of the night and to have a full day before them when they should arrive they landed at Bracken (now Augusta, Ky.,) and stayed until there would, in their judgment, be about time to float down to the Little Miami about daylight. Previous to leaving Maysville they had heard a report that some hunters had returned from a hunting tour who had seen five hundred Indians at the mouth of the Little Miami who heard that the white people were coming there to settle, and were waiting there to kill them as soon as they should land. On approaching the place of their destination about daybreak some of the females were very much alarmed on account of the report alluded to. To allay their fears five men volunteered their service to go in advance of the boats in a canoe. If they found Indians they were to pass on and join the boats below, if not they were to wave their handkerchiefs as a token for the boats to land. No Indians having been discovered, they gave the token for the boats to land, which by that time were nearly opposite the mouth of the Miami, and close to the Kentucky shore. As soon as could be, after the signal was given the boats were landed, but in rowing across the Ohio river were carried by the current about three-fourths of a mile down the river, and made a landing on the first high bank on the Ohio below the mouth of the Miami, a little after sunrise on the 18th of

November, 1788. After making their boats fast they ascended the steep bank and cleared a small space of ground in the midst of a papaw thicket. They then placed sentinels out to watch for the approach of Indians, and commenced a season of worship and thanksgiving to Almighty God, to whose providence they ascribed their success; first in a song of praise in which Mr. Wade took the lead, then in prayer upon their bended knees, in which Major Stites led, returning their thanks for the care exercised over them and in humble prayer imploring that protection which God alone could afford them. E. F.

Lawrenceburg, Dec. 30, 1850.

LETTER IV.

MR. TORBET—To avoid spinning out my last letter to too great a length, I broke off rather abruptly, leaving the little company of whom I was writing at the close of their morning worship. That exercise having closed, they commenced building Ft. Miami, as described in my first letter, and so successful were they, that before the usual hour of retirement they had erected the body of a block-house, hung the door and stopped the cracks between the logs, so as to have a place of defense to rest in. It being considered by them very important to finish their fort before the Indians should learn they were there, they persevered in their labor from day to day until it was completed, which was in about one month from their first landing, during all of which time they were careful to keep sentinels to give an alarm if the Indians should appear. The work being completed, they announced the event in military style, by firing a few rounds, using on the occasion their rifles and a brass blunderbuss with which Judge Symmes had kindly furnished them when they left Maysville. There were at the time some hunters on the Kentucky side of the river who heard the firing, and, supposing the Indians had attacked the new settlement, they returned with all possible speed to Washington to give the alarm, and in less than forty-eight hours from the firing, the company at the fort were surprised to see over fifty brave, generous-hearted Kentuckians come to their relief; among them, the celebrated Indian hunter, Major Simon Kenton. Though they did not need assistance at that time, it was a source of encouragement to know the willingness of their Kentucky friends to assist them if they should afterwards want help. They received them with heartfelt gratitude, which was increased to overflowing when they left, on hearing the assurance they gave, to hold themselves in readiness to respond to any call for help they might afterwards make on them. The fort being finished, and the best preparations made for defense they were able to make, not having seen any Indians, and being greatly encouraged by the arrival of Lieutenant (afterward general) Kingsbury, of the U. S. army, with a small company of soldiers, they began to think of making preparations to raise a crop of corn the ensuing season. For that purpose they appointed three of their company to select land which could be prepared for planting with the least amount of labor. The men then appointed selected an open piece of land up the Miami about one mile from the fort, which they called "Turkey Bottom," on account of the great number of turkeys seen there. On the land selected by them there was but little timber, except honey-locust, which easily deadened, the balance being mostly hackberry and box-elder, with a few very large sycamore, which they kept at a distance from in laying out their corn-fields. On their return to the fort, they unexpectedly found themselves in the midst of a party of Indians, superior in number to themselves, to whom they had so nearly approached that there was no chance for retreat. Mr. Heampsted raised his rifle, placing his finger on the trigger, and was in the attitude of shooting one of the Indians (Capt. Black Fish), when the latter threw the muzzle of the gun above his head, saying, "Do not shoot, I'm your friend." Ascertaining that one of the Indians could speak English, and that they were disposed to be friendly, they entered into a conversation with them about their new settlement and the advantages both parties might derive in the way of trade with each other from living near together. The Indians then proposed to go with the white men to the fort to see the white people, to which they consented, on condition that one white man and one Indian should first go into the fort and give notice that they were coming, and obtain consent of the white people. The other two white men were to remain with the Indians as a guarantee that the Indian going to the fort should be permitted to return unhurt. To this proposition both parties agreed, and one of each went into the fort and obtained permission for the Indians to make the desired visit, provided they would come in unarmed, so as not to alarm the women. On receiving the information they all proceeded to the fort, leaving their guns, tomahawks, etc., behind. After spending some time in friendly conversation, the Indians returned, both parties giving mutual pledges of friendship. The Indians, on leaving, invited the white people to visit them next day at their camp, east of the Little Miami, near the place where New Town now stands. The next morning Messrs. Ephraim Kibbey and Hezekiah Stites rode out to their camp, when they found about thirty Indians, including squaws and children, encamped for a winter's hunt, who gave them a very friendly reception. Kibbey and Stites were soon invited by two Indians to spend the day in hunting, to which they consented, and soon left camp for the woods, dividing into two parties, Kibbey going with one Indian and Stites with the other. The day proved unfavorable for hunting, so that they killed but one buck, though they remained in the woods until it was too late to return to the fort that night, and were compelled to remain with the Indians, in their camp, until the next morning, where, for fear of wearying the reader with too long a letter, I shall leave them until my next.

Yours truly, E. F.

Lawrenceburg, Ind., Jan. 10, 1851.

LETTER V.

MR. TORBET—I will now proceed with my narrative of the adventure of Messrs. Kibbey and Stites to the Indian camp. After their return from the woods the Indians provided them with as good a supper as circumstances would admit of, and, after eating, laid skins on the ground for a bed to sleep; so that they enjoyed a pretty good night's rest, and in the morning in like manner prepared for them a good, wholesome breakfast. After eating they saddled their horses to return to the fort, when the Indian who hunted with Kibbey the day before offered him all the meat he had killed; Kibbey, through modesty, at first refused to accept, but being told by one of them who could speak English that Indians always considered it unfriendly to refuse an offered gift, he accepted the offer and tied it across his saddle. On noticing this transaction the Indian who hunted with Stites went back of the camp and selected from some venison he had previously killed an equal quantity and presented it to him, which he thankfully received. They then invited the Indians to visit them again at the fort, and to bring their women and children with them, which they promised to do.

then bid them good-bye and returned to the fort. On their return the white people were greatly rejoiced, for they had, through the night entertained strong doubts about their safety. The next day the Indians came in with their women and children, were treated very kindly, and appeared much pleased with the friendly interview. The women amused themselves with many curiosities they saw about the fort, but nothing seemed to attract their attention so much as an infant child (daughter of Mrs. Rhoda Stites, wife of Elijah Stites,) two or three days old, called Jane (after marriage Jane Blue) and the first white child born in the Miami country. After remaining a few hours in the fort, in which they appeared to enjoy their visit, they began to make preparations to return to their camp, when Major Stites told them in a few days it would be Christmas, a day generally observed as a holy day by the white people, and invited them to come in and partake of a Christmas dinner with them, to which they assented, then bid them good-bye and retired. About this time the new settlers were encouraged by the arrival of several families who had descended the river to join them; among the families was Mr. Hugh Dunn, from New Jersey. Mr. Dunn had in his family two sons, Micajah and Samuel, and a nephew, Samuel Dunn, who were active young men, besides several younger children, among whom were Elizabeth, now Mrs. Elizabeth Mills, of Elizabethtown, Ohio, and Judge Isaac Dunn, of Lawrenceburg, Ind., who still enjoys good health and is active in his business pursuits. On the approach of Christmas, preparation was made to entertain the Indians with a suitable dinner, to which Lieutenant Kingsbury and his men were invited. The dinner consisted of a turkey pot-pie, cooked in two large pot-metal kettles, over a fire made by the side of a large sycamore tree which had been cut down outside of the fort, and a table was made in the late Kentucky barbecue style. The Indians came in, and everything moved on quietly until the dinner was made ready. When about to sit down at the table Kingsbury with his soldiers made their appearance, of which the Indians had not been apprised, and on their near approach, seeing them armed, some of the Indians, fearing it was a hostile move, became alarmed, and one of them giving a sign by whistling on his fingers, they started to run, but Major Stites by calling to them and assuring them that nothing unfriendly was intended, they returned and partook of the dinner prepared for them, well pleased, but could not account for the hot pungent taste of the pot-pie. From that time the Indians and white people kept up almost a daily friendly intercourse, until the former left in the spring to return to their village to prepare for a summer crop, but on leaving they stole and took away with them what few horses the white people had, which was at that time a severe loss.

During the remainder of the holidays there was but little for the white people to do but to amuse themselves in the best way they could, as a swell in the river cut off their communication with the woods and confined them to a very narrow circle around the fort. Unfortunately Lieutenant Kingsbury had selected too low a site for his fort, and was by this flood driven from his position. As all his begun works were submerged he immediately loosed his cable in search of a more suitable place, which he did not find until he passed the mouth of Deer creek, where he made a landing, immediately above the foot of Broadway, where the next day he commenced building a fort as near the bluff bank as he could place it, and in front of the site where Fort Washington was afterwards erected. This was known for several years as the Picket fort, and was used as a prison in which the captive Indians brought in by Generals Wilkinson and Scott in 1790 were confined. Mr. Hezekiah Stites, from whom I received the information of Kingsbury's removal from Columbia to

Cincinnati, and who accompanied him to the latter place, stated to me many years ago that it took place on the last day of December, 1788, and that then no previous improvements had been commenced in Cincinnati. This brings me to the close of the year, and so I conclude this letter that my next may begin with the new year.

        Yours truly,   E. F.

Published Jan. 17, 1851.

LETTER VI.

MR. TORBET—The year 1781 commenced with prospects more encouraging to the new settlement than had been anticipated; the dread of Indian hostilities had partially subsided, and though there was a scarcity of bread, deer, bear, turkeys and other wild game furnished an abundant supply of meat, and hickory and beech nuts could be had in any quantity wanted, at any time, by picking them up. Under the pleasing prospects before them the settlers commenced making preparations in Turkey-bottom to plant a crop of corn. In the meantime their numbers were increasing by the arrival of new emigrants; not only to strengthen but to establish two new settlements, one opposite the mouth of Licking river (now called Cincinnati), the other at North Bend. Among those who remained at Columbia were several families of the Flinns, one a very aged man, said to be ninety, with three sons, Thomas, Daniel and James; the two former had families, and were all good woodsmen. Other families soon followed, viz.: Captain Benjamin Davis, Mr. Newel, several families of the Clawsons, Biddles, Fletchers, Covalts, Gerrards, a Mr. Soward, and three young men without families, Luke, Gabriel and Zebulon Foster; Luke afterwards Judge

Foster, still resides on his farm in Springfield township, Hamilton county, Ohio, at an advanced age. All the above named persons arrived in time to assist in the preparations made for a crop. The arrangement among themselves was for each man to determine for himself the quantity of land he would clear, the whole to be enclosed in one common field, each one to make his proper proportion of fence. In prosecuting their work they were unexpectedly retarded by frequent swells of water in the Miami, overflowing the land, and removing the fence, after it was made, from its proper place. They, however, by continued exertions, prepared a large field for planting, which might probably have been planted in time had the Indians not stolen their horses when they left to return home to attend to their summer crop. The last named loss and the want of a sufficient quantity of seed corn were severely felt; so that it was too late before the corn was in the ground for it to ripen. During the summer, health and uninterrupted peace with the Indians prevailed, and the new settlements were continually increasing in numerical strength, but they labored under great difficulties in tending their corn for the want of teams, plows, etc., but autumn brought with it its difficulties. In September, some of the hunters reported signs of Indians, and as they did not come in to trade as they did in the previous winter, it was feared their designs were hostile; but soon all doubt was removed. Towards the close of September Mr. Soward sent two of his sons (John and Ziba) to the corn-field for some green corn, who on their way out were surrounded by a party of Indians, as was afterwards learned from Ziba. Not returning, the inhabitants of the fort became very uneasy, and preparation was made to go in search of them early in the morning, should they not return by that time. As soon as it was light, all the men that could be spared from the fort, went in pursuit of the missing boys, dividing into small parties. Messrs. Luke Foster and John

Clawson took the direct path that was usually traveled to the corn-field, within a short distance of which, in crossing a large tree that had fallen across the path, they found Ziba on his elbows and knees, with his forehead nearly imbedded in the earth, and his scalp, including all the skin with hair on it, stripped off, and the marks of three strokes of the tomahawk on one side of his head, each of which had perforated the skull and passed into the brain, who, though apparently insensible, was still living. Mr. Clawson, who was a remarkably large and strong man, proposed to Mr. Foster that if he would assist in getting him on his shoulders he would take him to the fort, which he did, carrying him in that way more than three-fourths of a mile. No physician could be had to dress his wound, but all that could be done with the skill they possessed was done to soothe his pains. After washing and dressing his wounds, he for a time revived, and told his friends that as he and his brother were going to the corn-field they were suddenly surrounded by a party of Indians; that they felt very much alarmed; that one of the Indians said to them in English: "Do not be frightened; you are safe;" that he then took a halter from his bosom and commenced to tie John, on seeing which, he started to run for home, and was followed by some Indians, but kept ahead of them until he came to the tree across the road, when he was knocked down, and knew nothing more. He lingered in his sufferings for a number of days and died. Three days after this distressing occurrence a Mr. Larkin, as he was returning from the woods, found the head of John stuck on the top of a hickory pole, which had been bent over, the top cut off and sharpened, and his body on the ground. This circumstance ended all friendly intercourse with the Indians until Wayne's treaty in 1795. Notwithstanding the dark shade this event cast over their prospects, there was no choice left them but to persevere in their efforts—retreat was impossible—danger must be met at every point; it was with them truly a critical period. They, however, breasted the storm, and, after years of toil, war and bloodshed, succeeded in effecting what they had undertaken.

Yours truly,   E. F.

Published Jan. 24, 1851.

LETTER VII.

MR. TORBET—Unlike farmers in old settled countries, after the corn crop was laid by, our new settlers had no labor to perform to occupy their time profitably to themselves. To remedy that evil Major Stites had nearly all the bottom lands at Columbia laid off in five-acre lots from the fort down to the plat of that part he laid off in half-acre for a town, and from the river back to Turkey Bottom, which he offered for sale on reasonable terms, giving every man an opportunity to become a land-owner, and, to such as did not wish to buy, he gave leases for three years on condition they would clear and fence the lots they leased. Many embraced the opportunity to buy or lease, and went to work to prepare for a crop the next season. Unfortunately, the crop then growing did not ripen before frost, so that it was scarcely fit for bread and totally unfit for planting. In anticipation of the difficulties that might result from that state of things, Mr. Hezekiah Stites, accompanied by two other men who wished to return to the old settlements, was dispatched on a trip to the Red Stone country for a supply of breadstuff and seed-corn, and did ascend the Ohio and Monongahela to that place, in a canoe, which they propelled with poles and paddles against the stream, undisturbed by the Indians, and returned the ensuing spring with his supply. In the meantime the tide of emigration was so great that the supply brought on by Mr.

Stites was entirely insufficient, and many of the settlers were driven to the necessity of going through the woods to Lexington, Ky., for seed-corn. In the early part of December seven persons, viz., Isaac Ferris, John Ferris, Jonah Reynolds, William Goforth, John S. Gano, Daniel Bates and Luther Kitchel arrived about the same time with their families; the two latter passed on to Cincinnati. With these families there were several men without families, viz., Benjamin Alcut, Libeus Marshal, Abraham Ferris and others; add to these, families almost daily arriving, and the fort would soon fill to overflowing, many of the small apartments being occupied by two and three families at one time. It was rather fortunate at that time that they were not cumbered with much furniture. For chairs, they used three-legged stools; for tables, chests or large boxes; and their beds at night were spread on the rough floor. I do not remember of but one chair in the fort. Forced by necessity, several cabins were built outside the fort. Major Goforth built a two-story hewed log-house, which was as well prepared for defense as the fort was. Among the outsiders I recollect Captain Davis, Mr. Newel, Mr. Mills and Mr. Isaac Ferris. About the close of December Mr. David Jones, a minister of the Baptist Church in Pennsylvania, who had been a chaplain in the Revolutionary under General Wayne, arrived at Cincinnati, in company with the reinforcement of soldiers (I believe under Major Daugherty), in the character of a chaplain, but finding no encouragement to preach there he came to Ft. Miami; he preached the first sermons ever preached in the new settlements. The sermon was preached in the block-house in the southwest corner of the fort—the congregation was large, but had to stand on their feet for want of seats. I was too young to comprehend and judge of the merits of the discourse, but recollect it was full of encouragement; the people were exhorted to put their confidence for defense in the arm of an Omnipotent God, and he would drive out their enemies before them and give them as an inheritance the goodly land. Mr. Jones, not liking the service, soon returned to Pennsylvania. This brings me to the close of 1789, a little more than thirteen months from the time the first five families landed to take possession of the country.

      Yours truly,   E. F.

Lawrenceburg, Ind., Jan. 26, 1851.

LETTER VIII.

Mr. Torbet—In sketching in former numbers my recollections of the early settlements of the Miami country I wrote mostly what has been communicated to me from others, of what they had heard and seen, hereafter I shall write mostly what I have myself heard and seen. The early settlers in the commencement of 1790 felt an increased confidence in their ability to repel any general attack the Indians might make upon them. The increase of numerical strength at Columbia, Cincinnati and North Bend—the settlement of Dunlap's station on the Big Miami, and Covalt's station on the Little Miami, left but little ground to fear that any serious attack would be made on the older stations. The winter was exceedingly pleasant, during the whole of which there was no snow, nor but very little frost, so that for a time there appeared to be no difficulty thrown in the way to hinder the most persevering industry in preparing the largest possible amount of land for cultivation for the ensuing season, but while dreaming of prosperity a dark cloud suddenly passed over. Mr. Abel Cook, one of the first party who had landed at Columbia to commence the new settlement there, while attempting to travel from Covalt's station, was waylaid and killed by the Indians. News of that sad event soon reached the fort, and a sufficient number of volunteers immediately started in search of his body, which was found a short distance from the path that had been marked out to guide the traveler in going to the station, and near where Armstrong's upper mills were afterwards built. The body of Mr. Cook was brought in and interred, but it was not known to what tribe the aggressors belonged, or how many there were in the party. It was supposed by the militia who went out to bring the body in that he was at first slightly wounded, and attempted to escape by flight, but was pursued and overtaken; that he made a desperate defense from the appearance of the ground around where the body lay, but was overcome by superior numbers, killed and scalped. This melancholy event taught them that whatever security they might have against a general attack, there was no safety for them when scattered in the woods. In the month of March the attention of the people was turned away from their corn-field to their sugar crops, for until that month the weather had not been cold enough for making sugar. Not long after the excitement occasioned by the above related circumstance was allayed another cry of Indian alarm called the people from their slumber; I recollect being awakened from my sleep by the noise and confusion, and that the first sound in my ears that I could understand was, "Turn out for the Indians are coming!" There was one universal rush among the militia from their cabins to the open space inside the fort. A messenger from Cincinnati had arrived bringing the intelligence that Dunlap's station was besieged by the Indians, that a Mr. Abner Hunt had been taken by the Indians the evening before, and that after an unsuccessful attempt to use him as an instrument to prevail on Lieutenant Kingsbury to surrender they had killed him and made a general attack, and that a Mr. John W. Wallace (I believe it was) offered his service to creep through the Indians, under cover of the darkness of the night, and make his way to the new settlements for assistance. He first arrived at Cincinnati, but it was thought there could not be a sufficient force raised there, not being able to judge the number of Indians engaged in the attack, and therefore he was sent to Columbia for further assistance. The first suggestion made was that it might be a feint, on the part of the Indians, to attack that place with a small party, to draw away the militia from the stronger points, where they could strike a more fatal blow, but there was no time for delay. In a short time the whole body of the militia, except a few of the most aged, who were left to protect the fort, were on their march for Dunlap's station. In about twenty hours they returned and reported that on their approach to the station the Indians fled, but on ascertaining the course of their trail it was feared they intended an attack either on Columbia or Covalt's station. A messenger was sent to the latter place to warn them of their supposed danger, and the night was spent in the fort to put it in a better condition for defense. The men reported that the people at the station had made a most gallant defense, and that the women had proved themselves heroines, that they not only personally visited the men at their posts, and furnished them with food and drink, but encouraged them to acquit themselves like men, and when their lead was like to fail melted their pewter spoons and plates and run them into balls. During the balance of the war the valor of the Colerain heroines was oft referred to as worthy of imitation, and as one of the means by which the inhabitants of that place were preserved from indiscriminate slaughter. Yours truly, E. F.

Published Feb. 7, 1851.

LETTER IX.

Mr. Torbet—In my last I made an allusion to the encouraging prospects the early settlers had when they entered upon the labors of 1790; but purposely omitted to speak of the productiveness of soil as one source of encouragement. The agriculturist whose principal hope (for the time being) depends on a good crop of corn can not be otherwise than pleased with a fertile soil, which, if properly cultivated, and Providence should send sufficient rain, gives full assurance of an ample reward for his labor. The soil at Columbia, though it had not been fairly tried with those domestic vegetables which constitute the usual variety wanted for the comfort and support of civilized men, was so rich and mellow, and had, without the aid of cultivation, produced such rich pastures and beautiful forests, that none could doubt that when subdued and brought into cultivation, it would more than amply reward all the labor bestowed upon it. By the dint of labor, they had cleared, fenced and prepared as much land of that character for cultivation as they, with the strength they then had, could work to good advantage, so that when the season should roll around, they had in prospect a full supply of bread as a stimulus to persevering industry. I have no doubt but many of the present citizens of Columbia and the surrounding country would feel an interest in reading a correct reply to an inquiry often made by strangers, when they happen to fall in company with any of the surviving pioneers of the Miami valley: "What was the appearance of the country at that time?" For the gratification of such, should this letter meet their eye, I will answer—romantic. It was then the temporary residence of the red wild man at certain seasons of the year, and at all times the range of the bear, the deer, the wildcat, the raccoon, the opossum and wild turkey, with numerous other animals ranging on the green pastures at all seasons, and during most of the fall and winter months glutting themselves with the rich fruits of the forests. On approaching the shore at the mouth of the Little Miami, you would see the banks of both rivers beautifully lined with rows of cotton-wood and water maple. Rising to the first level there was a mixture of the honey-locust, hackberry and box-elder, interspersed with very large sycamores, the latter most generally near the rivers. Rising to a still higher level you would enter an extensive plain covered over with as rich a growth of forest trees as the eye of man could wish to look upon. There was the oak, the ash, the walnut, the hickory, the beech, the sugar tree and the buckeye, all growing together, and towering toward the skies, as though they had been vieing with each other for ages which should rise highest in the air, so as to catch the first rays of the morning sun, or which should spread its boughs to the widest extent so as to form the coolest retreat for the weary traveler seeking a shelter from the scorching heat of the noon-day summer sun. Among the rest there was one sycamore that might with some propriety be called the king of the forest. This tree stood a few rods back from the bank of the Ohio river, about eighty rods below Fort Miami. Of its height I can not speak; but it must have far out-topped the most lofty of the other trees, for after resisting the pressure of the stormy winds (probably for centuries) it had been forced at last to yield to some furious tornado that had passed over the land; which separated the top and part of the trunk from the main portion of the body at (as I should judge) about the height of eighty feet, where I think it was still about six feet in diameter. The body of this sycamore was sixteen feet six inches in diameter near the ground and had a hollow of fifteen which continued in a proportionate size to where the top was broken off. It diminished in size as it ascended very gradually, and was remarkably straight, and had very smooth outside bark for so large a tree. On the northwest side of the tree there was an opening large enough for a man on horseback to enter. I knew a gentleman once to ride into the tree, with a lady on behind him, who turned around and came out again without any difficulty. It became a place of resort to the inhabitants of the fort, who, when they wanted to take a pleasant walk, and were not deterred by fear of Indians, more frequently visited this large tree than any other place. The description here given is taken from my own personal view and recollection of it, and in no way exaggerated. I suppose I have seen it more than a thousand times. But lofty, aged and strong as it was, when deprived of the protection it received from smaller surrounding trees, it was forced to yield to the pressure of an immense mass of drift which floated and lodged against it in the extraordinary flood of 1793, and accumulated until by the force of the current it was broken off at the bend of the ground and forced into the Ohio, from whence it descended to parts unknown.. This beautiful plain was covered in many places with an undergrowth, mostly of spice bark and papaw, and everywhere with a coat of wild grass and other vegetables which at all seasons of the year afforded a full bite pasture for all the cattle owned by the citizens until subdued and brought under cultivation, but could not be used for their horses without exposing them to be stolen and taken away by the Indians. Yours with respect, E. F.

Published Feb. 14, 1851.

LETTER X.

MR. TORBET—Many other circumstances, other than those heretofore named, operated on the fears and hopes of the early settler. Many of them had been raised in opulence, and had indulged in many of the luxuries and enjoyed all the necessaries of life; now removed far from their former homes, where nothing but the most common fare could be had, and that often in stinted measure, were cast down, "though not forsaken." I recollect hearing it said, and suppose it is true, that Mrs. Rhoda Stites (a mother who had three children) was one day so deeply affected with the danger of starvation, if they should escape the barbarity of the Indians, that she started to seek a place of retirement in the woods where she might alone give vent to her grief. While pursuing a narrow track a short distance from the fort, she approached within a few steps of an Indian before she discovered him, and was so affrighted that she turned around, as she was permitted to do undisturbed by the Indian (who, she supposed, saw her cheeks bedewed with tears), and made her way back to the fort, rejoicing that she had escaped the danger to which she had just been exposed. Add to the want of bread the mortification of an American mother, who had been in the habit at all times of clothing her children comfortably, and sometimes ornamenting them to please her own fancy, must feel to see them clad in rags and dirt, for the want of materials to make new ones of, or soap to wash them when dirty, and you will see enough to discourage and depress them. As yet there was no shoemaker, tailor, blacksmith, weaver, or any other mechanic's shop; nor was there a mill in the country to grind their grain, should they chance to procure any, save such as were turned by hand. But admit all these difficulties, they indulged a hope that better times awaited them. In the early part of this year they were visited by Elder John Mason, Baptist preacher from Kentucky, and the Rev. Mr. Rice, a Presbyterian from the same state, both of whom preached to the people in the fort. They were likewise encouraged with the prospect of a school for the education of their children. Mr. Frey, a young gentleman from

Freysburg, N. H., opened a school in one of the block-houses in the fort, which, when built, was designated for that purpose. This was the first school ever taught in the Miami country. Early in this year Governor Arthur St. Clair arrived in the Miami country accompanied with some judges, vested with authority from congress to establish a civil government in the northwestern territory. At Columbia he appointed Major William Goforth a justice of the peace, and Mr. Joseph Gerrard, constable, with instructions (if my recollection is correct) to perform the several functions of their offices in conformity with the laws of Pennsylvania until further provisions should be made. The governor also appointed Mr. James Flinn captain, Mr. John Ferris, lieutenant, and Mr. Elijah Stites engineer of a militia company at Columbia, with authority to enroll, discipline and call into service the militia when circumstances might require it; but what was more pleasing than all, they were now promised an army, which should come shortly with sufficient strength to chastise and drive back the Indians. The advance of this promised army, shortly after, arrived under command of General Harmar, which was hailed with enthusiastic joy, and greatly strengthened their confidence. All these circumstances taken together instilled fresh vigor into their minds, and with the means they had they went to work and raised a bountiful crop; which, but for the increase of emigration, would have more than supplied their want of corn. Another circumstance full of encouragement—a Mr. Coleman, who was an extraordinary genius for a man of his information, undertook, and actually built, a mill in a flat-bottom boat capable of grinding their corn. This boat was placed below a fish dam made by the citizens across the Little Miami about half a mile above its mouth, and fastened to the shore by a rope, so that when they wanted it to grind it was shoved out so that the water pitching over the fish pit in the dam would fall on the water-wheel and start the mill to grinding, and when they wanted it to stop they drew it to shore where the water was turned away from the wheel. This mill worked well for a time, but unfortunately in the fall of the year, and when most wanted, a flood in the Miami swept it out into the Ohio river and they saw it no more, and the citizens had again to turn to their hand mills. Harmar's campaign was, however, the all engrossing topic for the time. By it they expected to be delivered from all further danger of Indians, and permitted to pursue their labor in perfect peace.

The march, progress and termination of the campaign shall be the subject of my next letter.

      Yours truly,   E. F.
Lawrenceburg, Feb. 18, 1851.

LETTER XI.

MR. TORBET—In the following communication, I do not pretend to write from information received officially. There was at that time no newspaper in the country through which official communications could be made to reach the people; consequently they had to depend upon public rumor, and by it they formed their opinion of men and things, and, whether true or false, if believed, it had the same effect upon their hopes and fears. They knew it was a fact, that early in the year 1790, General Josiah Harmar arrived among them with a number of soldiers, which, rumor said, was but the advance of an army shortly to arrive, sufficient in number to drive the Indians back, and to compel them to ask for peace, and consent to a favorable treaty. Though General Harmar established his headquarters at Cincinnati, as it was then said, in accordance with the wishes of Judge Symmes and Major Stites, as being the most central place from which all the different stations could get help if attacked by the Indians, he often visited Columbia, it still being the most populous station among the new settlements—and by his appearance and the encouragement he gave for a prosperous campaign greatly strengthened their hopes; so that there was but one opinion about his final success. The expected result created great anxiety for the speedy accomplishment of what they so much desired, and every week's delay was a source of uneasiness. It was, however, understood that the general was authorized to raise one thousand mounted volunteer militia from Kentucky, and that he expected additional forces (and military supplies) down the river, the arrival of whom must necessarily occasion considerable delay; but still there was such an intense anxiety to see him march, that many complaints were uttered about his tardy movements. At length, after spring and summer had been spent in preparation, about the last of September the general took up his line of march with an army of about fifteen hundred men under his command, to the inexpressible joy of all citizens, and almost certain expectation of a triumphant victory. In the military forces of the Kentucky mounted men, they had unbounded confidence, and in the interview they had with General Harmar they had formed a very favorable opinion of him, and now their impatience was raised to hear the result. On leaving Ft. Washington the army marched up Deer creek to the first fork, then ascended the point of the hill near to the place where the Walnut Hill road leaves the Reading turnpike, and over the country between the waters of Mill creek and Duck creek, crossing Sycamore and Turtle creek in a direction east of north until they came to the waters of the Little Miami, near Deerfield, opening as they passed along a track for the army, afterward known by the early settlers as "Harmar's trace," which became the principal thoroughfare many years, for white men and Indians in passing out and in, from and to the river. After coming to the waters of the Little Miami, they passed up on the west side of the river near to the mouth of Sugar creek, where they crossed over to the east side of the river, and kept up the valley, several days' march, to an Indian village, called Old Chillicothe, where they changed their course, recrossed the river, and took a northwesterly direction, crossed Mad river, and the Big Miami on a direct course to the Miami villages on the St. Joseph, near to where the town of Ft. Wayne now stands. There they came to a halt, and, after a few partial engagements with the enemy, retraced their steps and returned to Ft. Washington early in November, being absent one month and five days. The news that the army had returned without any general engagement with the enemy produced one general burst of indignation. It was said that on several occasions a minority of the army had met the Indians, and in an unequal contest had been able to hold them in check until exhausted, when they were compelled to withdraw, leaving the enemy so crippled that they dare not presume to follow, while the main body of the army were retained in camp, and had no share in the engagement, and that while the officers who had been exposed to all the dangers of the contest were imploring further assistance, with the assurance of victory, if they could obtain but a small reinforcement, the general issued a general order to take up the line of march and return to Ft. Washington. All their reports, whether true or not, had their influence on the public minds, and excited the most intent opposition to the commanding general. The militia threw all the blame on the commander, while the officers of the regular army threw it all back on the insurbordination of the militia. The people believed the former, and seemed for a time prepared to make a sacrifice of him to appease their vengeance. The bearing of so unexpected a retreat (after an absence of only about five weeks), with the loss of about two hundred men, upon the future prospect of the country, it was thought would be very unfavorable. It is true it was afterward reported that the Indians lost as many as the white people, but that is all conjecture on our side, while the Indians knew, almost to a man, what our loss was. It was also said they had destroyed the growing crop and towns of the Indians ; but while some viewed that as favorable, others thought it would only exasperate them, and excite to a more cruel, barbarous and destructive warfare on their side.

The whole campaign was considered a failure, and it was thought the whole country was now exposed to invasions and continued depredations from an enemy so exasperated ; that he would struggle hard for revenge. The question was, what shall be done? To retreat was impossible; to collect the militia and place them in a situation to defend against the enemy would be to jeopardize every interest of the country, except personal safety ; and even that in the end would be lost by a state of starvation; the largest proportion of their corn being in Turkey Bottom, about a mile from the fort, and could not be gathered and brought in without being continually exposed to danger. While all these difficulties were staring them in the face, it seemed to be a source of consolation to many that, if they could do nothing more, they could at least, with their tongues, wreak their vengeance on the head of their unfortunate general. After a short time's consideration, it was found that the militia in Columbia had increased to one hundred and fifty, in Cincinnati to one hundred, at North Bend to eighty, Dunlap's Station to fifteen, and Covalt's Station to twenty. Two new companies were formed at Columbia, and Mr. John S. Gano was appointed captain of one, with Mr. Ephraim Kibbey, lieutenant, and a Mr. Hall, captain of the other, and they were ordered to muster their companies every week Orders were also given to see that

every person enrolled as a militiaman should carry his gun and be equipped ready for fight, at all gatherings, whether on the Sabbath or other days. Thus it will be seen that a dark cloud hung over the new settlements for a time, and eclipsed all the pleasing anticipations indulged in at the commencement of the year. Yours truly, E. F.
Lawrenceburg, Feb. 22, 1891.

LETTER XII.

MR. TORBET—In my last letter, in order to carry my recollection of the influence of Harmar's campaign on the minds of the people and its bearing on the prosperity of the settlements to its termination, I passed over other circumstances, worthy of a passing notice. The expected success of Harmar in driving the Indians back brought an increased number of emigrants to the country, among them the families of Broadwell, Buckingham, Light, Morris, Biddle, Clark, Crosly and others, whose descendants are still residing in the country, to witness the results of the enterprise and industry of their fathers. The school heretofore spoken of was soon broken up on account of a difficulty between Mr. Frey and his landlord. He was, however, soon succeeded by a Mr. Ayreheart, who continued the school for one quarter; then gave way to a Mr. Thomas Haman, an accomplished teacher and gentleman (from Ireland), who continued the school nine months longer to the satisfaction of all. I will here mention as a part of history that some may feel an interest in that in the month of March, 1790, Elder Stephen Gano, a Baptist preacher, then from the city of New York, who had come to the west to visit an aged father in Kentucky, came also to Columbia to visit a brother (the late John S. Gano), and there found nine persons who had been members of Baptist churches in the parts from which they came, and who wished to be organized into a church. He organized them as such, and on the ensuing Sabbath added to them three others, by administering to them for the church the ordinance of baptism. This was the first organized religious church in the Miami country, and still exists, and is known by the name of the " Duck Creek Church." The increase of emigration was so great this season that many families ventured to build cabins and remove down to the town, about one mile below the fort, and so great was the increase that before the close of the year the town outnumbered the fort in population. There was also another settlement made this year on the east side of the Miami, called Gerrard station, consisting probably of from ten to fifteen families. The season this year was very favorable for a crop, and the yield an abundant one, for the amount of land cultivated, and what was very extraordinary—in almost all their fields, but more abundantly in the lower lands near the Miami river, there was a plentiful crop of squashes, without planting, consisting of various species, not less that ten to fifteen, which were found to be very useful. These were preserved as a substitute for potatoes, and thought by many to be fully equal to them. There was also an extensive crop of excellent pumpkins, which, had they had flour for crust, and shortening, spice and milk, would have enabled them to indulge in the free use of pumpkin pies; but for the want of other materials they could only be used for pumpkin bread by mixing it with corn meal and baking it. The Indians were less troublesome this year than the several succeeding ones. I do not remember any other injury done by them, after the commencement of spring, than stealing a few horses about planting time. I believe there was one Indian scalp taken that year by a white man while out hunting. Taking the result of Harmar's campaign into view, in connection with all the circumstances that operated on the hopes and fears of the people, the same dark cloud that hung over their prospects in the commencement of the season still darkened their horizon, and they had to enter upon a new year in the same state of suspense they had entered the last one, excepting an increasing confidence (growing out of their numerical strength) that they would be able to resist any attack the Indians might make upon them.

      Very truly,   E. F.

Lawrenceburg, March 7, 1851.

LETTER XIII.

Mr. Torbet—The most gloomy apprehensions entertained by the people in the new settlements, about the results of Harmar's campaign, in 1790, were realized to the fullest extent in 1791. Emboldened by Harmar's precipitate retreat from the Miami town on the St. Joseph, back to Fort Washington, and the small loss of life the Indians reported that they had sustained in their successful resistance to his attack, they began early in the season to hover round the frontier settlements, and in the end there was more bloodshed and slaughter that year than any other during the seven years' war. Very early in the year they commenced their depredations by stealing all the horses they could possibly get hold of, and in this they were so bold that one night, the gates of the fort being left open through carelessness, they entered the fort and stole two horses that had been taken inside and tied by halters for safety. Early in the spring a Mr. Dimett, in company with Mr. Jonathan Coleman, in traveling from Columbia to Covalt's Station, were waylaid by a party of Indians, who killed and scalped the former, and, it was supposed, carried the other away a captive, as no trace of his body was found.

I believe he was never heard of afterwards by his friends. The Indians not only harassed the frontier settlements, but they collected in large numbers about the mouth of the Scioto river, as was supposed, if possible, to prevent emigration to the country. The first certain evidence had of their strength by the white people was in the slaughter of Colonel Strong's party of soldiers, the remnant of Harmar's army, whose term of service had expired. Colonel Strong had been ordered to march them to Fort Harmar, near Marietta, and discharge them; so it was reported. On their way up the river from Fort Washington they stopped the first night at Columbia, where, as far as they could, they exchanged the flour they had drawn for corn bread—by which many who had not tasted wheat bread for many a day had, an opportunity of having warm biscuit for breakfast. I very well recollect how I relished the rare treat. Colonel Strong had a keel-boat in which the provisions and camp equipage was transported, which was rowed up stream by a number of soldiers. There was a cabin in the boat fixed up for the officers in which, it was said, they rode, and the men traveled up the shore on foot, using the boat for a ferry in crossing the mouth of the streams of water in their way. I do not know that it was reported how many men there were, but should suppose, from my recollection of their appearance, there were not less than two or three hundred. A few days after passing Columbia, up stream, the keel-boat, with a few of the men, returned on their way back to Fort Washington, and landed again at Columbia and made the following report: On their way up they passed undisturbed until they approached the mouth of the Scioto, where the boat landed to ferry the men across, and when they were stepping into the boat a large body of Indians rushed suddenly from ambush and formed a line in their rear, and, with tomahawks and knives, making the most hideous yells, they rushed furiously on them, and commenced the work of slaughter. The soldiers made no resistance. Being instantly cut off from a retreat to the woods they tried to crowd into the boat until it was like to sink, and was, by order of the commandant, shoved off, leaving the most men on shore to the mercy of the savages—many of whom plunged into the river to swim for the boat, and were drowned, and those left on shore were indiscriminately slain. The Indians, or a part of them, followed the boat for some distance, keeping up a fire from their rifles; but she was soon rowed out of their reach, not, however, without receiving the impression of a great many balls shot into her sides. I believe there were some men killed and wounded in the boat. This was the most distressing slaughter of white people that had as yet been made and created great alarm.

A few days after the return of Colonel Strong, a flat-boat hove in view—the first that had made its appearance since the colonel's return. The boat was discovered by some of the school boys just as they were dismissed for dinner; I recollect hearing one of the school boys cry out, "Yonder comes a flat-boat," to which another responded, "She must have run the gauntlet to get here; let us go and see," at which word we all ran down to the river where the boat was landing. I was in the crowd, and so was Judge Isaac Dunn, who, with myself, is a living witness of the shattered and bloody appearance of the boat. On landing it was ascertained that the boat was owned by Mr. William Plasket, who had his family on board, and who made the following report: that he was descending the river in company with two other families by the name of Greathouse, each of whom occupied separate boats, and that in each boat there were several passengers, not belonging to the families, who were descending the river to see the country. At the time they drew near to the Scioto river the other two boats were something like half a mile in advance of his, and that, on looking out, he saw several canoes loaded with Indians go out and take possession of both boats without resistance, and that both of them were immediately landed. For him to retreat was impossible. If he attempted to land he could not make the shore much short of the spot where the Indians were, and as they were supplied with canoes, they could attack him on either side; so that in his mind the only question was, shall we fight or die? He chose the former and prepared for action. The first thing was to examine the guns on board, nine in number, and see that they were all loaded. He then, with an ax, split off the top of the board, next to the roof of the boat, so as to make room to shoot through if attacked. He then directed his son William to lie down in the bottom of the boat and load the guns after they were discharged, soon as handed to him. He next placed the men in a row in a position to fire, but not until he gave orders, and directed his wife and children to lie down on the bottom of the boat, and not to stir or make any noise on any consideration. As they came opposite the mouth of the river, three canoes, with three Indians in each, approached them from the shore, when Mr. Plasket directed them each to shoot so that no two should point at the same Indian, and to await his order before they fired. He permitted them to come so near that he supposed they had concluded he would make no resistance, and dropped their paddles and reached out their hands to take hold of the boat, when, at the word "fire," each shot, and killed six of the Indians; the other three tacked about and made for the shore, at which time as many (they supposed) as five hundred Indians appeared on the shore and commenced firing on them; but by exertions they soon passed some small stream below, and the Indians gave up the chase. In the struggle they had two killed and two wounded, and lost all the horses and cows they had. Before arriving at Columbia they had landed and buried the dead and threw their dead horses and cows overboard.

These melancholy events made the impression at first that immigration must be so interrupted as to prevent the arrival of any more families. But in this they were disappointed, for the Indians soon left the rivers and returned to their town; after, as was supposed, having massacred the two families they had taken. They were never heard of by the settlers in the new country. Yours truly, E. F.
March 14, 1851.

LETTER XIV.

The circumstances related in my last letter were of such a discouraging character that the most gloomy apprehensions were still pressing on the minds of the people, and left no other hope than that they would be able to defend themselves, which hope was strengthened by the continual influx of population. Among the arrivals which were daily taking place at all the stations along the river were John Smith and family, John Ludlow and family, Colonel Oliver Spencer and family, Francis Dunlevy, John Riley, and many others who were afterwards known as taking an active part in the public affairs of the new country. I recollect one arrival of nine families, viz.: David, Joseph, Daniel, Jacob and Stephen Reeder, who were brothers; Thomas Hubbell, who was a brother-in-law, and William Harper, Jeremiah Brann and Mr. Tingley, who had married daughters of the Reeders. To strengthen the hope growing out of the tide of emigration continually setting in, it was rumored that an expedition was preparing in Kentucky to march to the Indian towns and attack them in their own villages, and teach them the necessity of staying at home to protect their wives and children and fire-sides, and, by that means, draw them off from our frontiers. The rumor proved true, and, in the month of May, General Charles

Scott crossed the Ohio river at the mouth of the Kentucky, with eight hundred mounted men, and moved forward with such rapidity that he reached and attacked several of the Indian towns on the Wabash before they had notice of his approach. In this expedition General Scott killed a number of warriors, took fifty-four prisoners, destroyed a large amount of property, and returned in triumph with very little loss. The news of this brilliant affair, as it spread, infused joy and gladness into the minds of the people. It was soon rumored that the success attending this expedition had influenced General St. Clair to start a second one, under the command of General Wilkinson, which was confirmed early in August, by his arrival at Ft. Washington with five hundred mounted Kentucky riflemen. From thence he moved forward to the Indian towns on Eel river, near its mouth—took several of their villages by surprise, killed a number of warriors, captured thirty-four prisoners and returned with but very trifling loss—increasing the joy of the people to something like enthusiasm. Now, the people said, "The scale of war has turned, victory perches on our brow, and we hope soon to have peace." The prisoners taken by Scott and Wilkinson were brought to Cincinnati, where they were treated with all the kindness that circumstances would admit; but at what time, or how liberated, I do not recollect. It was next rumored that if the success of the two expeditions named failed to bring the Indians to terms, another grand expedition, under the command of General St. Clair, in person, would march into the heart of the Indian country, take possession of some of their principal towns, fortify themselves and continue a military force among them. This campaign and its results shall be the subject of my next letter.

Yours truly, E. F.

Lawrenceburg, March 17, 1851.

LETTER XV.

Mr. Torbet—In my recollection of the march, progress and final result of General St. Clair's campaign in 1791, I wish it to be understood that I do not intend to impute to any one the cause of the misfortunes attending that enterprise. That the general was a patriot I have no doubt; and that he was a man of superior mind and acquirements has been so well established that it need not be re-asserted; of his military skill I am not capable of judging, but know he was unfortunate. In the commencement of his campaign, following so soon after the brilliant victories of Scott and Wilkinson (which were said to have been projected by him), the people had an unshaken confidence in his prospects of success. No application for a treaty having been made by the Indians, early in September the army took up the line of march for the Indian towns, and on their way erected a fort on the east bank of the Big Miami, called Fort Hamilton, where the town of Hamilton is now located. After having finished that fort they again moved forward, and at the distance of about forty miles erected another fort, called Fort Jefferson. The site of this fort is within the present bounds of Darke county, and about six miles from the county seat. After having erected the last-named fort, they again continued their march for the Indian towns. Information of their progress had been heard by expresses arriving almost daily, and this was generally of an encouraging character; but after leaving Fort Jefferson it was reported that the terms of service of the men were daily expiring, and that they were demanding their discharges, and returning, so that the army was continually diminishing; and that provisions were short and that the men were put on half rations. Desertions and insubordinations were also spoken of, and, on the whole, the prospect was less encouraging than it had been; still, as to the final result, but little doubt was expressed. The Indians were to be humbled and compelled to sue for peace.

Thus matters connected with the movements of the army stood in the minds of the people at Columbia on the morning of the 8th of November. What was the feeling at Cincinnati, or the other stations, I know not, but so it was with us; yet final success was not seriously doubted.

On the morning of that melancholy day, as it proved to be, I was employed, by the direction of my father, in filling corn baskets with corn, on the outside of the fort, for a neighbor who had a husking the evening before, and was putting away his corn for safekeeping in an upper room, or, as they term it, the loft. While thus engaged a man appeared, coming from the woods, ragged and dirty, and, as he said, nearly starving with hunger, who reported that he had escaped the destruction of St. Clair's army. His story was, that on the morning of the 4th they were attacked by an overwhelming force of Indians, and that after three hours hard fighting, during which time the most of St. Clair's men were slain, the Indians rushed upon them, and that the whole army had been slain—that, so far as he knew, he was the only man that had escaped. He also said that he had eaten nothing since his escape but some haws he picked up under a haw tree he passed in the woods on his way, and a part of a dead turkey he had found in the woods on his way, without being cooked. The report brought by this man, passed with almost the rapidity of lightning through the fort; but its effects were in part stayed by the opinion of some woodsmen (or, as they were often called at that time, Indian hunters), that the man was a deserter, and had made up this tale to prevent being taken up as such; he, however, continued to affirm that what he had said was true. While questioning, and partly insulting the man, another appeared, telling the same tale, except that more than the first man had supposed had escaped the general slaughter; this last man was almost instantly followed by two others, who confirmed the same facts. Imagination can not describe the scene that ensued. Very few families were there who had not friends in the campaign, bearing the relation of husband, father, brother, or child. There was, indeed, weeping and wailing, and a refusal to be comforted. I had a brother with them, and, perhaps, my melancholy feelings were increased by the grief and wailings of a mother on his account. To me the heavens appeared to be shrouded in sable, and though the sun was shining the atmosphere around appeared like the "troubled waters"; all around was dark and gloomy. The state of suspense, however, hanging over the mind in relation to friends was gradually removed, and before bedtime that evening, so far as I can recollect, all that went from Columbia, except two (James Bailey and Isaac Morris, who were killed), had returned or were heard from. Captain Gano (as he was then termed) had a severe wound from a ball passing through one arm, but returned, in other respects, safe. He, it was said, manifested the bravery of a true soldier during the battle, and covered himself with glory. This, of all others, was, at Columbia, the most gloomy and trying time the inhabitants of the new country had passed through, and presented the most dark and gloomy prospect of any event that had yet occurred. Some thought, as they said, further resistance would be vain; that the Indians would be in on us in such numbers that we should be compelled to fly before them; but others thought best to strengthen the fort, and hold on to it as a place of retreat, if assailed, and that we should still be able to repel any invasion. But all agreed that the campaign was an entire failure, and that the people had nothing now to depend upon but their own personal and private resources. The unfortunate

general, who had a few weeks before marched out at the head of more than three thousand men, full of expectation, and had now returned with less than six hundred, having lost the balance by discharge, desertion and death in the field of battle, nearly (it was said) a thousand in the latter, while it was supposed the Indians did not lose more than about sixty, was now the object of their most bitter denunciations. This campaign, carried on at a very great expense, and attended with so great a loss of human life, was considered the most unfortunate attempt yet made to bring the enemy to terms; but I have already spun my letter to too great a length, and must therefore close. ·　　　　Yours truly,　　　　E. F.
Lawrenceburg, March 20, 1851.

LETTER XVI.

MR. TORBET—The most gloomy apprehensions among the people, about the result of St. Clair's defeat, were in a great measure realized. Marauding parties of Indians were soon hovering around all our settlements, stealing horses and killing our men, if they ventured from home, or capturing and carrying them off as prisoners. To prevent these disastrous consequences, block-houses were erected on the hills, beyond the outside limits of the settlement at Columbia, and the militia were called out in small parties to keep up a line of communication from one to the other, and, if possible, prevent Indians from entering the settlement and attacking the people without being first discovered; but all, apparently, to no purpose, for the Indians would still pass their lines undiscovered, commit depredations and escape unpunished. Notwithstanding all these discouraging circumstances, there were others of a cheering character. Among them, not the least important, a Mr. Wickerham had built a tub-mill east of the Little Miami, near the mouth of Clough creek, which was capable of grinding a large amount of corn; thereby, relieving them from the fatiguing labors of the hand-mill. There had also been brought to the country several lots of goods, mostly taken to Cincinnati, the headquarters of military operation. Among the goods brought on were some articles essentially necessary for the comfort and health of the citizens. Their wearing apparel, bed clothing, etc., brought with them to the country, were worn out, and in the country there were neither wool, cotton or flannel to make more. So that the opportunity of obtaining supplies was very convenient to those who had the means to purchase with. Others had to supply themselves with the skin of the deer from the woods, which they dressed for clothing. While some resorted to the coarse lint of the nettle weed, from which they made a very rough substitute for linen.

The most important event which occurred during the winter was the fitting out of another expedition to go to St. Clair's battle-ground and bring the dead. A rumor was circulated among the people that some hunters had ventured out as far as the field of slaughter, and had seen the buzzards, panthers, wolves and wildcats tearing out the eyes and glutting themselves on the flesh of the dead men, and, although no one could tell the origin of the rumor, it produced an intense excitement, and public opinion called for the burial. The governor himself first visited Columbia to raise volunteers; but he, like all other generals who had been so unfortunate as to lose a battle, was unpopular with the militia and could not succeed. Saturday, of the following week, which was muster day for training the militia, General Wilkinson visited Columbia and attended the muster of the three companies, who all met at one place, on the bank of the river, in the center of the population. These three companies were then commanded by Captain Kibbey, successor to Captain

Gano, who had been promoted to major, and Captains Flinn and Hall. Like other boys, I was fond of visiting such places, and was present. After the men were paraded, General Wilkinson appeared, with his hunting shirt, moccasins, belt, knife and tomahawk—a real woodman's dress. He commenced by inspecting their guns, powder-horns and bullet bags, to learn what their supply of powder and balls was, occasionally tapping a man on the shoulder, saying: "I see by the look of your eye you intend to go with me." After a most excellent and eloquent appeal to the feelings of the men, he asked them if they were willing that their brethren in arms, who had fallen in defense of their wives, children and firesides, should be eaten by the wild animals then glutting themselves on the slain in battle without a burying; and said, in a few minutes he would give an opportunity for all who were willing to go to manifest it by volunteering their services. At the proper time he gave orders, for all who intended to go with him, at the word "forward march" to step three paces forward. When the order was given, it was said that every healthy man in the three companies advanced three paces, and some who did not belong to the militia offered their services. After some directions were given them how they should prepare themselves, and when and where they should rendezvous, they were dismissed to give them time to prepare. That night, Sabbath and Sabbath night, were busily employed in making the preparations. Monday morning they left for Ft. Washington, from whence they took up the line of march and proceeded on the campaign, and were permitted, without being disturbed by the Indians, to prosecute their designs and bury the dead; and, after a short time, they returned without the loss of a man. On their return they erected another fort about halfway between Ft. Jefferson and Ft. Hamilton, to which General Wilkinson gave the name of Ft. St. Clair.

The result of the campaign, in a great measure, checked emigration, discouraged the citizens, and brought upon the infant settlement a train of evils by emboldening the Indians to venture into the very heart of all the new settlements, who were unchecked in their bloodshed by another army for near two years. During which time many citizens were slain, of which I will give you some account hereafter.

      Yours truly,   E. F.

Lawrenceburg, March 25, 1851.

LETTER XVII.

Mr. Torbet—In carrying my recollections back to the close of the year 1791, and the commencement of 1792, located, as I then was, in the midst of a population so deeply interested as the citizens of the Miami country were at that time, in every movement having for its object the driving back the Indians, I can not but feel astonished at the fortitude with which they bore the disappointment they felt at the result of St. Clair's defeat. It is true, they were somewhat cast down, but not in despair; and when the inquiry was made (as it often was), "What shall we do?" the answer was at hand: "We must breast the storm, and be prepared for every emergency." The minds of the people seemed to be prepared for the crisis, and notwithstanding all the discouragements thrown in their way they anticipated a final triumph. Among those most instrumental in keeping their hopes alive, if any one man deserves more praise than another, the highest honor was due to Captain Kibbey, who, by his vigilance in watching the movements of the Indians, and perseverance in pursuing after, and punishing them, when found hovering about our frontiers, gave a confidence in his bravery and skill that partly scattered the dark and gloomy cloud that was hanging over the country.

The first outbreak in the spring of '92, as far as my recollection serves me, was an attack upon a fatigue party sent out from Fort Jefferson, to perform some labor not far distant from the fort. While engaged in the labor assigned them they were taken by surprise and nearly all cut off, among them some valuable officers.

But the most important movement that year was an attempt at a negotiation for peace with the Indian tribes before resort w.s had to another campaign. To effect that object it was said that orders had been given to General St. Clair and General Wilkinson to select three men, to dispatch as commissioners to three of the most important tribes on our borders, to try, if possible, to restore the country to peace. Major Trueman, Colonel Hardin and Dr. Freeman were selected and commissioned for that purpose, and William Smalley, Joseph Gerrard and Thomas Flinn were employed to accompany them as guides and interpreters. Major Trueman also took with him a soldier by the name of William Lynch for a waiter; all of whom, after making the necessary arrangements about their business at home, and preparations for the hazardous adventure, left home on the mission to which they had been designated; none of whom, except William Smalley, ever returned.

This unfortunate mission, with its results, as related by Mr. Smalley after his return, will be the subject of my next letter.

       Yours truly,   E. F.

Lawrenceburg, April 21, 1851.

LETTER XVIII.

Mr. Torbet—In complying with my promise in my last letter, I find myself embarrassed with the fact that the history of the country, founded in part upon official documents, appears to contradict what I know to be true in relation to the hazardous mission in which Major Trueman and his associates were engaged. General Wilkinson says they were selected and sent out by him as the authorized agents of the government. This I believe to be true, connected with the fact that he was to consult with and act in the matter as an associate of Governor St. Clair. I am confident that neither Generals Harmar or Wayne, as stated by some historians, had anything to do in the matter, as Harmar had ceased to command and left the country before any orders for such a mission issued from the department, and Wayne had neither come into command, or to the country, until the unfortunate attempt at negotiation had proved itself an entire failure.

Another difficulty, growing out of the letters of General Wilkinson to the department, is his stating that Trueman, Freeman and Hardin were dispatched by him at different times, which, according to my recollection of the matter, can not be true, as I feel satisfied in my own mind that they all started at the same time. And, even admitting that I might be wrong in my recollection, I can not be mistaken in the narrative Mr. Smalley gave me of the whole affair after his return. Again, General Wilkinson, in his official letter, says nothing was ever heard of these unfortunate men, except some vague accounts collected from the Indians by Mr. May, whom he had directed to desert and go over to the Indians to ascertain, if possible, their fate. This, however, may be accounted for from the fact that Wilkinson wrote before Smalley's return. But how can it be possible that it should still be said by historians that the fate of this party is still unknown, or none of them ever returned, when it is and has been known to thousands that William Smalley did return; that his accounts were settled and paid at the department, and that he afterward lived with his family until extreme old age; was a man of good reputation, and died in the Wabash country four or five years past, and always seemed willing to communicate freely to all with whom he conversed upon the subject, all the circumstances relating to the whole affair? From all the circumstances, I feel justified in saying that on or about the 7th of April, 1792, Major Alexander Trueman, with William Lynch as a waiter, and William Smalley as an interpreter; Colonel Hardin, with Mr. Thomas Flinn as an interpreter, and Dr. Isaac Freeman, with Mr. Joseph Gerrard as an interpreter, left Columbia to visit several of the Indian tribes bordering on our frontiers on a mission, having for its ultimate object a treaty of peace, and that of these seven persons, none save William Smalley ever returned, as far as I ever knew or heard; and that William Smalley did return about Christmas of the same year, a fact in which I can not be mistaken, as I well recollect hearing the report of the guns fired as a salute when he came home; of seeing and talking with him, perhaps a thousand times after his return at his own house and at other places; of his appearing before Major William Goforth, a justice of the peace, at his request, and there relating to him, in the presence of all who wished to attend, all the circumstances connected with his travels during his absence, and the number of his companions, and of his own captivity and escape, answering all the questions asked him freely, except that he then declined relating the manner in which his escape from captivity was effected, and that afterwards (say in 1811) he related to me (with a view to its publication, if I should think proper at any aftertime to publish it) a narrative of all the circumstances connected with the whole affair, which I will give next week if health permits, and which, in combination of facts bearing upon my mind in relation to the whole affair, I fully believe is true.

Yours truly, E. F.

Lawrenceburg, April 29, 1851.

LETTER XIX.

MR. TORBET—As promised in my last letter, I now send you a narrative of the mission of Major Alexander Trueman and others, to the several Indian tribes, to whom they were sent, related to me by Mr. William Smalley, the only survivor of the company sent out by the government. Some time in the year 1811 I visited Mr. Smalley's family, and was detained for a night. I asked Mr. Smalley to relate to me the circumstances that occurred during the trip he had with Major Trueman, on his attempted visit to the Indians, which he gave me, as near as I can recollect, in the following language, which, after returning home, I penned:

"On the 7th of April, 1792, we (meaning Major Trueman, Colonel Hardin, Dr. Freeman, Thomas Flinn, Joseph Gerrard, William Lynch and himself) started from Columbia, and in the most convenient manner we could struck on to Harmar's trace, which we followed until a change in the course made it necessary to leave it to pursue a more direct route to the towns to which we were sent. We continued to travel together in company, carrying with us a white flag, until about the middle of the afternoon of the eighth day of our travel, when a halt was called, and a consultation was held about the propriety of separating, that each of the commissioners might take a direct course to the town or tribe to which he was sent. It was the opinion of Mr. Flinn, Mr.

Gerrard, and myself, that we could not travel any longer together without some of the company going very much out of their course; so we parted. Major Trueman, William Lynch, and myself, took our course toward the Delaware towns, and about sunset met three Indians on the waters of a stream called Hog creek. We presented our flag, and I hailed them saying: 'We are on an errand of peace; the white people want to have peace, and have sent this man (meaning Major Trueman) to make proposals for peace': and proposed that we should camp and spend the night together; to which, after consulting among themselves a short time, they agreed. After making a fire, Major Trueman directed William Lynch, his waiter, to prepare some chocolate for supper; which he did, and Trueman invited the Indians to sup with him; to which they consented, and expressed a great fondness for the new kind of supper. After supper, as neither Trueman or Lynch could speak the Indian language, I entered into a conversation with them upon the subject of our visit, and attempted to show the advantage the Indians would gain by having a market for their furs on the Ohio river instead of Detroit. I told them the white people were anxious to have peace, and open a trade with them, and to exchange powder and lead with them for their meat, to all of which they listened, and appeared well pleased—occasionally asking me to make certain inquiries of my captain (meaning Major Trueman), which I did, and interpreted to them the answers. About 11 o'clock, as I supposed, Major Trueman, having a very bad cold, occasioning a severe cough, proposed to lie down, which I communicated to the Indians; on hearing which the oldest Indian said, 'Ask your captain if he will let one of his men be tied, as you are stronger than we are, not counting my boy (a lad about fourteen) and he is afraid to lie down'; to which Trueman replied he might tie Lynch. The Indian then went a little from the fire, and stripped the bark from some small hickory sprouts, with which he tied Lynch's arms above his elbows, fastening the bark across his back, but not so as to render it very inconvenient to him. Lynch then lay down back of the fire, and Trueman spread some bear skins on the ground in front, and lay down on them, covering himself with a blanket; I lay down on some bear skins with my head raised by placing my elbows on the ground, with one hand each side of my face, in such a posture as to have Trueman and the Indians before me; the latter still sitting up. In this position we entered into another conversation about the success they had had in hunting the past winter. The old Indian complained of having very bad luck, and said he believed it was partly owing to his gun-lock, at which moment he reached out his hand and took hold of the gun, and showed me that he had lost the screws that fastened the lock on, and had to tie it with a leather string. While he was showing his gun, and continuing his complaints, Major Trueman had a very severe spell of coughing, and as soon as the phlegm seemed to rise turned his head over to spit when the Indian shot him, the ball entering about the point of the shoulder-blade and passing out near the nipple on the opposite side, which killed him instantly; so that he did not turn his head back. I sprang up in a moment and ran for the woods, and when, as I suppose, I was about two rods from the fire the other Indian shot at me, but without effect. The Indian boy, like myself, made for the woods, and the old Indian, who first shot, ran back of the fire and seized Lynch, who had raised to his feet and got partially untied, and hallooed to the other Indian to help him, saying: ' This man is stronger than I am, and will get untied and escape'; at which call he went round and struck him on his head with a tomahawk several times. During this time I remained stationary, reflecting on what I should do. I felt as though the joints of my loins were loosed, my knees were knocking together, and teeth rattling. I felt as though to escape was impossible. I was eight days travel from home, had no gun to kill game with to subsist on, and should have to lie by in daylight and travel at night, so that I must starve before I could get home. I concluded I was in the hands of God, and must submit to my fate, and in an instant became composed. After a short time the old Indian called to me, and told me to come to the fire. I refused, saying, 'You will kill me'; to which he replied, 'We will not.' I told him he had promised not to hurt the other men; to which he replied, 'I wanted his gun.' After further conversation, knowing they had not loaded their guns, I placed my butcher-knife in a concealed position, so that I could use it if necessary, and told them if they would put their guns and tomahawks out of reach I would return to the fire; which they did. I then advanced about half way to the fire and halted—the Indian still urging me to come to the fire; I told him if they would sit down I would; they then sat down, and I went up to the fire. They requested me to sit down, which I did." And there he said he passed such a gloomy night that a house full of gold would not be a temptation to go through another such, and continued his narrative.

Not to make this number too long, I must defer the balance for another. Yours truly, E. F.

Lawrenceburg, May 5, 1851.

LETTER XX.

Mr. Torbet—I now proceed with the narrative where I left off in my last.

"I began," said Mr. Smalley, "to reflect on myself for consenting to accompany him on so hazardous a business, knowing, as I believe I did, and as I often told Major Trueman, that we should all be killed. But the fear of being called a coward had spurred me on, to leave for the time my wife and children and home, to throw away my life, merely to escape the reproach that I feared would follow a refusal to go. I next began to charge my misfortunes on the president and congress, and wished, for the moment, they were all with me to share my fate, and lastly, I reproached the society of Friends, who, I understood, had petitioned to congress to make an attempt at negotiation before sending out another army to fight them. I then again concluded all these movements were directed by an overruling Providence, and it was my place to submit, and that, trusting in Him, I might yet be preserved and restored to my family. I concluded that, prepared, as I was, with a knife, I should be able to kill one, and possibly both, and, in the latter case, could have the advantage of the provisions we had with us, and a gun and ammunition, as well as of a pony Major Trueman had brought along to pack his baggage on, so as to render it probable to make my way back to Columbia. I also took into consideration how far I would be justifiable, as a professed Christian, as a last resort to save my life, to deceive them by making false statements about my intentions in coming among them. I thought of my relation to God and to the Baptist Church, as a member with them, and came to the conclusion that neither God nor the church would condemn me for such resort, when impelled to it by the most urgent necessity. I then commenced telling them I was sorry they had killed these men, not that I cared anything about them, but because I wished the Indians well, for whom I had more friendship than for the white people, and thought it would be for their best interest to have peace. I told them I had been raised among their tribe, been adopted into one of their families, and when I left them had an Indian father and brother whom I loved, and that I left them by consent, with the privilege of remaining among the white people or returning to them, as I should choose; that I engaged to do an errand for them at Pittsburg (then called Ft. Duquesne), after which I visited George's creek, the place where I was captured by the Indians when a boy. I told them on my arrival at that place, my friends were all dead or gone, and that from that time I had determined to return to the Indians, and had embraced the opportunity of accompanying these men, as the first ever offered, by which I could elude the watchfulness of the white people, who were always jealous of me as being more friendly to the Indians than to them. I told them if I could find my Indian father or brother, they would confirm all I had said upon the subject. While we were engaged in talking, as above stated, the Indian boy returned from the woods, when the old Indian told him to kill that man behind the fire, "for he disturbs me with his groanings;" adding, "it is very disagreeable to me to hear him;" upon which order the boy immediately killed him by striking him on the head. He then bid the boy scalp him, which he did, and brought the scalp to the Indian, who threw it at me, and told me to dress it, which, with me, was the most trying and terrifying event attending the whole scene. I had to brace up my nerves so as to show no regret, or else I should expose to them the falsity of all I had said, which seemed to require more courage than I had. Several times I found myself drawing my arm, and preparing my mind to plunge my knife into the vitals of one of them, when again I was checked by the consideration that to me it would be immediate death; so that with a mind changing with almost every breath, I passed one of the most gloomy nights that was ever witnessed by man, through which I must have been overwhelmed, had it not been for the help of God and the encouragement given me by the repeated and positive pledges of the Indians that I should not be hurt, until delivered up to the Indian chief next morning, at the town where he resided, which promise they fulfilled, and the next morning conducted me safe to the town, and delivered me into the hands of Boconjehaulis, the principal chief of that tribe, who had me placed under the guard of a number of warriors until further orders."

Finding I can not condense so as to give the transactions before the chief, without tasking the reader with too long a letter, I defer that for another number.

Yours truly, E. F.
Lawrenceburg, May 12, 1851.

LETTER XXI.

MR. TORBET—Mr. Smalley continued: "After being detained a short time by my guard, I was ordered to appear again before Boconjehaulis, who was then considered by the Indians their king. Assuming a rather pompous attitude, he asked me in a very stern way what I had come there for, to which I replied, 'To live with the Indians.' He then inquired, 'And what did these men with you come for?' To which I answered, 'To try to make peace,' they said. 'I think,' said he, 'they were very impudent to attempt to come here; I had given them no leave to come.' In answer I said, 'I do not know anything about it, only what they said; but they told me if I would come with them, as a pilot and interpreter, I might stay with the Indians; and that was all I knew about it.' I then repeated what I had told the Indians in the camp the night before about my Indian father and brother, calling them by name, and rehearsed the circumstances of my captivity and adoption into the family, and of my leaving them with the privilege of remaining with the white people, or returning to them as I might choose, declared my intention of now remaining with them, and repeated the statements I had made of having no relations or friends among the white people. After I had concluded, an Indian rose up in the crowd, and said he knew both the men I had claimed as my father and brother, and knew where they now lived, not more than between one and two days' travel off. I requested to have them sent for, to which the king consented, and I prevailed on the Indian to go after them, who started immediately, and I was returned to the care of my guard. During the absence of the Indian I had sent for my father, I was brought each day before the king, and, as I thought, examined to try to make me contradict myself; consequently, I was very careful to repeat, in the same words, my friendship to the Indians, and reasons for returning to live with them again. The second day of my captivity, I saw, at a distance, the head of a white man, brought into the town by some Indians, elevated on a pole, which I believed was the head of Mr. Joseph Gerrard, who had accompanied Dr. Freeman. But as I had not told the Indians of any other company besides Trueman, Lynch and myself, I dare not show an anxiety about Mr. Gerrard, lest I should betray myself, and did not ascertain to a certainty, but believe it was Mr. Gerrard's head, and am the more confirmed in it now, as he was never afterward heard of by me. I was detained in a very restless state of suspense until the arrival of my Indian father and brother, with the return of the Indian I had sent after them, who interested themselves as much for me as any natural father could have done—attending me every day when examined by the king, continually pleading my cause for me, and confirming all I had said about my former residence with them, and the circumstances connected with my return to the white people. I was detained fourteen days as a prisoner, and examined each day about my professed attachment to the Indians, when I was given up to my Indian father, on his becoming responsible for my conduct, and submission to the chief of the town where I was going to reside with him. Being in part relieved from my anxiety about my own personal safety, I set out immediately to accompany my Indian father home. But new difficulties presented themselves to my mind. My most faithful father and friend had involved himself so far for me as to endanger his life if I should escape without leave of the chief, and I was still kept at a distance from my wife and children, and could devise no means to communicate to them my situation, without having the false statements I made to the Indians exposed; which I knew would cost me my life. While reflecting in my own mind about these difficulties, and suffering from the anxiety I felt about my family, I saw, at a distance, Mr. Patrick Moor brought in as a prisoner, only thirteen days from Columbia. This increased my alarm, for I feared he might say something about my family before I could see him, or that should I meet him in the presence of the Indians, he might speak of my wife and children. No person unacquainted with my situation can imagine how I felt; an old acquaintance near at hand, who I knew could tell me about my beloved family, from whom I had been so long separated, and yet I dare not approach him. I then concluded if I was at home again the world would be no temptation to draw me into the difficulties I was then involved in. Providence, however, so overruled matters that I again escaped; had an interview with Moor—heard from home—but had no opportunity to communicate to my wife the fact that I was still living. In the midst of my anxiety I made known to my adopted father that I had a wife and children at Columbia, and wanted to return to them, who, without hesitation, promised me all the aid he could give. 'It will not do,' said he, 'to attempt it now, but we will watch for an opportunity more favorable, and as soon as it can be done without endangering your life, and my own, I will assist you to return.

Finding my letter will be too long if I follow up the narrative to his return, I defer the balance for another number.

Yours truly, E. F.

Lawrenceburg, May 19, 1851.

LETTER XXII.

MR. TORBET—I will now present your readers with the escape of Mr. Smalley from the Indians, and his return to his family. He continued:

"I remained in a state of painful anxiety about my family and hr .ne, and often conversed with my Indian father upon the subject, who, after due consideration, made the following proposal: 'That we should obtain from the chief of the village permission to go out upon a hunting tour, and while absent I should desert and make the best of the way I could home.' In pursuance of that plan, he applied to the chief, who readily granted his request, but required us to return at night, which we did, as it was thought one day would not give me a sufficient advantage of time to make sure work in eluding their pursuit. During the summer similar applications were made and granted by the chief, who still restricted us to only one day's absence, which we always complied with in the most punctual manner. In the fall, when the weather began to be somewhat cold, we made application for permission to be absent three days, urging as a reason that the game was so scarce near the village that we could expect but little success in hunting unless permitted to go farther in the woods than we could do in one day and return at night; this request, appearing reasonable, was granted, and we went out and returned accordingly. While out on the three days' tour we made the final arrangement for my return home, as follows:

"We concluded to make application for a fall hunt, to be absent eight days, and should we succeed in obtaining permission, my Indian father and brother agreed to accompany me seven days in a direction towards Columbia, where we were to part, and I was to make my way home and they return and report that I had deserted; and as an excuse for their long absence, to say they had pursued after me as long as they dare venture, on account of their near approach to the settlement of the white people, and in that manner conceal from the Indians my escape until I could reach home. We succeeded in our application, and set out on our journey, and my mind was elated with the prospect of reaching home in a few days; but, unfortunately, the first night my prospects, for the time being, were blasted by my Indian brother being attacked with a most distressing pain in his hip, shooting down to the knees, which proved to be a white swelling, and rendered him unable to travel. Being detained several days in the woods taking care of him (for I felt my obligation binding on me too strong to be broken off), we concluded to try and remove him to the lake shore, where there was a Frenchman from Canada living, from which place I could have an opportunity to escape across the lake. By great exertions we succeeded in reaching the Frenchman's house, where we had again to make an appeal to a stranger to aid me in an attempt to cross the lake. My Indian father approached him by asking him if he could confide in him without fear of being betrayed, to which he answered he could. He then said to the Frenchman, 'this man' (meaning me) 'is a prisoner, and has a wife and children at home, and wants to return to them, and we are trying to help him into Canada.' To which the Frenchman replied, 'I dare not help him, for the Indians would kill me, but,' pointing to the shore, he said, 'there is a canoe that belongs to me, but I dare not assist him.' He was then asked how we could pay for the canoe, to which answer he replied by asking, 'can your white man make an ox yoke'? On being told he could, 'I want a yoke,' said he, 'and there is the canoe, but I dare not sell it to him.' We understood him, and I made him a yoke. We afterward concluded it would not do to cross the lake in, as it could not ride the waves if there should be a storm. We again changed our plan, and I concluded to make my way along the lake shore to Preskiel in Pennsylvania. This plan being settled on, my Indian father said to me: 'I will go up the lake to find a suitable place to make a camp for hunting, and leave you to take care of my son, and if while I am gone you should take the canoe and go off, we can say I was absent, and my son was so lame he could not follow you, so that they could not attach any blame to either of us.' Accordingly he went to the woods, and I, after procuring some bread and meat, took possession of the canoe without leave, and steered my course for Preskiel (Presque Isle, now Erie), Pennsylvania. After a few days' paddling my canoe a part of the way along the lake shore, and walking through the woods, I reached my native state, and once more enjoyed the inexpressible happiness of being again in civilized society. From Preskiel I made my way through the wilderness across to the waters of the Allegheny, and down that river to Pittsburgh, thence down the Ohio to Columbia, where I was once more permitted to meet my old neighbors, who, when they saw me coming, appeared so overcome with surprise and gladness that they ran out to meet me from every direction, and take me by the hand to welcome my return, partially obstructing or retarding my way to my family, so that I had almost to force my way through the crowd to my own dwelling, where I found my beloved wife and children in good health, who were overjoyed to receive me, as one who had returned from the grave. Others may imagine, to some extent, but can not realize, the joy I felt in finding myself once more in the bosom of my family—by my own fireside—and my thankfulness to that kind Providence that had watched over my path, and again brought me home in peace, after an absence of eight months and twenty-three days, in time to spend the holidays with those whose happiness and welfare had created so much solicitude in my own breast during my absence, and who had never heard from me from the time I took them by the hand and bid them farewell."

I have now given the substance of the narrative as related to me by Mr. Smalley, and have the utmost confidence in the correctness of what he said. I wish, however, to have it understood that it was a verbal communication, and not penned until some time after; also that I have abridged his statements considerably. And here, permit me to say that although Messrs. Gerrard and Flinn never returned to their families, their memory should be equally cherished by the pioneers of the west as patriots who sacrificed their lives upon the altar of their country, and, had a favorable result followed their adventures, they would have shared in the benefits since enjoyed by those hardy sons who risked their all to settle this goodly land. Yours truly, E. F.

Lawrenceburg, May 26, 1851.

LETTER XXIII.

MR. TORBET—In the spring of 1792, the inhabitants of the new settlements were again reduced to a very scanty allowance of bread, most of them having exhausted their crop of corn in the winter; and for meat they were entirely dependent on the game in the woods, which was brought in daily by the hunters. To show the dangers the hunters were exposed to, and the uncertainty of regular supplies, I will relate the following facts:

Mr. Patrick Moor, a young man from Ireland, who had made his way to the new settlement in the west, undertook the business of hunting and killing meat. One morning, he went out as usual, in search of game, but returned no more for more than twenty years; nor was he heard from during that time, so far as I know, except the account given by Mr. Smalley after his return Mr. Moor gave the following account of his captivity:

"I was," he said, "passing through the woods in search of game, when suddenly I was surprised by the report of a gun, shot at me by some Indians, the ball of which passed through my side, but gave me only a flesh wound. I immediately turned towards home, and exerted myself to escape; and for a time thought I should succeed, being about thirty yards ahead of my pursuers. I kept my distance very well, until I came to a long tree, which had fallen. In attempting to cross it, the Indians gained some advantage of me in distance, but the Indians, like myself, being very much exhausted by the chase, the first one who attempted to cross the log, fell back, whereupon, seeing their leader fall, one ran round one end of the tree; seeing that move, I wheeled immediately off, and ran for the other end, so that while they were running round the tree, I gained so much on them that they gave up the pursuit and stopped. Being very much exhausted when I saw them stop, I did the same to collect a little air in my lungs; but at that unfortunate moment my hopes were all ended by seeing three Indians in advance of me, who were waiting for me to come up to them. I knew that, fresh as they were, I could not get out of their way, and surrendered myself as their prisoner. The Indians who had at first shot and pursued me, came up and claimed me as their prisoner, saying, 'if they had not run me down the others could not have taken me;' to which the others replied, 'You had given up the pursuit, and had it not been for us he would have escaped.' Both parties were very stubborn, and in their quarrel came very near taking my life. One Indian raised his tomahawk to strike it in my head, and thus put an end to the quarrel; but the other knocked it off with his hand, and said, 'Take him, we will not kill a prisoner;' so I escaped death, and was carried off a captive."

The same summer, Mr. Francis Griffin started for Lexington, Ky., to procure corn for his family, and a few days after was found dead, lying on his face with the blade of a war club sticking in his flesh between his shoulders, which was all that was ever heard about the way he came to his death.

Thus, the inhabitants had to learn "that in life they were in the midst of death." Yours truly, E. F. *Lawrenceburg, June 2, 1851.*

LETTER XXIV.

MR. TORBET—As, in my last letter, I related two circumstances to show the extreme danger the inhabitants of the new settlements were exposed to, when they ventured abroad in search of bread and meat, I will now give you a fact, to show how insecure they were at home.

In the winter of 1791-2, there were a few families ventured to form a settlement at the upper (or north) end of Turkey bottom, so as to be nearer their work in tending their cornfields in the bottom. For their security, they built a small fortification, consisting of a block-house with pickets around the door, to which they might retreat, in case of an attack from the Indians. Among these families there was one by the name of Gordon, in which there was a boy named James, perhaps fourteen years old, and a younger daughter whom they called Nancy. During the season of making sugar, Mr. Gordon tapped some trees on the side hill to obtain sugar water for the use of his family; but the weather being rather too cold the trees produced but little water, and that, in the night, froze nearly solid, leaving a small quantity of water in the middle of the ice, very sweet. One Sunday, James and Nancy invited a boy named John Webb to go with them and get some sweet sugar water; to which young Webb replied, "That his mother had told him he must not run about or play on the Sabbath day; "but, on being told by James, "she would never know it," he started with them, having about forty rods to go; but about half way of the distance he said "a thought came into his mind that he ought not to disobey his mother, if she did not know it," and he turned back and left them, but James and Nancy went on. On arriving among the sugar trees, they each selected a trough, broke the ice, and bent over to drink the sweet water. While in the act of drinking some Indians approached suddenly, and one Indian advanced toward each of them. Nancy was taken prisoner, and carried into captivity as was supposed, and never more heard from by her parents. But James, seeing the Indian coming toward him, ran for the fort. He said, in the race (the Indian being close in his rear), he saw no way of escape but by leaping a sappling that was bent over his path too low to run under; and he concluded if he could get the foot foremost that he commonly started to jump on he could leap it—the Indian being in his rear, with his arms spread to grasp him, when he should come up to the sappling. James, however, succeeded in making his leap, and the Indian being bent forward, with his arms spread to lay hold of him, not expecting he could pass over, struck the little tree so hard with his breast that it knocked him back, and he fell on the ground, and James made his way to the fort.

Mr. Webb is still living, and ranks among the most respectable farmers of Hamilton county, and no doubt remembers better than any other his narrow escape, by honoring the instructions of his mother, not to desecrate the Sabbath day.

Yours truly,
E. F.

Lawrenceburg, June 7, 1851.

LETTER XXV.

MR. TORBET—After the almost annihilation of St. Clair's army in November, 1791, and the discharge of the Kentucky militia, the country was left nearly without means of defense, and the Indians seemed to have come to the conclusion that they might, with impunity, hover round our settlements, as there were very few soldiers to pursue after them, and as there was, as yet, but little talk of another army until the result of the trial at negotiation with the Indian tribes should be certainly known. From the foregoing causes the settlements were continually annoyed with marauding parties, stealing their horses, and killing or carrying off the inhabitants into captivity. We had frequent reports of murders by the Indians at North Bend, Cincinnati, and other out stations; but, as I was small and lived at a distance from the scene of action, I can not recollect the names. I remember a man being killed in the vicinity of Cincinnati, on the west of Mill creek, while hunting his cows, on one Sunday morning, and another while choping cord-wood in the back part of the town, between the Hamilton road and Mill creek, and, at another time, a man was driven from his team while plowing a lot not far from where the center of the city now is, and his horses were cut loose and taken off. In the same year a Mr. Van Hyse was taken prisoner by the Indians. He, however, was not detained long before he returned, and it was believed among the people that in consequence of the kind treatment the Indians heretofore spoken of received when prisoners, that Mr. Van Hyse was very much favored, as he resided in that place when at home. Of these difficulties I heard as a boy, and being at a distance, was not so deeply affected by them. I, however, proceed to give an account of a most melancholy event that occurred partly under my own notice, being in the daily habit of seeing the sufferers before they went out.

Mr. William Lytle, then of Kentucky, afterward Gen. Lytle, of Cincinnati, visited Columbia to employ some men to accompany him in an exploring tour on the Virginia military county lands, east of the Little Miami, to find where he could locate some land warrants to the best advantage. Among others, he engaged Benjamin Alcott, James Newel and Henry Ball, three respectable young men, to accompany him on horseback, who were to meet him next day at Covalt's station, a small settlement about twelve miles above Columbia, on the Little Miami. Thinking it would be safer, these young men concluded they would not leave home until near night, so that when they should have to pass the narrows on the river below Round Bottom it would be dark, and by riding fast they would be exposed to less danger, that being considered the most dangerous place on the way. According to arrangements, they started a little while before night, but had traveled but about three miles, when crossing the point of a ridge between two small ravines, near where Madisonville now stands, they were fired at by the Indians. Mr. Alcott was wounded in the arm, but remained on his horse, but both Newel and Ball fell to the ground. Alcott wheeled his horse, and the other two horses followed him, I recollect being out with a number of boys playing, when suddenly our attention was arrested by the noise of the horses advancing in full speed. Those that had lost their riders seemed to be trying to escape with the same speed as the others. As they passed our little crowd, Mr. Alcott cried out, "Run home, the Indians are coming; I am wounded, and Newel and Ball are killed or taken prisoners." We all hastened home to tell the news. The alarm was spread, and by morning a party of the militia were ready to start in search of the missing. They soon reached the fatal spot, and found Newel still living, but most horribly and barbarously mangled, but could not find Ball. Newel was brought into his widowed mother, brother and sisters, a melancholy object to fix the eye upon. The whole hairy scalp of his head was taken off, and several strokes of a tomahawk had passed through his skull into the brain, A surgeon was sent for, who attended, but said, "it would be in vain to attempt to do anything, as he could not possibly survive his wound." He lingered through most of the day and died. On examination, it was found that his gunshot wound was but a slight one. Mr. Newel was not able, after being found, to give an account of this sad affair.

Many years afterward Mr. Ball returned, and gave an account of the whole transaction. He said they were riding in a brisk trot, when they were unexpectedly fired on by a number of Indians; that Mr. Newel was slightly wounded and fell from his horse; that they shot at him and missed, but his horse wheeled about so suddenly that the girth of his saddle broke, and he fell with the saddle, and made an attempt to escape, but had not more than got on his feet before he was seized hold of by some Indians, who, perceiving that Newel was wounded, did not give any attention to him until they had him (Ball) tied. They then began to search for Newel, but he was gone, and as it was now nearly dark, they started off without finding him; but after traveling a few rods they saw Newel's dog standing and looking up a small bushy topped tree. They at first passed by it, but after going a few rods further, one of the Indians said, "The white man must be up that tree, or the dog would not be there whining," on which suggestion they returned and got Newel down, but as he was too badly wounded to travel well, they scalped and tomahawked him.

Soon after this sad affair, rumors were afloat that another army was coming, to be commanded by Gen. Wayne, which gave great encouragement that they would be relieved from the almost continued encroachments of the Indians.

Yours truly,   E. F.

Lawrenceburg, June 17, 1851.

LETTER XXVI.

Mr. Torbet—I fear I shall weary the patience of the reader by the monotony there is in so many Indian tales following each other.

Shortly after the death of Mr. Newel, as related in my last letter, it was generally supposed that the Indians had retired from our frontiers to attend to their crops at home, and as fur skins and meat killed in the woods in warm weather were of but little value, consequently there was but little inducement to stay where they could do nothing but hunt. The inhabitants, generally, were permitted to pursue their business through the spring and summer with but little difficulty from the Indians. They, however, this season, suffered very much from the destructions of the cut-worm, which, for a time, seemed to shut out all prospect of a crop, except in ground worked for the first time that season. The approach of hot weather, however, subdued them, and by replanting there was something more than half a crop of corn; but a considerable portion did not get ripe, which caused a scarcity again the ensuing spring equal almost to any former time.

Rumors were frequently heard during this season of military preparations being made to drive the Indians back. Wayne, it was said, was coming, and at his presence it was supposed the Indians would flee. The movements of the army were tardy, and they remained at Legionville, near Pittsburg, that winter. Early in the fall it was reported that the Indians were again on our frontiers, and that it was dangerous for the white people to venture far from home. They, however, did very little mischief in the early part of the season, and it was supposed their object was to hunt; but towards spring they became more troublesome, and occasionally stole horses from the white people. In the latter part of the winter there were some young men about Gerrard station, on the east of the Miami, who concluded to play what they called a "trick" on them, as horses were their object. They accordingly took a white horse from a drove of poor, worn-out pack-horses that belonged to the contractor, and had been sent there to recruit in the woods, as they could neither buy hay nor corn, and hoppled him near to a place where three large trees had blown down and fallen across each other, so as to make three sides of a pen; and after they had hoppled and cross-hoppled the poor horse, so that he could not move, they put a bell on him, and concealed themselves behind the fallen trees. They had not been long concealed before they saw an Indian advancing towards the horse. It being very bright moonlight, his first move was to stop the clattering of the bell, which he did by stuffing it with dry leaves. He then bent down on his knees to untie the hopples, when the boys shot at him, and he fell on his face, but immediately arose to his feet and ran. They dare not follow after him that night, fearing there might be more Indians near at hand. But in the morning early they went to the place, and found that he had bled profusely, and had left his gun behind. They followed his tracks a few miles, and came to a camp in the woods, where, they supposed, about five Indians had been staying for a length of time; but they were all gone, and the pack of one was left behind with some bloody clothes. From that time the people about Gerrard station were upon the lookout—expecting the Indians would retaliate.

In the spring of that year three families had settled in small cabins on the bank of the Ohio river, about a half mile from the station, above the mouth of the Miami, near to each other. The name of one family was Raridon, one Reynolds and one Smith. Early in March, one evening after they had barred their doors, one of the small boys, with a good deal of surprise, cried out, "There is an Indian looking down the chimney." All about the fire immediately looked up, but saw no Indian. They then commenced expressing an opinion whether the boy had seen an Indian, some thinking one way and some the other; but all concluded it was best to stay in the house and keep the doors shut. The next day the people at the station were notified of what the boy said, but they generally concluded he was mistaken. The following evening Mr. James Welch, who was making sugar in his house, and gathering his water from trees on a side-hill near at hand, went up the side-hill after water between sundown and dark, followed by a little dog, but had been gone but a few minutes before the dog returned apparently very much alarmed. He turned round from the house, looked up the hill and barked as though greatly distressed. Mrs. Welch commenced calling Welch, but obtained no answer. She continued calling louder and louder, until she became almost frantic. The neighbors ran together, and concluded he was either killed or taken prisoner, but that it would not be safe to follow after him before morning. In the morning they assembled together, and went in search and soon found the buckets, but found nothing of Welch. All they knew about him afterwards, until his return, was mere conjecture. Some time in October or November following, Welch returned and gave an account of his captivity. He said as he was passing up the hill he was seized by three Indians, one to each arm, and another behind him, with a tomahawk in his hand, and marched immediately off six or eight miles to an Indian camp, where there were twenty-five or thirty warriors awaiting the return of the three men who had captured him. He learned that they were about making an attack on the three families on the bank of the Ohio, and had sent some spies down the night before to ascertain how many men there were in the three houses; that the spies had returned and reported, and also reported that one of them had been discovered by a boy, and related the talk that had taken place in the house growing out of what the boy had said, and said that he had laid still on the roof until the people in the house went to sleep, and had then crawled down. On hearing this reported, they had sent three men to learn whether the boy's story had created any alarm, with the intention, if it did not, to make the attack in the after part of the night. These men reported that there was no alarm among the people; that they were all at home pursuing their usual business, and how they had taken Welch. Their first conclusion was to kill him and make the attack, but as soon as this conclusion was announced an old Indian arose, saying, "You are wrong; there's an alarm now; you have taken this man and now they are all alarmed, and will be ready for you; they ought not to have disturbed this man." They then tried the question over, and determined it would be best to make their way home, and immediately shouldered their sacks and were off, taking Welch with them as a prisoner, and kept him through the summer to raise corn, and treated him to about the same fare with themselves. In the fall he fell in company with a Canadian who had come among the Indians to buy furs, and had a boat up one of the rivers to convey them across the lake. Welch made a bargain with him to meet at the last point of high land before entering the lake, from which place the Canadian agreed to take him across the lake. Welch succeeded in taking an Indian canoe and passing down the river. Though he was discovered and closely pursued, yet he eluded their pursuit by running his canoe into the bullrushes and hiding himself in the grass, and finally got into the Canadian's boat, who hid him under some furs until next morning and took him over into Canada, from whence he made his way home. Mr. Welch had not been heard from from the time he was taken prisoner until they saw him coming home, where he found his family all in good health, and glad to see him. Yours truly, E. F.

Lawrenceburg, June 24, 1851.

LETTER XXVII.

MR. TORBET—In carrying out my designs in writing a series of letters containing some historical sketches attending the first settlement of the Miami country, I can not (though tired of relating Indian stories) pass by the following lamentable circumstance as being one that affected me more than any other during the war. Mr. O. M. Spencer, one of the sufferers, lived in the same place with myself. We were about the same age, and had been to school together. In addition, I heard the lamentations of his father and mother over their lost son in the day of their affliction, and, though a boy, I could not but sympathize with them.

About the 3d of July, 1792, some officers from Fort

Washington visited Columbia in a keel-boat rowed by soldiers. As was usual with all the officers of the army, they called on Colonel Spencer, and, while there, invited his' daughters to accompany them to Fort Washington to attend a Fourth of July celebration to take place the next day, promising to see them safe home on the 5th. By consent of their father and mother they accepted the invitation, and their brother Oliver was permitted to accompany them. On the 5th, they made the necessary preparations to return, but Oliver was missing, having wandered off with some boys he had fallen in company with. After waiting as long as they could for his return, without making it too late to row the boat to Columbia and back that night, they started and left him behind. When Oliver found he was left, he was very uneasy, as he said his father had enjoined it on him very strictly to return with his sisters; and he sought an opportunity to go home with other company, and finally found a canoe belonging to (or in possession of) two men by the name of Light and Layton, who had gone down to Cincinnati that morning, taking with them a Mrs. Coleman, who had some marketing to sell to the soldiers. He made application, and was permitted to return with them. On his way up, he complained of being so cramped by the way he had to sit in the canoe that he asked permission to get out and walk a part of the way, which they allowed him to do. About a mile below Crawfish they were attacked by the Indians, and Light and Layton were both shot—the former wounded, and the latter killed instantly; both fell and turned the canoe over, and, with Mrs. Coleman, were all thrown into the river, and young Spencer was taken captive. Some person at Columbia heard the guns and saw the men fall, so that the alarm was given immediately that the Indians had killed a canoe-load of people coming up the river below Columbia. The militia, who were always on the alert, ran for their guns, and, without waiting for orders, repaired to the spot as quickly as possible. On arriving at the place, they found Light and Layton in the river where the canoe had upset (the water being shoal), and Mrs. Coleman a short distance below holding on to a snag. They took them out of the river, found Layton dead, Light wounded in the arm, and Mrs. Coleman unhurt. Light and Mrs. Coleman remained in the water thinking it would be more safe, as they did not know but the Indians might still be lurking in the woods. Mrs. Coleman said she got hold of the snag, and turned her eyes toward the Indians before they had taken young Spencer; that he did not try to escape, but that when the Indians came up to him he clasped his hands and drew them over his head; that they did not hurt him as long as she could see him, but led him in great haste up the bank to the woods, and that she saw but two Indians. Colonel Spencer himself was on the ground, of course greatly distressed, but very much composed, considering the circumstances he was placed in. Several of the militia volunteered to pursue immediately after the Indians, and recapture Oliver if possible, but the colonel objected. He said, "If they have determined to keep him prisoner, he may some day return; but if pursued and overtaken, their first object will be to kill him, then run;" so that it was concluded best not to pursue after them. This circumstance created great alarm. It had hitherto been considered that there was little or no danger that season of the year, as the Indians were generally at home tending to their crops. And it was also thought that as Cincinnati had now grown to be more populous than Columbia was, and that as there were so many soldiers about, the Indians would hardly dare venture between the two places. I recollect the Sunday following, as the people were collecting for worship at the meeting-house on the point of the hill, some neighbors, meeting Colonel Spencer, began to condole with him on account of his loss, to which, with deep emotion, he commenced a reply by complaining of the suspense in which his mind was held. "My oldest son," said he, "left home, leaving a wife and one infant son behind, to make a voyage at sea, and we never heard from him again; and now my youngest and only remaining son is either slain or captive among the savages. It would be some relief to know what his fate has been;" and, as if overcome with grief, he could say no more. The narrative of O. M. Spencer's captivity, treatment, and final return, as published by himself, renders it unnecessary that I should say anything further up on the subject.

The attention of all the inhabitants, from about this time, was taken up with speculation and rumors about the preparations that were then being made to raise a powerful army to be placed under the command of General Wayne, in whom, notwithstanding all their former disappointments, they had the most unshaken confidence. The last consideration, in part, made up for the gloomy prospect of a corn crop produced by the ravages of the cut-worm, which were sorely felt the ensuing winter and spring.

Yours truly,   E. F.

Lawrenceburg, June 30, 1851.

LETTER XXVIII.

MR. TORBET—I have not in my recollection any more Indian massacres that occurred in 1792 to record, but there were other difficulties thrown in the way of the new settlements that were almost equally distressing to the inhabitants. After contending with the forests for years, and reclaimed so much that with the same yield of corn they had had in past times they might look for a full supply of bread, and to be reduced by the depredations of the cut-worm one-half, was truly a loss, and severely felt, as the number of the customers was so greatly increased, and the opportunity of obtaining supplies from the fields so much diminished. But these things had to be borne, and very often nettles and pursley (and sometimes without salt or vinegar) had to supply the place of bread and meat. There was, however, one fact that encouraged them, and enabled them to bear up under all these discouragements. There was occasionally a boat load of soldiers arriving (always said to be the forerunners of a numerous army coming on) sufficient to protect all the new settlements. Our information at that time was neither received by lightning or government mails (for we had neither), but by express sent from one military station to another to inform them what was going on, and from the commandants of military posts was communicated, as far as proper, to the people. One of these expresses arrived probably early in July, bringing the gratifying news that Wayne was actually on his march across the mountains with his army on his way to Fort Washington. This news was received with joy, and the arrival of the army expected and waited for with intense anxiety. From the first news of the army having taken up the line of march until it was heard they had gone into winter quarters at Legionville, a short distance below Pittsburg, every ear was open to hear the news from the army, and the time of their expected arrival at Cincinnati was the subject of general conversation; so that for the balance of that and the two succeeding years, Wayne and his army were too intimately connected with the history of the new settlements not to be seen in every page. It was a subject of great regret among the inhabitants that they should have stopped short of Cincinnati, but their confidence in final success was not diminished.

The people were not so much annoyed by Indians during the winters of 1792–3 as they had previously been. Some,

I recollect, assigned as a reason, that they were directing their attention to the headquarters of the army, to ascertain, if possible, Wayne's intended movements, and by what route he would probably invade them.

The spring of 1793 brought with it a calamity unlooked for in the memorable flood of that year. Not knowing the height to which the Ohio had been sometimes swollen, many of the settlers had built their cabins on low ground, where they had made gardens and corn-fields, enclosed with common rail fences. But in April the river rose to such a height that many of them were driven from their places of residence, and had the mortification to see their fences taken off, and in some instances their houses floated down stream with the flood. Fortunately, however the rise in the water was very gradual, and the weather mild, so that they were all able to save what little stock they had. This flood was several feet higher than any that has ever taken place in the Ohio river since, except the floods of '32 and '47.

Soon after the flood had subsided, and the waters were again reduced to their banks, the long looked-for army arrived, making a very formidable appearance as they floated down the Ohio. They passed Columbia on Sunday, I think, about the last of April, but it might have been in the beginning of May. Gen. Wayne and suite first arrived in a keel-boat and landed at Columbia, where he probably tarried about an hour, until the fleet came up. He then started in advance of them, passed Cincinnati and took up his headquarters in a beech woods above the mouth of Mill creek, to which he gave the name of Hobson's Choice, by which name it was called for many years, as all the old pioneers of the country can recollect. This event was hailed with joy, and the people now felt as though they were secure.

       Yours truly,   E. F.

Lawrenceburg, July 9, 1851.

LETTER XXIX.

MR. TORBET—Soon as it was announced to the new settlements that General Wayne had established his headquarters at Hobson's Choice, and encamped his army on the bank of the Ohio river, between Cincinnati and Mill creek, the anxiety to visit his camp became almost, or quite, universal. Like other boys, I partook of the same feeling, being then ten years of age. It was not long before I gained the consent of my father to accompany a neighbor to the camp, who was going down to sell some vegetables to the soldiers. We descended the river in a small canoe, passed Cincinnati to the east line of the camp, where we were hailed by a sentinel and ordered to land, and questioned what we had on board. The sergeant of the guard was called for, and, on satisfying himself that we had no spirits on board, we were told to pass on to the camp. On landing and ascending the bank of the river, I had before me the most attracting scene I had ever beheld—well calculated to fill with amazement any person, man or boy, who had been four years in the woods, seldom seeing any buildings better than the inferior order of log cabins, except Fort Washington and a few hewed log, and unpainted frame, houses, boarded up on the outside with oak clap-boards from the woods, shaved smooth with the drawing-knife, that were then to be seen in a very scattered condition in Cincinnati. In the encampment there was perfect order. In the first place, the beech trees, which were far the most numerous of any other species, were nearly all of a size and height, spreading out their branches so as to interlock with each other, and form one of the most beautiful arbors I have ever seen, with but very little undergrowth; and what had been there the army had removed as far as the encampment extended—the whole of which, in point of cleanliness, would compare with the door-yards of any of our neat farmers in the present day. In an exact line with the river, and in rows as straight as a line, the whited tents were fitted up in the neatest style, extending, I suppose, at least a half a mile along the river, leaving a space next to the bank of the river about the width of Front street in Cincinnati, and in the same manner rows were formed in the rear of each other, until space enough was occupied for the whole army. In the rear of the encampment there was built a row of shantees by setting posts in the ground and siding up and covering them over with boat-plank, which were used as stables for their horses. Near the center of this encampment, up and down the river, General Wayne had his markee. If I remember right, in the second row from the river, leaving an open space in front, and at the proper places throughout the camp, the markees of the different officers were to be seen—the whole presenting a scenery (taking into consideration the state of the improvements of the country in 1793) more attracting than our most magnificent cities present now. Besides here, so far as human effort was concerned, was to be seen the hope of the country in an army who were destined in another year to drive back our savage foes, to retrieve the character of our past failures in arms, and restore the country to peace. Although it is now fifty-eight years since my first visit to Wayne's camp (as it was then commonly called), the prospect then presented seems as vivid, and the flights of imagination that flashed upon my mind as I looked over the whole scene, as lively as it did on that day.

Yours truly,   E. F.

Lawrenceburg, July 15, 1851.

LETTER XXX.

MR. HIBBEN—Since I suspended some numbers I was addressing to Mr. Torbet, containing reminiscences of the early settlement of the Miami country, I have learned that you have become proprietor and editor of the *Independent Press*, the paper in which they were published. The cause of the suspension having been removed, at the request of a number of your subscribers (by your permission) I purpose to address to you a few more numbers for the same paper.

In the winter of 1792-93 the fact that Gen. Wayne, with his army, had taken up winter quarters near the head of the Ohio river, and would descend in the spring to Cincinnati, encouraged a number of adventurers in Columbia and Cincinnati to venture back in the country to settle lands they had purchased, but had not ventured to settle on through fear of danger from the Indians. It was generally supposed by the inhabitants that soon after the army should arrive the campaign would be carried into the Indian country, and give security to the new settlements. The character that Gen. Wayne had acquired as an officer in the Revolutionary war forbid all idea of another failure, and led to a confident belief that the Indians would be driven back, and compelled to sue for peace. Columbia and Cincinnati, at that time, were crowded with a population that only intended to make these places a temporary residence, who were anxious to remove to their own lands. Col. Israel Ludlow, who had previously commenced an improvement on Mill creek, but on account of its exposedness to danger, had abandoned it for a time, reoccupied it that winter, and three miles higher up the creek Capt. Jacob White, from Columbia, with a few families, settled another station, and still higher up the creek Tucker's and Cunningham's stations were settled. The same winter Mr. John

Beasley erected a large block house near the bank of the Little Miami, to which he removed his family preparatory to building a mill at the place (now known as Armstrong's lower mills). In the spring of 1793 a number of families from Columbia, Cincinnati and North Bend made a settlement at the mouth of the Big Miami, which was called the point. Among the families from Columbia I recollect those of Mr. Hugh Dunn, Mr. Benjamin Randolph and Mr. Isaac Mills. In addition to these there was also a settlement made at Round Bottom, a short distance below Covalt's station and above Newtown, which had been settled the previous year. The arrival of Gen. Wayne and army in the spring increased the confidence of the new settlements, and caused other families to join them. They argued that the presence of so large an army at Cincinnati would deter the Indians, and keep them at a distance. But some, who thought they understood the Indian character better, said they would constantly keep small parties of their most daring warriors hovering about our frontiers to watch the movements of the army, and that the exposed frontiers would be more liable to attacks. With the last opinion Mr. William Smalley, who had escaped from his captivity among the Indians, and returned home about Christmas, agreed, he having accompanied Major Trueman, Hardin and Freeman on their visit to the Indians with a flag of truce, and witnessed the murder of Major Trueman and his waiter, and being satisfied that Hardin and Freeman, with whom they had parted the afternoon before Trueman was killed, had shared the same fate. Mr. Smalley warned the people that they would have no abatement of hostilities until the Indians were whipped. He said they as much expect to defeat Wayne as they were certain that they had Harmar and St. Clair. The first circumstance confirming the correctness of either opinion was an attack on Mr. Beasley's block house. He employed the time, after removing his family (or rather his two families, for, having a large family of his own, he had married a Mrs. Prichet, with one equally large, so that the two united could furnish seven good fighting men for defense), in collecting materials for his mill. Among other materials, he had drawn a large pile of stone for a foundation, lying from the river bank back to near the upper corner of the house. One Sunday evening the dogs, of which he had a number, appeared to be very much disturbed, and would frequently move a short distance from the house toward the hill, and bark furiously, which gave suspicions that there were Indians about. The barking of the dogs increased with more fury after dark, and continued through the night. Toward day they appeared frantic, and changed their course toward the pile of stone. On observing the fury of the dogs, Mr. Beasley, as I heard him say the day following, concluded he would venture out into the yard to see if he could make any discoveries. He accordingly opened the door and walked out in a direction toward the river bank, but observing the dogs run towards the pile of stone and jump back, he concluded there might be Indians there, and that he had better return to the house. On turning round, he was alarmed by the report of a gun from behind the stone pile, the ball of which nearly grazed his head. He quickened his speed, and saw a number of Indians running toward the door, as though trying to cut off his retreat. He, however, succeeded in getting there first, and having secured the door with bars, he, with his boys, took their stations at the port holes in the upper part of the house, where they saw the Indians in the woods concealing themselves behind the trees. Mr. Beasley said he noticed one place himself behind a large tree, and immediately pointed his gun through a port hole in a direction toward the tree, waiting an opportunity to shoot; that he soon saw the Indian's head, and his gun pointed at him, and was in the act of shooting, when he received a ball in his right wrist, which for a moment paralyzed his finger, then on the trigger, but that he immediately recovered the shock, and shot and killed the Indian, after which they (the Indians) made no other exertion, only to escape in the safest way they could. When I saw Mr. Beasley, and heard him relate the story, the ball was not yet extracted.

    Yours with sincere respect,   E. F.
Lawrenceburg, September 15, 1851.

LETTER XXXI.

MR. HIBBEN—After the attack on Mr. Beasley's blockhouse, noticed in my last, with the exception of stealing a few horses, the new settlements were but little disturbed by Indians until near the close of summer. Sometime about the last of August, as Mr. Moses Prior and his brother-in-law, Mr. Goble, were digging some potatoes to take to Wayne's camp, the next morning, to sell to the soldiers, they supposed they heard turkeys calling in the woods on a side hill a little above the place where they were working, and Mr. Goble said he would go and shoot one. About this time, Mrs. Prior had gone to the bank of Mill creek to milk the cows, taking her second child with her, leaving the youngest sleeping in the cradle, the oldest being with his father in the field, which was near by. Mr. Goble had left but a very short time, until Mr. Prior said he heard the report of a gun, and supposed he had shot at a turkey, but as he did not hear any fall concluded he had missed, and commenced working again; but almost instantly turned his eyes in that direction, and saw a number of Indians, armed with guns and tomahawks, rushing out of the woods, making their way with all possible speed towards his house. In the confusion and hurry of the moment, he forgot his little boy, and ran toward the house, but, finding himself cut off from that retreat, he thought of his son, and turned round to try and save him, when he beheld him already in the possession of the Indians. He then retreated across the creek to Captain White's block-house, where he found Mrs. Prior, who had been more fortunate than himself; for, on hearing the alarm, and seeing the Indians already in possession of the house, she seized the little boy she had with her, and plunged into the creek, where the water was up to her shoulders, and made her way with him to the block-house before her husband had arrived there. The Indians entered Prior's house, killed the little child left in the cradle, and destroyed the bedding, and some other property; then crossed over to the west side of the creek, and made a regular attack on the principal station. They took their first stand behind some trees, at what was supposed rather beyond the reach of gun-shot from the block-house; and sent an Indian with the little boy in his arms, held in such a position that would endanger his life if the white people shot at him. In this way he approached within speaking distance, and summoned them to surrender; promising as a condition to spare their lives; but, finding his summons was disregarded, he soon stepped backward, keeping the boy between himself and danger, until, supposing he was beyond the reach of their bullets, he took little Jack by the heels, and, with a swing, beat his head against a tree and killed him. Some person in the block-house who saw him perform this brutal act, shot through a port-hole and killed the Indian. Seeing one of their number fall, the Indians seemed more determined to rescue his dead body than to make any further attempt to take the station. And, approaching from tree to tree, they made a rush, and seized the body of the dead Indian, and commenced bearing it away; but, in the attempt, a second Indian was killed. They, however, succeeded in bearing them both away a short distance, and then disappeared.

As soon as it was supposed they were gone, one of the men at the station started for Cincinnati and Columbia to give the alarm, and ask for assistance; fearing they might return again and renew the attack. Early the next morning they were sufficiently reinforced by the militia from both places, who were always ready to go when called for. Among those who went to their assistance from Cincinnati was Mr. Stephen Ludlow, one of our most enterprising farmers, living, at this time, in the neighborhood of Lawrenceburg, and who is still actively engaged in superintending his farming operations. Mr. Ludlow was the first man who found the bodies of the two Indians killed, where they had been left, in Captain White's corn-field. The militia, in their search, found the remains of Mr. Goble, who had been shot, and of Mr. Prior's two children. This was considered by the white people a very bold attempt on the part of the Indians. To attack White's station, within nine miles of Cincinnati and five of Columbia, with several other stations further advanced into the country, filled the inhabitants of the new settlements with more consternation than any former attempt they had made. But lest I should be too tedious, I will close for the present.

Yours with much respect, E. F.

Lawrenceburg, September 25, 1851.

LETTER XXXII.

MR. HIBBEN—After a long suspension, occasioned by a severe indisposition, which at one time seemed to threaten my life, I now resume the series of letters I promised your readers.

In my last I gave an account of the attack of the Indians on White's station, and the panic it produced in the minds of the inhabitants of the out stations. I will now proceed to an account of a different character, which diffused gladness into the hearts of all the inhabitants of the Miami country, and inspired them with a confidence that their warfare was soon to end. On Sunday morning, September 7, 1793, in pursuance of a general order from the commander-in-chief, the army of General Wayne took up the line of march for the frontiers, and, it was then thought by the people, for an immediate attack on the Indian towns. In their march they passed up the valley of Mill creek, following the trace of General St. Clair's army in their march in 1791, crossing the big Miami at Fort Hamilton. They continued their course, by way of Fort St. Clair, and after a march of seven days, arrived at Fort Jefferson on the 13th, at which place the general made a halt for a short time. But, not being pleased with the location, after a short stay he moved the army six miles north and built another fort, which, in honor of General Green, of the revolutionary army, he called Greenville. At this place the army went into winter quarters, except a regiment (designated the rowdy regiment), which was ordered to encamp on the first high ground on the west bank of the Big Miami, about its junction with the Ohio, to afford protection to keel-boats which might descend the Ohio with supplies for the army, to ascend the Miami up to Fort Hamilton, that being the best way at that time to convey heavy articles from Cincinnati to that place. The above named place of encampment is still known as the rowdy camp in the neighborhood of Lawrenceburg up to the present time. In the latter part of October, General Wayne was reinforced at Greenville by the arrival of General Scott from Kentucky with a thousand mounted militia. But, having determined not to proceed against the Indians until spring, they were sent back and dismissed until that time. During that winter every exertion that could be was made to forward as large an amount of provisions as possible to the outposts, that the army might not be embarrassed, as St. Clair had been, for the want of full rations. In December General Wayne sent a detachment from his army to St. Clair's battle-ground, which they took possession of on Christmas, and proceeded to erect a fort, which was called Fort Recovery, affording an opportunity of sending on supplies in advance of the army, so that by spring he had an abundance for any force he might want to collect on the frontiers. General Wayne, in all his arrangements, gave evidence that he was not only brave but also prudent and skillful in the discharge of all the duties confided to him, and gave to the people increased confidence of all final success.

Fearing I shall weary the patience of your readers, I will close for the present, and subscribe myself

Your friend, E. F.

Lawrenceburg, December 8, 1851.

LETTER XXXIII.

MR. HIBBEN—The infant settlements in the Miami country did not enjoy that repose from Indian alarms and depredations that, from some former circumstances, they had anticipated when the army removed to Greenville. Small parties of Indians still hovered round the settlements with hostile designs, as the history of their following movements will show. The first I recollect was the following: Some time toward the last of October, or beginning of November, Mr. Benjamin Olcott (being a constable) was called on business to that part of the town of Columbia called the hill, between which and the river there is a tract of low land subject to frequent inundations of water, so as to prevent any families from settling on it. On his return home, Mr. Olcott had to pass through a long, narrow lane, connecting at that time the two parts of the town, as it was then called. In traveling home, though about the full of the moon, it was a part of the time very dark, owing to the scuds that frequently obscured the moon. Mr. Olcott afterwards said that, turning his head around after one of these scuds had passed the moon, he thought he saw an Indian following him. He felt alarmed, but he thought it would be unsafe for him to make any delay, in order to ascertain the fact, and so he hastened his pace home on horseback. On riding up to the door (which was but a very short distance from my father's house), he threw his bridle over a stake in the fence, took off his saddle and went into his house, took it up a ladder, and threw it into the loft, as all the upper floors of all their cabins were then called. He returned to put his horse in the stable, but he was gone. He said he felt for the stake, thinking he might possibly have slipped the bridle, but it was not there. He had strong suspicions of what had become of his horse, but dare not tell, fearing that he might be wrong and subject himself to the charge of cowardice.

He then returned to the house, and told his wife that his horse had got loose, and gone, and he would let him go until morning. Next morning, being Sabbath morning, search was made in vain for the horse, and after reasonable attempt was made to find him and failed, Mr. Olcott told what he thought he had seen the night before, while passing down the lane, and what he then believed had become of his horse, in which opinion all appeared to concur. At the usual hour for public worship, the people assembled at the meeting-house, built on the front of the hill by the Baptist church (being the first house built for the worship of God in the Miami country). About the time for public worship to commence, two men came down the hill with Olcott's horse and an Indian scalp. The scalp seemed to electrify the congregation, and without attending to the forms of worship most of them made their way home in the most speedy manner they could. The two men named had gone to the woods the day before, in search of some hogs that had wandered off to the woods during the summer in search of food, and, not succeeding, they wandered about until it was so late they could not find their way home. On their way home in the morning they saw the Indian riding the horse (very carelessly as they thought), and hid behind trees until he nearly approached them, when they shot and scalped him, and brought the horse and scalp in with them. The result was, the Indian lost his scalp, the worship for the day was suspended, and Olcott's horse was returned to him. Yours,

(*Published Dec. 26, 1851.*) E. F.

LETTER XXXIV.

MR. HIBBEN—Soon after the removal of Wayne's army from Cincinnati to Greenville, in 1793, the settlements were visited by a calamity which (as far as human life was concerned) was far more destructive than the Indians had been. In December the small-pox, in its most malignant form, made its appearance among them, and spread with such rapidity that its progress could not be arrested until it had reached the remotest station. But this calamity, severe as it was, brought with it some consolation. Many indulged the hope that the Indians, in their intrusions, would catch the disease and convey it home, to the destruction of their people there. All business was suspended, as well as all assembling for public purposes, or military trainings, and the whole attention of the people was directed toward finding out the best and most speedy way of eradicating the disease from the country before spring. Houses most detached, where they could be had, were selected for pest-houses, and all who were willing to risk the process of inoculation were encouraged to resort to them as speedily as possible, where men were prepared to inoculate them without charge. Among others, the house of Mr. John Smith (pastor of the Baptist church) was selected, it being an entire frontier house, and Mr. S. being a very friendly and benevolent man, great numbers resorted to it.

After the disease had subsided, the families who had used Mr. Smith's house met to assist his family in cleaning up, as they called it. Every part of the house, where it was thought any part of the contagion could have been deposited, was scoured, and all their wearing apparel and bed clothing were washed. To make the cleansing as effectual as possible, the family clothed themselves for the day in old and worn-out garments that had been laid aside, intending to burn them the next day, when they should put on their clean clothes. In order to avail themselves of a white frost expected that night, the whole were left out, and the want of bed and bed clothing made up for through the night by a good warm fire. A family thus situated would of course be like those who are watching for the morning. The reader can judge in part of their surprise when it was announced at the dawn of the day that their clothes were gone. "Gone! where to?" said one in surprise. "We can not tell," was the answer. It was of no use to inquire; they were all gone, and no one would suspect any neighbor for having done it, for they could neither be worn nor concealed without exposure. All that could be learned was that two men, shod with moccasins, had passed along the fence where they were spread out early in the evening. They knew it must have been early, as their feet made deep indentations in the soft ground, which they were certain could not have been done long after dark, as it froze hard at an early hour. Here, for the present, I must leave Mr. Smith and his clothing in rather a bad fix, his neighbors, though they might wish to relieve him, could not for want of means. A few days after, some Indians penetrated the very heart of the settlement of Columbia and stole two horses from the stable of Mr. Thomas Hubble close by his dwelling-house. To reach Mr. Hubble's stable, they had to pass through the settlement, at least about a mile, at a place where I suppose three hundred men, armed and equipped for fight, might have been raised by the sound of a horn in one hour. In addition to other facts there was something more daring in this, from the consideration that they had, with their tomahawks and scalping knives, to cut away the check of the stable door before they could reach the horses. The alarm was given in the morning as soon as the fact was known, and large numbers assembled to determine what should be done. Mr. Hubble was highly esteemed, and there was a great deal of sympathy for him, but more indignation for so daring an outrage, and determination to punish it. Each of the militia Captains Flinn, Hall and Kibbey, proposed to raise volunteers and follow after, but finally agreed to go together and act in concert. As soon as they had time to fill their sacks with parched corn they were off on the trail of the horses, which it was ascertained had crossed the Miami at Flinn's ford, opposite Turkey bottom, and passed up on the east side of that river. On the second day, Capt. Hall was of the opinion that the prospects were not sufficiently flattering to continue the pursuit and returned. On the third day Capt. Flinn, who was the oldest officer, and considered an excellent woodsman, expressed the opinion that they were risking too much for any probable success they might expect to meet with; but Capt. Kibbey, though he would not oppose Capt. Flinn's opinion, said that if seven others would follow him he would keep up the pursuit another day, whereupon John Clawson, Richard M. Gano, Isaac Ferris, Jr., Thomas McCardle, Sylvanus Reynolds, Benjamin Stites, Jr., and

Ephraim Simpson agreed to follow Capt. Kibbey, and Capt. Flinn and the balance returned home. The next day, being near the Indian town called Old Chillicothe, on the Little Miami, Capt. Kibbey and his men thought it the most prudent to return, accordingly they turned about and followed Harmar's trace home. On the second morning of their return, soon after taking up the line of march, they saw two men at a distance coming towards them on the trace, apparently heavy loaded, and ascertaining that they were Indians they hid behind trees until they came opposite them, when they shot, and killed them both. After scalping them they examined their packs, and found them to contain Mr. Smith's clothes, which, with the Indian scalps, they brought in with them. Capt. Kibbey and his men were very much applauded for this affair, and Mr. Smith proposed to give them ten dollars each for his returned goods, but I believe few, if any, received it.

The goods were uninjured except an attempt to unravel one or two new coverlets to plait bats of woolen yarn, that had been used for filling, it being of various beautiful colors.

Lawrenceburg, Dec. 29. E. F.

N. B.—I may be mistaken as to two or three of the names of Captain Kibbey's party.

LETTER XXXV.

MR. HIBBEN—The excitement produced by the return of Captain Kibbey's party with Mr. Smith's goods, and the scalp of the Indians who stole them, had not subsided, when the following occurrence took place.

About the time that General Wayne arrived, with his army at Cincinnati, Mr. Henry Tucker removed from Columbia, with several families accompanying, on to Mill creek, and established what was then called Tucker's station. Mr. Tucker had two very valuable horses, which, after the summer was over, he sent back to Columbia for safe-keeping. Mr. Tucker had, at Columbia, a very strong stable, from which, it was thought, the Indians would not be able to steal his horses, the horses and stable, if I remember right, were placed in the charge of Mr. Joseph Lambert, and thought to be entirely safe. One morning, about the 1st of April, the alarm was given that the Indians were about, and that Mr. Tucker's horses were stolen. Mr. Tucker was sent for, and, in the meantime, before his arrival, large crowds of the militia had assembled at the stable, to find out, if possible, how the stable door was opened. Mr. Tucker, on his arrival, offered a reward of eighty dollars for the return of the horses, and the militia were soon off on the pursuit of them. They had no difficulty in keeping the track of the horses and Indians through the day; so that they could follow on as fast as their strength and activity would permit, but at night the Indians had the advantage. They could make tracks, but the white people could not follow them until morning, and, had they improved the opportunity, might easily have escaped. Directly after starting on the track the second morning, some of the white men discovered a smoke ahead, which they soon learned was an Indian camp. An arrangement was made to approach it with all possible caution, but the Indians were too vigilant. One of them saw the white people coming, and gave the yell, when they all broke for the woods but one, who, being a little more resolute than the rest, made for the horses, and, with his scalping knife, cut the rope with which they were tied fast to a tree and made an attempt to mount one of them, but they were very tall and he failed. He next tried to shelter himself between the horses, but, finding the white men were pressing too hard on him, he took to his heels and made his escape, although several guns were shot at him, and most of the white men believed he was wounded, but thought it more prudent to return with the recaptured horses than to risk anything further in pursuing after the Indians. Thus, after an absence of four days, Mr. Tucker's horses were returned to him at an expense of eighty dollars, and the Indians taught that they could not longer, with impunity, intrude on the property of the white people.

     Yours,   E. F.
Lawrenceburg, Jan. 5.

LETTER XXXVI.

MR. HIBBEN—The depredations of the Indians on the inhabitants of the Miami country in the winter of 1793–94 were not confined to the settlement of Columbia, but other stations were made to share in the evil. In the spring of 1793, as related in a former letter, a number of families from Columbia and other places made a settlement on the east side of the Big Miami, a little above its junction with the Ohio, near a place called the Goose Pond. During that season a Mr. Rittenhouse built a mill to grind corn on a small stream passing down the hill to the Miami, through where the town of Cleves now stands. The mill was a wet weather concern, the stream being small; but it was a great accommodation to the people at that time. In the after part of the winter, or beginning of spring, after a rain sufficient to supply the mill with water, a Mr. Demos, with a young man by the name of Micajah Dunn, and another young man whose name I can not recollect, went from the settlement before named to Mr. Rittenhouse's mill, with each a bag of corn to have it ground into meal, and were detained so as not to start home until after dark; that, however, produced but little inconvenience, as it was very bright moonlight. A short distance after leaving the mill they came to the residence of a Mr. Wheeling; and, seeing several persons there, Mr. Dunn and the other young man with him rode up to the door to make some inquiry, but Mr. Demos rode on, expecting soon to be overtaken by them. While sitting on their horses talking at the door (as they supposed about twenty minutes after Mr. Demos left them), they heard a firing of guns in the direction he had gone; that, however, created no great alarm, as the white people were in the habit of going out such moonlight nights to kill wild game. They immediately started on hearing the guns, and, after riding as briskly as their horses could well travel with the load they had to carry, about the distance to where they supposed the firing was, they found Mr. Dennis lying across the path dead, and the bag of meal by his side. It would be useless to attempt to describe their feelings in that trying moment, traveling a narrow path in the woods, surrounded by a large growth of trees, behind which they might easily imagine their enemies were concealed, ready to shoot at them the fatal balls by which their leader had just been shot down, without means of defense and not knowing whether by advancing or retreating they would be exposed to the most dangers. Their course was onward, and proved to be a safe one, for they reached their home, gave the alarm, and a party was roused to go out after, and convey, the corpse of Mr. Demos to his family. who, instead of returning with his bag of meal, as was expected, to supply their daily wants, was brought in a mangled, lifeless corpse, that they might behold him once more, take a last farewell view, then commit him to the silent grave, to be seen by them on earth no more. The bloody scene above narrated took place almost within the hearing of the guns at Lawrenceburg, had there been any person there to have heard, a remembrance of which presents to the mind a wide contrast from the state of things as they now exist.

Who that is not void of feeling can reflect on the sufferings that have been endured, on the labors, toils and sweat, the dangers and untimely deaths that have been passed through, to provide in this goodly land for those who might follow after a peaceful home, surrounded more abundantly with all the necessary articles of life, probably than any other country in the world has ever been blessed with, without feeling his heart swell with emotions of gratitude at the remembrance of the names of those early pioneers, who had abandoned all the charms connected with their former peaceful homes, and sundered all the delightful ties that bound them to their former associations that posterity might enjoy the blessings procured for them at so great a cost. The Mr. Dunn above alluded to was the oldest brother of Judge Isaac Dunn, now living in this place, and the father of a respectable family raised in our country, most of whom are still among us.

Lawrenceburg, Jan. 15. E. F.

LETTER XXXVII.

MR. HIBBEN—In my last three letters, I tried to show the dangerous situation the citizens of the Miami country were placed in by reciting several hostile acts committed by the Indians on individuals, in person, and on their private property. I now invite your attention back to the movements of the army; which was the all-important topic of conversation in that day. The transfer of the army, and of General Wayne's headquarters, from Hobson's Choice to Greenville, made a great change in the business of the country. The latter place became the resort of those who were seeking a market for the little amount of surplus produce they had to spare, and the track opened by General St. Clair, which had previously been used only as a military road, became a great thoroughfare, thronged by citizens and soldiers, going to and from headquarters. The change gave the Indians an opportunity to waylay the road and kill and plunder as circumstances would permit, and though generally escorted by detachments of soldiers they were frequently attacked and plundered. Among the number killed was Mr. Moses Pryor, who had lost two children killed by the Indians at the time they attacked White's Station, leaving Mrs. Pryor, with one little boy she had saved by her own exertions at the time, to mourn his loss, and that little fellow fell a victim to fever the next fall, so that she was, indeed, a lonely, forlorn widow, far away from her relatives and former associates, left to buffet alone the storms of adversity with which she had been so often assailed.

Colonel Robert Elliott (attached to the army) was another victim to savage barbarity. He was traveling on horseback (in company with a soldier who served him as waiter) from Cincinnati to Fort Hamilton, and at a place then called the Big Hill, in Springfield township, was fired on and killed by the Indians. The soldier escaped, followed by Colonel Elliott's horse, and made his way to Fort Hamilton. The next day a party was raised (and a coffin provided), who went with the soldier to the spot, and found the body of Colonel Elliott, placed it in the coffin, and started to Cincinnati to bury it. They had traveled but a short distance before they were attacked by the Indians, by whom the soldier was killed, and the coffin, with the remains of Colonel Elliott, taken. In a very short time the white people rallied, and retook the body of Colonel Elliott, with his waiter, and proceeded with them to Cincinnati, where they were buried the next day.

The spring opened with an encouraging prospect of an early, vigorous, and successful campaign, and rumors were continually afloat of boats loaded with soldiers, descending the river to Fort Washington, and making their way from that place to headquarters. A company of spies were called for from Columbia, which was soon raised, and organized by the appointment of Ephraim Kibbey, captain, William Brown, lieutenant, and Ashbel Gray, ensign, and ordered to march with all possible dispatch for headquarters. While contemplating the pleasing prospect before them, with a glowing delight, an express arrived from the army, bringing news of a most unpleasant character. General Wayne had been using every possible exertion, through the winter and spring, to get as large an amount of supplies on to the frontiers as possible, and had, in the latter part of June, ordered between two and three hundred horses (loaded I suppose) on from Greenville to Fort Recovery, and had detached one hundred and forty men under the command of Major McMahen, to escort them. The major arrived at Fort Recovery on the evening of the 29th, and it may be supposed the supplies forwarded were deposited in the fort, but the place being too small to hold the horses, and it being desirable to let them graze as a matter of economy, the escort encamped outside the fort. Early on the morning of the 30th they were attacked by an overwhelming force of Indians, and, after a brave and desperate struggle, Major McMahen, Captain Hartshorn, Lieutenant Craig and Ensign Torry having been slain, and fifty-one privates killed, wounded and missing, they were compelled to retire into the fort, abandoning their horses to the victors, who hung about through the day, and made several ineffectual attempts to storm the fort; but, seeming a little modest about pressing the matter too far, they, in the course of the following night, retired with the horses they had captured. News of the above misfortune hung like a dark cloud over the mind for a few days, but it soon passed off. The people had too much confidence in Wayne to be shaken by one adverse wind, and the circumstance was almost forgotten in a short time by the joy that was felt on the arrival of General Scott, from Kentucky, with sixteen hundred mounted volunteers, who passed immediately on for headquarters, where they arrived on the 26th of July, and were reported to Wayne, at which time he announced himself ready to march in search of the enemy. Here I will come to a close, after expressing my regret that I should, when writing my last letter, have forgotten the name of Thomas Fuller, the young man who was with Micajah Dunn at the time Mr. Demos was killed by the Indians. E. F.

Lawrenceburg, January 19, 1852.

N. B.—The reader will please read Demos for Dennis in my last letter.

LETTER XXXVIII.

MR. HIBBEN—On the 28th of July, 1794, Major-General Anthony Wayne was in command of an army of efficient, well-disciplined, brave men, powerful enough in numbers to have awed the Indians into submission, had it not been for the folly of their advisers. The army numbered (as was generally understood) over five thousand effective men, equipped for war, well supplied with military stores and provisions, the larger portion of them regulars, divided into two brigades—one under the command of Brigadier-General James Wilkinson, the other commanded by Brigadier-General Thomas Posey; the militia were under the command of Major-General Scott. This army, through the persevering, untiring industry of General Wayne, had been drilled until it is probable the United States never had had together at one time an equal force of brave men, better disciplined and prepared for action. Thus prepared, with Captains Debutts and Lewis, and Lieutenant William Henry Harrison for his aids-de-camp, Wayne moved with his army, on the 28th of July, in search of the enemy, and, from reports circulated among the people, was equally cautious, as he had been on his march to Greenville, to have his camp well guarded, so that there was no night on his march in which he could have been attacked by surprise. After leaving Fort Recovery, about twenty-four miles in his rear, he built another fort, which he called Fort Adams. From Fort Adams he directed his course toward the junction of the Maumee and Auglaize, where it was expected the Indians would make a stand, but being disappointed in this (as they all fled at his approach) he made another halt of several days and erected another fort, which he called Fort Defiance. From Fort Defiance he crossed over the Maumee, and marched down the course of that river on its left bank towards the rapids, and on the 18th lost one of his spies (William May), taken prisoner by the enemy. On the 19th, believing the Indians were so closely pursued that they would either come to a fight or disperse, Wayne had another fort erected, called Fort Deposit. In this fort he ordered the heavy baggage that it would be inconvenient to be encumbered with in time of an action to be deposited, leaving a sufficient force to protect it. The next morning (August 20th) at an early hour the army was put in motion in search of the enemy, prior to which the commander-in-chief issued a general order directing the manner of conducting. They had not moved far before they had sufficient indications of an intention on the part of the Indians to join issue with them, and to prepare for the conflict. Every necessary arrangement was made that could be made while on their march, so that they should not be surprised or thrown into confusion whenever the attack should be commenced; that is, they were prepared for the engagement at any time the enemy might choose to make the attack. They moved on until approaching some fallen timber calculated to obstruct their march; an advanced corps of mounted men were fired on from a thicket of undergrowth, and driven back to the advanced line of the regular troops, which soon brought on an engagement with as large a portion of our army as the nature of the ground would admit of. The Indians kept up a very brisk fire for some time, but finding the battle to be rather hot they gave way and began to fall back, closely pursued by our men, until they came to an open space, when they dispersed and fled in every direction, many of them toward the British fort, followed by our army until it was seen they received no protection from the garrison, when they gave up the pursuit. Thus in the space of an hour, or probably less, a victory almost bloodless (compared with some of the first engagements) was obtained over the combined forces of the Indian tribes, a victory as important to the interests of the west as was that gained by Washington at Yorktown over the forces of Great Britain under Lord Cornwallis to the united colonies. When the news of this victory reached the settlements, to use a common expression, it spread almost with the rapidity of lightning, and to judge of its effects in Columbia, diffused universal joy into all minds throughout every station then settled. The people were almost frantic with joy, and the first thing heard when they met was congratulations on account of the late triumph of our arms over the savages. To a people, many of whom the last five or six years had been penned up in a small fort, or the more circumscribed limits of a log cabin, beyond which they could not go but at the risk of life, whose last act when they retired to rest at night was to see that every avenue by which their dwelling might be entered was sufficiently barred to prevent the entrance of the midnight assassin, with his tomahawk and scalping knife, from breaking in to execute his murderous intentions, to be at once relieved of all apprehensions of danger, so that they could repose in safety at home, and without fear attend to their business abroad, it was indeed transporting, and calculated to call into lively exercise every emotion of gratitude and joy hitherto latent in the breast. The length of my letter admonishes me to close.

     Yours with respect,   E. F.
Lawrenceburg, January, 1852.

LETTER XXXIX.

MR. HIBBEN—After the victory obtained by the United States army, commanded by General Wayne, on the 20th of August, 1794, the commander observed the same prudence and manifested equal skill as before the battle. As it had been understood from various rumors that the Indians were daily in expectation of reinforcements, Wayne remained on the battle-ground three days to await a second attack, should they be disposed to another engagement. At the close of three days, no enemy appearing, he conducted his victorious army back to Fort Defiance, at which place he remained two or three weeks to strengthen his works there, when he removed to the Miami village, near where the town of Fort Wayne now stands, to select the site for another fort in the heart of the Indian country, in which he determined to leave a sufficient force to check any hostile movements of the enemy in the bud. After having determined on the situation and the plan of the fort intended to be erected, he left the prosecution of the work in the charge of one of his officers, Colonel Hamtramck, and removed with the main body of the army back to Greenville, where he again established his headquarters, having previously ordered the militia back to Fort Washington to be discharged and mustered out of service. On their return, every portion of the army, and every individual who had belonged to it, was cheered in the most enthusiastic manner by the citizens, and to have belonged to Wayne's army was enough to elevate any individual (in the estimation of the people) almost to the pinnacle of fame. The officer to whom the erection of the fortification was committed, after having performed the work, named it Fort Wayne. During the winter, preliminaries of peace were signed by General Wayne and the chiefs of the principal tribes, and an arrangement made to hold a treaty at Greenville the ensuing spring to establish a definite and lasting treaty of peace. By the preliminary arrangement both parties were to cease all acts of hostility towards each other, and all prisoners held by either parties were to be delivered up as soon as practicable. The anticipation of peace expressed by the people on hearing of the victory of the 20th of August now began to be realized; the howling of the wolf or the hooting of the owl could no longer be in imagination turned into human voices imitating those animals as an artifice, by which the Indian, unsuspected, could approach the dwelling of the white man from the different points where he had stationed his forces, so as to make a simultaneous attack on every side and cut off all opportunities for a retreat. The writer of this article has often known whole neighborhoods terrified at the report of some one who supposed he had heard the Indians imitating the sound of one or both the animals above named, begun at one point and answered from another, until at about an equal distance from every surrounding point the token was given to move forward and commence the attack, and, as a living witness, can testify that the distress produced on the mind for the time is equally as terrifying as if the danger were near. He remembers (no doubt in common with hundreds of others) often to have lain down at night with the impression deep upon his mind that the probabilities were stronger that before morning he should be a victim of savage cruelty than that he should live to see the light of another day. Can it then be thought a matter of surprise that persons so long suffering so many dangers, privations and fears should be a little enthusiastic in the praise of their deliverers, almost bordering on man worship? I sometimes feel to the present time, when I look over the dangers of past days (old as I am), as though I could throw my hat in the air and raise a hurrah in honor of Wayne and his victorious army, more fortunate, but possibly not more patriotic, than those who had gone before them. But after all, I must say to God be the praise, and to them the honor of being employed by him to bring about so glorious a result. E. F.

Lawrenceburg, February 6, 1852.

LETTER XL.

MR. HIBBEN—The citizens of the Miami country did not realize that exemption from difficulties and dangers on account of Indian depredations at as early a period as they had anticipated; after the victory of the 20th of August, several persons were killed, and other damage accrued in the course of the fall and winter; but it was generally believed that it was the acts of marauding parties, who were out from home and did not know of the truce that had been agreed upon between the hostile parties. The first person killed by the Indians about Columbia, after the battle, that I recollect of, was David Gennings. The circumstances connected with his death by the Indians were so very remarkable that I would not publish them to the world as facts were I not personally acquainted with Mr. Gennings and many of the circumstances, as to leave no doubt, in my own mind, that all I am about to relate to you is true. Mr. Gennings was a respectable farmer, living in Fayette county, Pennsylvania, near where the town of Brownsville now stands, then called Red Stone Old Fort, and in the neighborhood from which Major Benjamin Stites and his party emigrated in 1788, when they descended the river to make the first settlement ever made by the white people in the Miami country. Having heard of the arrival of Major Stites and party, and of their success in making their settlement before they were discovered by the Indians, and of the extraordinary fertility of the soil, Mr. Gennings determined to move his family to Columbia in the spring of 1790, and accordingly made the necessary preparations the preceding winter. At the time he made his arrangements to start, he had had all his effects that he intended to take, except such as were wanted for their comfort in cooking and sleeping the last night, placed in the boat the previous day, so as to make an early start the next morning. In the night he dreamed he had performed his trip down the river in safety, but, after arriving at Columbia, had been most horribly killed and mangled by the Indians. He awoke from sleep and told Mrs. Gennings his dream, and appeared, as she said, very much disturbed, and in the morning told her he had concluded to abandon his intention of removing to the Miamies. Mrs. Genning, being a very resolute woman, told him it would be folly in the extreme to abandon the idea of removal on account of a dream, after they had sold their farm, and other property, but all to no purpose, for the more he thought of his dream the greater his reluctance to remove. Finally, finding she could not remove his difficulties by anything she could say, she addressed him thus: "Well, David, if you think you can not with safety go, do you stay here and make another crop, and I and the boys will go to the Miami country, and raise one, and we shall be able to leave if there is danger, and will send you word, and, after hearing from us, if you think you can venture you can follow the next season." The last proposition was agreed to, Mrs.

Gennings, with the family, descended the river, having three sons young men, and Mr. Gennings following in the winter of '90 or '91. After arriving in the country Mr. Gennings was very unhappy on account of his dream, and frequently said to those he talked with upon the subject, that he had no other expectation but that the Indians would kill him. I recollect hearing him express himself, in a conversation with my father, that he expected to be killed by the Indians, and being a very pious Christian he spoke of not being so much terrified at the thought of dying as he was of the cruel, barbarous manner he expected to die. My father then said to him, "If I were in your situation I would take the advice your friends are giving you, to go back to the old settlements, and stay until the Indians are driven back, or make peace." He finally concluded to adopt that course, and made preparations to return to Pennsylvania with a party that expected shortly to start through the wilderness for Wheeling, but when the time to start came he shrank back, fearing he would be killed on the way. He afterwards, apparently with less fear, continued in the country until after Wayne's victory, when he, with most others, thought there was but little more fear from the Indians. Sometime near the 1st of October (breadstuff being very scarce) he gathered a grist of corn and started with it to Round Bottom, to mill, and to avoid danger, if there was any, he crossed the Miami and went through Newtown, and continued his course undisturbed, until he had nearly approached the ford, where he expected to cross the river again, to get over to the mill. As he was passing a grove of papaw bushes he was fired at by two Indians; the ball shot by one of them passed through one lobe of his lungs, but he did not fall, and the horse turned immediately round, and conveyed him home unconscious of much danger; he saw the Indians fly in much haste, instead of following him. After he had arrived at home, though his wound was not considered dangerous, the family and neighbors thought it best to send to Cincinnati for a doctor (for there was none in Columbia). The physician came (I believe Dr. Sellman), and, on examination, told them the wound would prove fatal; he said the ball had passed through his lungs, as was evidenced by the breath passing through the wound as often as he breathed. In the course of the night an inflammation took place, and the next morning he died.

In the confident belief of entering into glory, his death produced a deep sensation upon the minds of those who had often heard him talk of apprehended danger. He was buried in the burying ground attached to the Baptist meeting-house on the hill at Columbia, where, no doubt, his ashes still repose. The funeral sermon was delivered by Elder John Smith, pastor of the church to which he belonged, and was attended by a very large concourse of people, who appeared to feel that a strange, mysterious Providence was connected with the whole affair.

Yours with much respect, E. F.
Published Feb. 20, 1852.

LETTER XLI.

MR. HIBBEN—The confidence reposed by the people, generally, in General Wayne's ability to subdue or bring the Indians to terms of peace drew a large emigration to the Miami country, during the winter of 1793–94, and the ensuing spring. With the new emigrants, the old settlers, as on former occasions, were willing to divide, as long as they had any provisions, so that before the close of spring corn became very scarce. Of meat they had none but what was taken from the woods. In consequence of the scarcity of corn the people sowed oats as a substitute for corn and hay, and as soon as it sprang up, and grew to a sufficient height, cut it as food for their horses, and other stock used in raising another crop. All other stock not kept at labor, including swine, had to depend on the woods, as their owners had nothing to give them for food. The oats, although a poor substitute, green as they were, were made to answer their purpose until their corn was laid by. Columbia at that time contained a large population, and nearly all the land was cleared and fenced, and nearly all planted, and in corn. The streets were so bare that there was no chance for grazing short of the woods, to which their stock had to go for self-preservation, where many of them met with an untimely death by the wolves and bears. After the new corn had ripened so as to answer for food for hogs, probably about the beginning of November, Mr. Paul and his son, and Mr. Robert Giffen, whose hogs had strayed off during the summer, concluded to go to the woods in search of them, and, according to agreement, started next morning, traveling up the valleys until they passed Turkey bottom, and came to Duck creek, when they took up the creek, and spent most of the day in unsuccessful search after their hogs. Despairing of success, in the after part of the day they undertook to retrace their steps, and make their way home, returning down the creek, nearly on the track they had made in the morning. In traveling home they came near to a large sycamore tree which immediately above the ground had divided into three branches, which had grown to a very large size. Behind this tree, although unperceived by them, was a party of Indians concealed, and immediately after passing it they were fired at, and Robert Giffen and young Paul fell, being shot, and, it was supposed, died immediately. Old Mr. Paul escaped unharmed, and brought in the unfortunate news, which produced a great alarm. The militia, on hearing the news, repaired to the spot, and brought the dead bodies in to their friends.

This melancholy event, following so soon after the death of Mr. Gennings, shook the faith of many about the prospect of a speedy peace, and, the last murder committed by the Indians about Columbia, it kept the people for a long time in a state of alarm. Connected with the above account are some facts calculated to show the uncertainty of all schemes however well they may be planned. Mr. Robert Giffen came to the country in advance of his father to raise a crop for his family use when they might arrive. This was a prudent measure, which all wise men would approve of. Robert Giffen thought it best to raise a few hogs that they might have meat as well as bread when they might arrive. This was also wise management, but wise as it was to human view, it was the very means of producing in the family one of the sorest trials they could have been afflicted with, filling every heart with anguish. If Robert had not come to the country in advance of his father he would not have had any stock to stray off, and draw him to the woods in search of them, and if he had not gone to the woods on that day he would not have been exposed to the fire of the Indians, so that prudent and well arranged as his plans were, they resulted in an evil which, above all others, he would have wished to avoid; thus, being sent for good, the whole plan resulted in evil, showing how weak, and what short-sighted, frail mortals we are.

Yours, E. F.

Published Feb. 25, 1852.

LETTER XLII.

MR. EDITOR—When in the state that nature had formed it, and before it had been subdued by the hand of man, the big bottom had, in addition to the common trees of the forest, including the thickets of plumb and haw trees, a very luxuriant growth in a vegetable sometimes called the hog-weed, but commonly the horse-weed. This weed was thick on the ground, and in a few weeks in the summer would grow to the height of from ten to fifteen feet, bearing a seed which, when ripe, was eaten by hogs. Soon after the settlement was made by the white people, on the east side of the Big Miami (at the point), some of their hogs crossed over the river to graze and feed in these thickets, and some of them remained so long that no one continued to exercise ownership over them or their increase, until, like the deer in the woods, they became the property of any person who could find and take them. Late in the fall of 1794,[1] several persons from the settlement on the east side of the river crossed over into the bottoms in search of hogs, to use as meat for the ensuing season. Among them were Isaac Mills, Isaac Dunn, Benjamin Cox, Thomas Walters, Joseph Randolph, Joseph Kitchel and Garret Vanness. After an unsuccessful search for the most of the day, it was proposed by some of them to return home for the night and renew the search the next morning; but Cox and Walters thought it would be best to encamp on the ground, so as to have the advantage of an early start in the morning. The balance, disagreeing with them, returned home, and they stayed in the woods. After circumstances made it appear that after the others were gone they followed Double Lick Run down about a hundred yards below the place where the road from Lawrenceburg to Elizabethtown crosses it, when they selected a place to stay for the night, and made a fire to sleep by on the ground. Toward midnight the people at the settlement were very much alarmed at the report of several guns heard in the direction that Cox and Walters were left by the company, and entertained strong fears about their safety, but could not go for their relief until morning.

[1] NOTE—This date is erroneous. The tragedy occurred February 2, 1795. See Centinel of the Northwest Territory, February 7, 1795.

Early next morning a number of persons started to ascertain the fate of these men. They repaired to the place where they were when the company left them the last evening, but not finding them there they scattered through the woods in search of them, and in a very short time Mr. Garret Vanness and Mr. Isaac Dunn, who were following down the creek, came upon the body of Mr. Cox by the side of the place where they had built a fire to sleep by. He had been shot and scalped and otherwise mangled. The balance of the company were called together, and after a little search found Mr. Walters dead in the weeds, seventy or eighty rods from where he was first shot, and from the appearance of things concluded he had been first wounded and made an attempt to escape, but was followed, killed and scalped. These bodies presented a horrible appearance, and though they were the last persons killed in the Miami country, the barbarity of the savages exercised on them gave but little evidence of a disposition on their part to make peace. The traveler, passing from Lawrenceburg to Elizabethtown, as he crosses the run near the stone building lately the residence of the late Thomas Miller, may at any time, by turning his head to the right, glance his eye over the spot where Benjamin Cox and Thomas Walters, the last victims of savage barbarity in the war, closing with Wayne's treaty, were cruelly murdered. Yours, E. F.

Published March 3, 1852.

LETTER XLIII.

MR. EDITOR—I now proceed to give an account of the last act of hostility committed by the Indians on any of the inhabitants of the Miami country, coming within the reach of my recollection. There was formerly a large white (or as it is sometimes called) water elm tree, standing on the north side of a path leading from Columbia to Cincinnati, through the woods and along the bank of the river. The roots of this tree were of a peculiar growth, rising above the ground, as they spread out from the trunk of the tree, sometimes to the height of six or seven feet, uniting at the top with the body of the tree, and forming a shelter for man or beast in time of a storm. There was on the back or north side of the tree one of those open cells, formed by nature, of an unusual size.

Sometime late in the autumn of 1794, Mr. Reason Baily, one of the first company that landed at Columbia, 1794, to make a settlement there, was traveling on foot from Cincinnati to Columbia, and as he was passing the tree he was seized by three Indians, one taking him by the coat collar, and one by each arm, and led away about five miles north, to an Indian encampment on Harmar's trace, where, he supposed, there were about thirty Indian warriors. After arriving at the camp, an Indian who could talk English began to inquire of him about the military strength of Columbia; to which he replied that he did not know how strong they were, that he was a stranger, and had only lately come there. As he uttered the last words the Indian stared him in the face and pronounced what he said ''a lie,'' and said: ''I saw you there when the white people first came to Columbia;'' to which Baily replied, ''It is true I was there, but have been away and just returned.'' ''That may be,'' rejoined the Indian. Baily was then ordered to strip himself, and commenced by taking off his coat and handing it to an Indian, two Indians still holding on to their grip of him, one, after his coat was off, to the collar of his shirt, and the other to one arm, leaving an arm loose. He was then ordered to lay off his vest, which he said he threw over his shoulders, and then, making a stop, put his loose hand in his pocket, pretending to take something from it, and hand it to the Indian holding him by the arm, who immediately let go his hold of the arm to receive the thing offered him, at which moment Baily sprang with so much force as to leave his shirt collar with the other Indian and escaped. One Indian followed immediately after, the others stopping to arm themselves. After running a few hundred feet the Indian caught Baily, and a struggle ensued, in which they both came to the ground; while struggling the Indian attempted to draw Baily's knife he had belted around him, from the scabbard, but getting hold too low Baily grabbed the handle above his hand, and, drawing it out, supposed he had cut the Indian, who gave a yell, shook his hand and let go. Baily took the advantage for flight, but by this time found the other two were close at his heels, but, it being dark, the Indians had to stop and listen for the noise he made in the fallen leaves while running, to learn which way he was winding his course, which gave him the advantage. Having gained considerably on them, and being very much exhausted, passing through a very heavy, dark piece of woods, he stopped suddenly, and hugged closely to a tree, and the Indians passed him. After they had gone, as he supposed, about eighty steps beyond him, they stopped about a minute to listen, and then started again in the pursuit. Mr. Baily continued stationary, and in about half an hour heard the Indians returning; as they passed within about two rods of him, heard them talking as though very much displeased, and neither heard or saw them more. After he felt satisfied the Indians were gone, he moved very cautiously for home, but could not stir without making a noise among the leaves of the trees that had fallen to the ground. He, however, succeeded in arriving safe at the frontier house of Mr. John Smith, where he knocked for admittance, but was refused until he told his name and the cause of his calling at that time of night. On telling them he had been taken captive by the Indians, and had escaped, they caught the idea that he was still a prisoner, and that the Indians were using him for the purpose of getting into the house and charged it upon him, but he affirmed so positively that it was not so that they finally let him in.

This act closed the hostile scenes of a six years' sanguinary war that the early pioneers of the Miami country had to wade through, while contending with the forests, to reclaim and bring them into subjection for the use of man.

Yours, E. F.

Published March 24, 1852.

LETTER XLIV.

MR. EDITOR—In my last letter I gave an account of the closing hostile scene of a six years' bloody war the early settlers of the Miami country passed through, with all the evils attending such a savage warfare, viz.: a continual fear of danger, producing disquietude, frequent alarm, bloodshed, murders, widows and orphans, with penury and want, followed by a state of peace, connecting with it freedom from alarm, domestic security, ease and contentment, health and prosperity, with a fair prospect of an abundant supply of all the comforts of life, with increasing motives to industry, inviting emigration in an earnest ratio and introducing a new era in the history of the country. The prospect of peace engrossed the attention of all, and was the subject of general conversation, and many of the pioneers, as well as late emigrants and strangers from all parts of the United States, were engaged in making preparation to attend the treaty of Greenville the approaching summer. At the appointed time the parties met, a treaty of peace was concluded, signed, approved and published, and all apprehension of further danger put to rest. The joy on receiving the news of peace was universal, and from that time the inhabitants began to scatter over the face of the country. New villages and farms seemed to be brought into existence as by magic, so that the traveler might pass over a district of country and find it an unbroken wilderness, and in a few months repass and find in almost every direction the big work of opening a farm or building up a village, or a town commenced; and such was the progress in improvements and prosperity that, with the exception of a scarcity of bread for a few years, owing to the rapid increase of emigration, and the great amount of labor necessary to open new farms, no country in the world can boast of an equal increase in all the substantial articles necessary for the comfort of man, nor is there a spot on earth where the inhabitants are more secure from danger of being attacked by foreign foe. There, six years after entering the country in pursuit of a future home, the little band of pioneers had found themselves delivered from the fear of their savage foes, with the bright prospect of permanent peace, and a certainty of soon realizing more than their most extravagant imaginations had ever calculated upon. When I attempt to retrospect the events that have passed under my own observation since I landed at Columbia, on the 12th day of December, 1789, and call to mind the situation of the country at that time, then cast my eyes abroad over the same region and see what it is now, I am lost in astonishment, and feel that every attempt to limit the capacity of man to achieve whatever he, in the exercise of reason, may undertake, is severely rebuked, except the power of omnipotence should obstruct his progress.

    Yours with much respect,   E. F.

Published March 31, 1852.

GENERAL INDEX.

Agricultural Society, State, early work of, 186.
Amusements of early settlers, 55, 164, 167, 172.
Anderson, Indian chief, residence of, 174.
Andersontown, description of, 173–174.
Appropriation, for Indiana Historical Society, 40.
Archaeology, importance of study of, 218; divisions of, 220; first period of man, 221–222; era of mound-builders, 223; races of men, 224–226; mental development, 227–229; ancient buildings, 230; mounds, 231–235; skulls, 236–237; errors in, 238–240.
Auglaize river, mention, 349.
Augusta, Ky., mention, 256.
Australoid races, characteristics of, 225; habitat of, 226.

Beasley's block-house, built, 330; attack on, 331, 332.
Beaver, Indian custom in killing, 126.
Benevolent institutions, popular pride in, 186.
Big Hill, Indian attack at, 346.
Big Miami river, Indian villages on, 123; exploration near, 255, 268; mention, 278; Ft. Hamilton built on, 288; settlement at mouth of, 330; Wayne's army crosses, 335; settlements on, 343.
Big reserve, mention of, 121.
Blackford's reports, high reputation of, 186.
Blue river mentioned, 154.
Bluffs of White river considered for site of capital, 153.
Bracken. See *Augusta*.

Cahokia, Ill., mounds at, 232.
Cannon at Kaskaskia, 74, 76.
Cave-dwellers, age of, 220–222.
Cayugas, mention of, 125.
Centinel of the Northwest Territory, mention, 359.
Chicktaghicks, mention of, 126.
Chillicothe. See *Old Chillicothe*.
Christmas celebrated by settlers at Columbia, 261.
Church, influence of in history, 100–104.

GENERAL INDEX.

Churches, first established in Indianapolis, 162; pioneer preachers, 163–164; first established in Miami country, 246, 280–281; Baptist in southeastern Indiana, 246; anecdote concerning, 247.

Cincinnati, O., first settlement at, 262; growth of, 263, 268; Indians near, 270; Gen. Harmar at, 276; militia at, 279; Indian captives at, 287; Indian troubles at, 314; Indian attack near, 322; Wayne's army at, 326; Elliott killed near, 346.

Clark, Geo. Rogers, orders for campaign of against Kaskaskia, 74–76.

Cleves, O., mill at site of, 343.

Clough creek, mention, 292.

Columbia, Ohio, settlement of, 257; Lt. Kingsbury arrives at, 258; growth of, 263; lots laid off, 266; growth of, 268; natural advantages of, 271, 272, 273; social conditions of, 274; school at, 275; mill at, 275; General Harmar at, 277; militia at, 279; schools at, 280; Indians near, 282; news of St. Clair's defeat at, 289, 290; Wilkinson's visit to, 292, 293; peace commissioners start from, 297, 298; return of Smalley to, 309; massacre near, 315; crops at, 317; Indian attack near, 322; Wayne's army passes, 326; Indian depredations near, 337, 340; small-pox at, 338, 339; horses stolen at, 342; company of spies raised at, 347; rejoicing at over Wayne's victory, 350; Gennings killed near, 353–356; scarcity of food at, 356–357; Bailey captured near, 361.

Commission to locate capital of Indiana, members of, 153; journal of, 154; report of, 155.

Conner's station, capital commission meets at, 153; description of, 172–173.

Constitution, of Indiana Historical Society, first, 10–12; signers of, 12–16; amended, 30, 45.

Contracts, origin of provision against impairing obligation of, 72, 74.

Corydon, court at, 208; legislation at, 210.

Courts, first organized in Marion county, 158; trials in, 159, 160; of justice of the peace, 161; scenes in, 192–193; circuit traveling, 210, first justice court in Miami county, 275.

Courtship, frontier, 159.

Covalt's station, settlement of, 268; militia at, 279; Indian attack near, 315; mention of, 330.

Crawfordsville, political debate at, 194.

Crusades, causes and effects of, 113–115.

Cunningham's station, settlement of, 329.

Darlington, old town of, 209.

Deer creek, mention, 262; road up, 277.

Delaware Indians, purchase of lands of, 152, 158.

Double Lick Run, Indian attack at, 359.

Duck creek, mention, 277; church established at, 281; Indian attack near, 357.

GENERAL INDEX. 367

Dunlap's station, settlement of, 268; Indians attack, 269, 270; militia at, 279.

Early settlers (American), houses and forts of, 52; customs of, 54; amusements and schools of, 55; in Indianapolis, 156; newspapers of, 157; courts of, 158-161; hunting by, 164; food of, 165; amusements of, 167, 170, 172; privations of, 251, 274; crop failures, 266; furniture of, 267.
Eel river, Indian villages on, 139; Wilkinson's expedition against Indians on, 287.
Elizabethtown, Ohio, mention, 261, 359.
Elkhart river, Indian villages on, 139.
English communicate with Indiana Indians, 124.
Evansville, growth of, 209; early court at, 210.

Ferris letters, occasion of their publication, 245; sketch of author, 246, 248.
Feudalism, influence of in history, 105-112.
Finances of Indiana, creation of debt, 184; maintenance of credit, 185.
Five Nations. See *Iroquois*.
Fletcher, Calvin, memorial on, 56.
Flinn's Ford, mention, 340.
Floods, in Ohio river 1788-'89, 262; in 1793, 273; in Miami destroys mill, 276; in Ohio 1793, 326.
Food, of early settlers, 165; in time of crop failure, 263; at Columbia, 281, 325, 356.
Fort Adams built, 349.
Fort Defiance, built, 349; Wayne returns to, 351.
Fort Deposit built, 349.
Fort Duquesne, mention, 303.
Fort Greenville, built, 335, mention, 345; Wayne returns to, 351; mention, 352; treaty at, 363, 364.
Fort Hamilton, erection of, 288; mention, 293; Wayne at, 335.
Fort Harmar, mention, 283.
Fort Harrison, battle at, 178.
Fort Jefferson, erection of, 288; mention, 293; massacre near, 295; Wayne at, 335.
Fort Miami, description of, 250; cause of settlement at, 251-253; building of, 257; first sermon at, 267.
Fort Recovery, built, 336; battle at, 347; Wayne advances from, 349.
Fort St. Clair, erection of, 293; Wayne at, 335.
Fort Washington, site of, 262; Harmar marches from, 277; Harmar returns to, 278; Wilkinson at, 287; Fourth of July celebration at, 322; soldiers arrive at, 347; militia discharged at, 351.
Fort Wayne, mention, 278; General Wayne at, 351.
Forts (prehistoric), 235-236.

Forts built by early settlers, 52; attack on Fort Harrison, 178.
Fourteen Mile creek (Clark county, Ind.), stone fort at, 235.
Fourth of July, first celebration of at Indianapolis, 164; celebration at Fort Washington, 322.
Freeman case, trial of, 192.
French settlers, to be promised security and protection by Clark, 75; location of first uncertain, 123; character of, 208, 209.
Furniture used by early settlers, 267.

Game, abundance of, 164–165; in Miami country, 263, 271.
George's creek, mention, 303.
Gerrard station, established, 281; Indian shot near, 318.
Goose pond, settlement at, 343.
"Governor's Circle," early condition of, 161; religious services in, 162.
Grave creek, W. Va., mounds at, 232.
Greenville, treaty at, 136. See *Fort Greenville*.

Harmar's campaign, 276–280.
Harmar's Trace, course of, 277; mention, 298, 341.
"Harmonists," settlement of in Indiana, 237.
Harrison, Wm. Henry, movement for bringing remains of to Indiana, 47.
Henry, Gov. Patrick, orders of to George Rogers Clark, for Kaskaskia campaign, 74–76.
History, importance of study of, 81–82; moral effects, 83–87; sacred and secular, 88–90; teaches content, 91–92; use to public men, 93–96; origin of, 97; development of, 98–99; the church in, 100–104; feudal system in, 105–112; crusades, 113–115.
Hobson's Choice, named by Gen. Wayne, 326; Wayne's camp at, 327, 328; mention, 345.
Hog creek, mention, 299; massacre at, 300.
Honorary members, provision for electing, 17; elections of, 18, 29, 30, 31, 37.
Houses of early settlers, 54.
Hunting, early modes of, 164.

Incorporation of Indiana Historical Society, resolution for, 18; law for, 24.
Independent Press, establishment of, 245; sale of, 329.
Indiana, early settlers of, 52; log houses in, 54; early schools, 55; territorial stages of, 151–152; purchase of Indian lands, 152–153; railroad development in, 175–176; Indian warfare in, 178–182; growth of, 184; finances of, 185–186; social development, 186–187; attractive to young men, 207.
Indiana Historical Society, sketch of, 5–8; organization of, 9; first constitution of, 10; signers of constitution, 12–16; first circular of, 21; act for incorporation of, 24; second circular of, 31; third circular of,

38; appropriation for, 40; room obtained for, 61, 65; Dane's comment on, 69.

Indianapolis, commission to select site of, 153; journal of commissioners, 154; survey of site, 155; sale of lots in, 155; pioneer settlers of, 156; first newspapers, 156-157; mail facilities, 157; circuit court in, 158; justice of the peace courts in, 161; first churches in, 162; first Sunday-schools in, 162-163; first Fourth of July celebration, 164; game and food at, 164-165; militia at, 165; first theatrical entertainment, 167; early merchants, 168-169; transportation to, 168, 169, 175, 176; mock legislation at, 169-171; court-house at, 170; amusements at, 172; schools at, 174; first railroads of, 175-176; slave trials at, 193.

Indianapolis Gazette, established, 156; manner of printing, 157.

Indians, attacks of on settlers, 52, 53; treaty of removal with, 121; location of Indiana tribes, 122-123; missions to, 123-128; La Salle among, 129-130; use of liquor by, 131-138; villages of, 133; obstacles to civilization of, 137-140; Dillon's view of, 140-143; purchase of lands of, 152-153; removal of, 174; battles with in Indiana, 178-182; friendly near Columbia, Ohio, 259, 260; attack settlers at Columbia, 264, 265; kill Cook, 268; threaten settlements, 269, 270; Harmar's campaign against, 276-280; attack Dimett and Coleman, 282; massacre by at mouth of Scioto, 283-285; campaigns against by Scott and Wilkinson, 287; St. Clair's campaign against, 288-291; Wilkinson's expedition to bury dead of St. Clair's campaign, 292-293; peace commission to, 295-299; murder of commissioners, 300; captivity and escape of Smalley, 301-310; captivity of Patrick Moor, 311-312; kill Francis Griffin, 312; capture Nancy Gordon, 313; depredations near Cincinnati, 314; attack at Round Bottom, 315-317; troubles near Gerrard station, 318; captivity of Welch, 319-321; capture of Spencer, 322-324; attack Beasley's block-house, 331, 332; kill Goble, 332; attack White's station, 333, 334; Wayne marches against, 335; steal horses, 337, 340; steal clothing, 339; pursuit of, 342; kill Demos, 344; kill Pryor and Elliott, 346; attack Fort Recovery, 347; Wayne defeats, 349-350; terrors inspired by, 352; kill Gennings, 355, 356; kill Giffen and Paul, 357; kill Cox and Walters, 359-360; capture Baily, 361, 362; Wayne's treaty with, 363.

Intoxicating liquors, use of by early settlers, 55; use of by Indians, 131-138.

Iroquois Indians, Governor Dongan's speech to, 124; interfere with French, 125.

Iroquois river, Indian villages on, 139.

Kankakee river, Indian villages on, 139.

Kaskaskia, Clark's campaign against, 74; supplies and stores at, 75; mission at, 128.

GENERAL INDEX.

Keel boats, on White river, 155; for transporting merchandise, 168.
Knighthood, institution of, 110-112.

Lamasco, location and origin of, 211.
Law, Judge John, memorial on, 49; sketch of, 203; ancestry, 204; education, 205; removal to Indiana, 208; official positions, 210.
Lawrenceburg, newspaper at, 245; religious movement at, 246-248; mention, 261, 334, 344, 359, 360.
Legionville, mention, 318.
Legislature, assembly of first territorial, 152; first sessions at Indianapolis.
Lexington, Ky., mention, 267, 312.
Library, state, establishment of, 187.
Limestone. See *Maysville*.
Little Miami river, 250, 252, 255; Indians at, 256, 259, 268; scenery on, 272; mill at, 275; Harmar's course to, 277; mill on, 292; Indians capture settler at, 319, 320; settlements on, 330.
Louisville, death of Marshall at, 194; extracts from newspapers on death of Marshall, 195-199.

Madison, Marshall's home, 191; reception to Webster at, 194; mention of, 208.
Madisonville, Ohio, mention, 315.
Mad river, mention, 278.
Mail, early provisions for in Indiana, 157, 172, 173.
Man, ages of primitive, 220; original condition of, 221; present divisions of, 224-227; no deterioration in, 229; comparison of crania of, 236-237.
Marietta, Ohio, mention, 283.
Marion county, first courts of, 158; first court-house built, 170.
Marshall, Joseph G., sketch of, 191.
Maumee river, Indian villages on, 123, 133; battle on, 349, 350.
Maysville, Ky., mention, 252, 254, 255, 258.
Merchants, pioneer in Indianapolis, 168-169.
Mexico, antiquities of, 230, 231, 234.
Miami. See *Big Miami, Little Miami*.
Miami Indians, treaty with, 121; first location of, 122-123; missions to, 123; English communicate with, 124; religious instruction of, 125-128; first post among, 129; priests visit, 130; drunkenness of, 131-135, 137, 138; organization of, 132; villages of, 133; attitude of in 1814, 136; characteristics of, 137-140; purchase of lands of, 152-153; campaigns of Scott and Wilkinson against, 287; St. Clair's campaign against, 288-291; Wayne's campaign against, 347-350.
Miami reserve mentioned, 152.

Miamisburg, Ohio, mounds at, 232.
Michilimackinac, mention of, 130.
Militia, organizations of, 165-167; in Miami country, 275; after Harmar's campaign, 279; volunteer for Wilkinson's expedition, 293; discharge after Wayne's campaign, 351.
Mill creek, mention, 277; Indian attack near, 314; Wayne's army at, 326; description of camp, 327, 328; settlements on, 329; Indian troubles on, 332; Wayne's march up, 335; Tucker's station established on, 341, 342.
Mills, first on Little Miami, 275; tub-mill on Little Miami, 292; at site of Cleves, 343.
Mississinewa river, Indian villages on, 139.
Mississippi delta, geologic age of, 220.
Mohawks, mention of, 125.
Monachism, rise and influence of, 103-104.
Mongoloid races, characteristics of, 225; habitat of, 226; movement to America, 227-229.
Monongahela river, mention of, 250, 266.
Mound-builders, age of, 223; work of in United States, 231; work in Indiana, 232-234.
Mound City, O., mounds at, 233.
Mounds (prehistoric), universality of, 223; extent of in United States, 231; in Indiana, 232; character and contents of, 233.

Negroid races, characteristics of, 225.
Nettles eaten by early settlers, 325.
New Harmony, footprints in stone at, 238-240.
"New Purchase," meaning of term, 158.
Newspapers, establishment of first in Indianapolis, 156; manner of printing, 157; *Press* established at Lawrenceburg, 245.
New Town, Indian camp at, 259; settlement at, 330; Gennings killed near, 355.
North Bend, settlement of, 255; growth of, 263, 268; militia at, 279; Indian troubles at, 314.
Northwest Territory, character of settlement of, 69; ordinance for government of, 70; Jefferson's resolutions, 71; changes in ordinance, 72; growth of slavery clause, 73; author of slavery clause, 74; division of, 151.

Ohio river, fort contemplated at mouth of, 75; mention, 250, 252, 266; Scott crosses, 287; great freshet of 1793, 273, 326.
Old Chillicothe (Indian village), mention, 252; Harmar at, 278; mention, 341.
Oneidas, mention of, 125.

Onondaga, mention of, 124.
Onondagas, mention of, 125.
Ordinance of 1787, origin of, 70; compared with resolution of 1784, 71, 72; slavery clause in, 73, 74.
Ottawa Indians, mention of, 124.
Ouiatenons, villages of, 133; mention of, 134.

Paoli, mention of, 208.
Pensions for Revolutionary soldiers, Judge Law's bill for, 212.
Peorias (Indians), mention of, 134.
Piankeshaws, location of, 133; mention of, 134.
Picket fort (at Cincinnati), establishment of, 262.
Pigeon Roost massacre, description of, 53.
Population, of Indiana Territory, 152; growth of in Indiana, 184, 186.
Pottawattamies, mission to, 129, 130; location of in 1817, 139; purchase of reservation of, 153.
Prehistoric man, ages of, 220; first stage of, 221; in South seas, 228; buildings of, 230; mounds of, 231-234; stone forts of, 235-236; limit of geologic age of, 239.
Presque Isle (Preskiel), mention, 309.
Printing, pioneer method of, 157.
Pueblos, relation of to mounds, 230, 231, 235, 236.
Pursley eaten by early settlers, 325.

Railroads, early development of in Indiana, 175-176, 186.
Red Stone Old Fort, mention, 354.
Religious instruction, of Indians, 124-125, 126-128, 131; of pioneer whites, 162; at Columbia, 267.
Round Bottom, mention, 315; settlement at, 330; Gennings killed near, 355.
Rowdy Camp established, 335.

St. Clair's campaign, 288-291.
St. Joseph river, Indian villages on, 123, 139, mission at, 128, 129.
Salem, mention of, 246.
Scenery in the west at time of settlement, 272.
Schools, of early settlers, 55, 162-163; in Indianapolis, 174; school system organized, 186; Gov. Jennings recommends, 187; first at Columbia, 275; later at Columbia, 280.
Scioto river, Indian villages on, 122; massacre at, 283, 284.
Scott's campaign, 287.
Senecas, mention of, 125.
Settlements, by French, date of uncertain, 123.
Shockeys (Saukies-Sacs), mention of, 133, 134.

Signals of the Indians, 352.
Slavery, in Northwest Territory, origin of clause for exclusion of, 69-74; trial involving question of, 192-193.
Small-pox, outbreak of in 1793, 338.
Springfield, old town of, 209.
Strawtown, post-office at, 173.
Sugar creek, mention, 278.
Sunday, how observed by French settlers, 209.
Sunday-schools, first established in Indianapolis, 162; growth of, 163.
Supreme Court of Indiana, first justices of, 208.
Sycamore creek, mention, 277.
Symmes's purchase, origin of, 252-254.

Terre Haute, fight with Indians near, 178.
Theatrical entertainments, first in Indianapolis, 167.
Thorntown reserve mentioned, 152.
Tippecanoe battle ground, donation of to state, 179.
Tippecanoe, battle of, 179; poetical description of, 179-182.
Tippecanoe river, Indian villages on, 139.
Titles to real estate, origin of laws of Northwest Territory for, 72.
Tribune, New York, publication of Dane's letter in, 69.
Tucker's station, settlement of, 329, 341.
Turkey Bottom, location of, 258; planting at, 263; danger at, 279; Indian troubles at, 312, 313; mention, 339, 357.
Turtle creek, mention, 277.
Twightwees. See *Miamis*.

Utawawas. See *Ottawas*.

Vincennes, Post, mention of, 133; Indians at, 134; capture of by Gen. Clark, 178; Judge Law settles at, 208; land court at, 211; mounds near, 232.
Virginia, claim of to Northwest Territory, 75.

Wabash river, treaty at forks of, 121; Indian villages on, 133, 139; footprints in stone at New Harmony on, 238; expeditions against Indians on, 287.
Washington, Ky., mention, 252, 254.
Wayne's campaign, arrival at Columbia, 326; camp at Hobson's Choice, 327; advance to Greenville, 335; attack on Fort Recovery, 347; army of, 348; defeat of the Indians, 349, 350.
White river, Indian villages on, 139; navigability of, 154, 155; fish of, 165; amusements on, 172.
White's station, settlement of, 329; Indian attack on, 333; mention, 346.
Weas. See *Ouiatenons*.

Western Censor and Emigrant's Guide established, 156.
Wilkinson's campaign, 287; expedition to bury dead of St. Clair's campaign, 292-293.

Xanthochroic races, characteristics and habitat of, 226.

Yellow river, Indian villages on, 139.
Youghiogheny river, mention of, 250.

INDEX OF NAMES.

Abbett, Lawson.............. 15
Abbott, Dr. Charles C........ 222
Adams, John Quincy.......29, 205
Adams, Benjamin..........13, 20
Alcott, Benjamin,
    267, 315, 316, 336, 337
Allouez, Father......123, 128, 130
Ames, E. R................. 14
Ayreheart.................. 280

Baddolet, John.............. 18
Bailey, James............... 290
Baily, Reason. (See, also,
    Bayley.).............361, 362
Baker, Conrad............... 49
Baldwin, Elihu.............. 30
Ball, Henry.............315, 316
Ballard, Bland.............. 199
Ballard, G. M............... 16
Bancroft, George............ 31
Barbour, Lucien............. 193
Bartholomew, Joseph......... 153
Bassett, E. E............15, 62
Bates, Daniel............... 267
Bates, Hervey............... 158
Battell, C. I............13, 29
Bayley, Groenbright......... 255
Bayley, James F............. 256
Bayley, Reason. (See, also,
    Baily).................. 256
Beach, Wm. B................ 14
Beard, E. L................. 14
Beasley, John.......330, 331, 332
Beecher, Henry Ward..13, 30, 31
Beecher, Lyman.............. 31
Bell, P..................... 154
Bell, William A............. 16
Benton, Thos. H..........69, 71
Bergier, Father............. 123
Berry, Capt. John........... 174
Biddle...................... 280
Binetenu, Father............ 123
Black Fish, Capt............ 259

Blackford, Isaac..10, 13, 16, 19,
    22, 28, 29, 30, 31, 34, 35. 36,
        37, 149, 186, 207, 208
Blair, James................ 12
Blair, Solomon.............. 14
Blake, James...5, 12, 17, 22, 24,
    26, 29, 34, 35, 36, 162, 172
Blake, John L............... 31
Blake, John W......15, 62, 64, 65
Blake, William M............ 15
Blue, Jane.................. 261
Blythe, Benj. I..........153, 169
Blythe, Dr. James........... 30
Boconjehaulis (Buckongahelas) 304
Bodley, W. S................ 198
Bolton, Nathaniel..38, 149, 156, 157
Bolton, Mrs. Sarah T........ 149
Borden, James W............. 14
Bradley, Henry...........13, 163
Branham, David C............ 63
Brann, Jeremiah............. 286
Brent, Daniel............... 70
Broadwell................... 280
Brown, E.................... 13
Brown, George............... 15
Brown, George P............. 15
Brown, Henry L.............. 245
Brown, Hiram.............13, 169
Brown, James................ 159
Brown, R. T................. 14
Brown, Lt. William.......... 347
Brown, Wm. J.............38, 149
Bruté, Simon Gabriel........ 30
Bryant, J. R................ 14
Bryant, Wm. P............... 170
Buckingham.................. 280
Burns, Wm. J................ 14
Buxton, Edmond.............. 256

Cady, Charles W.,
      13, 30, 31, 34, 35, 36
Cain, John...............13, 170
Call, Jacob................. 210

INDEX OF NAMES.

Campbell, Alexander......... 246
Campbell, John L.,
    15, 43, 44, 46, 48, 49, 189
Canby, I. T................... 13
Carr, George W......15, 46, 51, 56
Carrington, Henry B........15, 43
Cass, Lewis.......18, 152, 153, 173
Chandler, John J............. 207
Chardon, Father..........123, 130
Charlevoix, Father........130, 131
✓Clark, Alfred M............15, 44
Clark, Gen. George Rogers,
              74, 178, 184
Clark, H. W................15, 43
Clark 280
Clawson, John 264, 265, 340
Clemens, C.................... 43
✓Coburn, Henry 15
Coburn, H. P......12, 30, 31, 35
Coburn, John, 14, 38, 39, 42, 43,
    46, 61, 62, 63, 64, 193
Coe, Isaac................13, 162
✓Coleman, Jonathan........... 282
Coleman, Mrs............322, 323
Coleman...................... 275
Coles, Edward 18
Collett, John.......15, 43, 232, 233
Collins (Collings, Wm. E.) ... 53
✓Conner, James D.............. 14
Conner, John................. 153
Conner, Wm.........153, 172, 173
Connor, Wm................... 13
Cook, Abel.........256, 268, 269
✓Cox, Benjamin......256, 359, 360
Cox, E. T.....15, 44, 48, 49, 51,
        62, 63, 64, 215
Cox, Joseph 256
Craig, Lt.................... 347
Cravens, Rev. Wm............. 163
Crawford, Randall 199
Cressy, T. R................. 14
Croghan, Col. George 153
Croly 280
Cummins, John J.............. 16
Curry, W. W....15, 43, 44, 46, 47
Curtiss, George L 15, 44

Dablon, Father..........123, 130
Dalton, Thomas J............. 133
Dane, Nathan..6, 26, 27, 29, 69, 71
Daniel, Richard.............. 210
Daugherty, Joseph F.......15, 62
Daugherty, Maj............... 267
Dawson, John W............... 14
Day, Henry................... 15

Debutts, Capt 348
Demos,——..........343, 344, 348
Defrees, John D........13, 69, 74
Denby, Charles............49, 201
De Pauw, John................ 13
De Ville, Father 123
Dewey, Charles,
   13, 30, 31, 192, 207, 208, 210
Dewey, Orville 29
Dillon, John B..6, 7, 13, 31, 35,
    36, 37, 38, 39, 40, 42, 43, 44,
    47, 48, 49, 61, 62, 63, 64, 119, 154
Dinett 282
Dongan, Gov. Thos 124
Dowling, Thomas.............. 14
Drake, Daniel 31
Drake, J. P.................. 12
Dumont, Ebenezer............. 14
Dunbar, W. E................. 13
Duncan, R. B..........15, 61, 62
Dunham, Cyrus I.............. 14
Dunlap, Dr. Livingston...156, 163
Dunlevy, Francis............. 286
✓Dunn, George H..12, 17, 19, 21,
  22, 23, 28, 29, 30, 31, 34, 35, 36, 199
Dunn, George G............... 60
Dunn, Hugh..............261, 330
Dunn, Isaac..261, 284, 345, 359, 360
Dunn, J. P................... 16
Dunn, James W................ 14
Dunn, Micajah,
      261, 343, 344, 345, 348
Dunn, Samuel................. 261
Dunning, Paris C............. 14
Durbin, John P............... 60
Durham, Jesse B.............. 153

Edson, Hanford A............. 15
Elliott, E. N................ 13
Elliott, Col. Robert......... 340
Ellis, Abner T...........13, 29
Ellis, F. W. H............... 14
Emerson, Thomas.............. 153
English, Wm. H............7, 10
Evans, Charles...........15, 62
Everett, Edward..........27, 29

Furnham, John H..5, 9, 10, 12,
  16, 17, 19, 20, 22, 24, 25, 28, 29
Farrington, James........13, 30
✓Ferris, Abraham............. 267
Ferris, Ezra. (*Sketch*)....13, 245
Ferris, Isaac................ 267
Ferris, Isaac, Jr............ 340
Ferris, John............267, 275

INDEX OF NAMES. 377

Finch, Fabius M 170
Fisher, S 14
Flaget, Rt. Rev 28
Fletcher, Calvin,
    12, 38, 56, 57, 58, 59, 159, 160
Flinn, Daniel 263
Flinn, Capt. James,
        263, 275, 293, 340, 341
Flinn, Thomas,
        263, 295, 297, 298, 310
Flint, Timothy 29
Fogg, W. H 16
Foley, James P 13
Foote, Obed 13, 161, 168
Frazee, John M 13, 170
Freeman, Dr. Isaac,
    295, 296, 297, 298, 305, 330
Foster, Gabriel 263
Foster, Luke 263, 264
Foster, Zebulon 263
Frey 274, 280
Frisbie, Samuel 13
Fuller, Thomas 348

Gabriel, Father 130
Gano, John S.,
    256, 267, 279, 280, 290, 293
Gano, Richard M 340
Gano, Stephen 280
Gennings, David,
      353, 354, 355, 356, 358
Gerrard, Joseph,
    275, 295, 297, 298, 305, 310
Gibson, David 15
Giffen, Robert 357, 358
Gilleland, John 153
Gilman, Samuel 29
Gist, Christopher 132
Given, James 168
Given, John 168
Goble, James E 245
Goble, —— 332, 334
Goforth, Wm 267, 275, 297
Gooding, David S 15
Gookins, J. F 16
Gookins, S. B 14
Gordon, James 313, 314
Gordon, Major Jonathan W ... 7-14
Gordon, Nancy 313
Graham, Wm 9
Gravier, Father 123
Gray, Ashbel 347
Gray, Francis C 29
Grenthouse 284
Gregg, Harvey 12, 156

Gregory, James 169
Griffin, Francis 312
Griffith, And. Ch 13
Griffith, Israel 170
Grimes, Samuel 14
Guilford, Nathan 29

Hagar, John 168, 176
Hager, J. H 14
Hale, Salma 31
Hall, James 18
Hall, Samuel 12
Hall, Capt 279, 340
Haman, Thomas 280
Hamilton, Allen 13
Hammond, P. D 15
Hamtramck, Col. John F 351
Hand, Gen. Edward 76
Hanna, Gen. Robert 169
Hanna, Samuel 14
Hannah, Samuel 14
Hannegan, Sen. Edward A.,
          186, 194, 211
Hardin, Col. John,
    295, 296, 297, 298, 330
Harmar, Gen. Josiah,
    275, 276, 277, 281, 282, 296
Harper, William 286
Harrison, A. W 13
Harrison, Christopher 155
Harrison, John Scott 47
Harrison, Temple C 15
Harrison, Wm. Henry,
    18, 47, 49, 135, 151, 152, 348
Hart, David 210
Hartshorn, Capt 347
Hasty, George 15
Hassey, C. G 13
Hayes, Joseph M 13
Heampsted, —— 256, 259
Henderson, Samuel 13
Hendricks, Thomas A.,
      15, 43, 47, 49, 56, 61
Hendricks, Wm 152
Hennepin, Father .. 123, 126, 127, 129
Henry, Patrick 74, 76
Heylin, Isaac N 13
Heylin, Dr. Isaac 26
Heylin, Newton S 170
Heylin, Rowland 29
Hibben, Rev. W. W 245
Higgins, A. M 14
Hinkley, Willard H 16, 64
Holliday, F. C.,
    15, 42, 43, 44, 46, 48, 56, 59

Holliday, Wm. A............ 14
Holley, Horace.............. 191
Holman, Jesse L.,
    10, 12, 16, 17, 19, 22, 208
Holman, Wm. S..........14, 42
Hooper, W. De M............ 16
Hough, Daniel...15, 43, 44, 46, 51
Howard, Tilghman A........ 13
Howe, Daniel Wait.......... 16
Howell, David.............70, 73
Howk, Isaac......13, 16, 17, 22, 23
Hubbell, Thomas. (See, also,
    Hubble).................. 286
Hubble, Thomas. (See, also,
    Hubbell)................. 340
Hunt, Abner................ 269
Hunt, F. W................. 13
Hunt, George............... 153
Hunt, Wm. Gibbes........... 29
Huntington, E. M........... 12
Hurst, Henry............... 13

Ingram, Andrew W.......... 170

Jefferson, Thomas,
    70, 71, 72, 73, 74, 151
Jennings, Jonathan,
    27, 152, 153, 154, 187
Joliet, Father............. 123
Jones, Barton D............ 15
Jones, David 267, 268
Judah, Samuel.............. 13
Julian, George W........15, 49
Julian, J. B............15, 43

Keenan, Henry F....15, 43, 47, 49
Kennedy, P. L.............. 15
Kent, James................ 29
Kenton, Simon.............. 258
Kerr, M. C................. 15
Ketcham, John.............. 193
Kibbey, Capt. Ephraim....256,
    259, 260, 279, 292, 294, 340, 341, 347
Kimberly, George W......... 170
King, Rufus.............70, 74
Kingsbury, Lt. Jacob,
    258, 261, 262, 269
Kinnard, George L.......... 167
Kinney, Amory.............. 13
Kitchel, Joseph............ 359
Kitchel, Luther............ 267

Lambert, Joseph 342
Lane, Amos................. 13
Lane, George W............. 14
Lane, Henry S.,
    14, 38, 39, 42, 49, 191, 192
Lane, General Joe.......... 185
Lanier, J. F. D............ 14
La Salle, Sieur de......126, 130
Lasselle, H., Jr........... 14
Law, John..13, 16, 17, 18, 19,
    20, 22, 23, 30, 31, 34, 35, 36, 38,
    49. (*Sketch of*)......203– 213.
Law, Lyman.............204, 205
Law, Richard............... 204
Law, Wm.................... 211
Layton, ——............322, 323
Lemon, Peter H............. 16
Levette, G. M.............. 15
Lewis, Capt. 348
Light.................280, 322, 323
Line. A. B..............14, 38
Linton, Wm. C..........10, 13
Livingston, Edward......... 29
Lizius, Charles B.......15, 41
Logan, Thomas J............ 16
Love, John................. 15
Ludlow, Col. Israel........ 329
Ludlow, John............... 286
Ludlow, Stephen 153, 334
Lubbock, Sir John, quoted.... 220
Lynch, Thomas,
    295, 297, 298, 299, 300, 303, 305
Lynch, Thomas H.........15, 43
Lytle, Gen. Wm............. 315

McCall, James B............ 211
McCartney, Wm.............. 158
McCarty, Enoch............. 13
McCarty, Nicholas.......... 168
McCarty, W. M.............. 14
McChesney, Jacob B......... 14
McClung, Rev. John 162
McClure, Wm................ 18
McCormick, ——.........154, 155
McCoy, Isaac............... 20
McDonald, David............ 199
McIlvaine, James 158
McKinney, J. T..........12, 30
McLean, John............31, 199
MacMahen, Major 347
McPherson, Wm.............. 13
Mace, Daniel 14
Maguire, D.,
    13, 30. 31, 156, 157, 162, 170
Mambre, Father 123
Manson, Mahlon D........... 15
Marest, Father............. 128
Marquette, Father.......... 123

INDEX OF NAMES.

Marshall, J. G. 14, 46
(*Sketch of*) 191-200
Marshal, Libeus 267
Marshall, Rev. Robert 191
Marshall, Rev. Samuel 191
Marshall, Wm 13
Martin, E. B. 13
Mason, Elder John 274
Mather, Cotton 124
May, —— 296
Mears, George W.,
    14, 35, 37, 38, 39, 44, 48
Mermet, Father 123
Merrill, Samuel,
  13, 17, 18, 19, 23, 28, 29, 30, 31
Miller, Thomas 360
Millison, James 16
Mills, Elijah 256
Mills, Mrs. Elizabeth 261
Mills, Isaac 350, 359
Mills, Jacob 256
Milroy, R. H 14
Minnich, J. A 16
Mitchell, Dr. Samuel G .. 13, 156
Mitchell, Wm 14
Moor, Patrick 306, 311
Moore, Joseph M 170
Morgan, Dr. Lewis C 235
Morris, A. W.,
  12, 26, 27, 28, 169, 171
Morris, Bethuel F.,
  5, 13, 17, 22, 24, 26, 29, 163
Morris, Isaac 290
Morris, Morris 169
Morris, Samuel V. 15, 62
Morris, Thomas A 170
Morris, ——.. 280
Morrison, James 13
Morrison, Samuel 15, 43
Mothershead, J. L 14
Muir, P. B. 198, 199
Murray, Elias 13

Naylor, Isaac 13
Neely, John J 13
Nelson, Thomas 199
New, Wm 170
Newberry, Samuel 13
Newel, James 315, 316, 317
Noble, Benjamin S 170
Noble, James 152
Noble, Noah 12, 169
Noble, W. H. L 44
Norris, John 53

Olcott, Benj. (See *Alcott, Benj.*)
Oliver, D. H 15
O'Neal, Hugh 170
Orr, Joseph 12, 169
Osbourne, Samuel 14
Otis, Samuel 70
Otto, William T. 14, 199
Owen, David Dale 239
Owen, Robert Dale 30
Owens, John 12

Palmer, N. B. 12
Parke, Benjamin,
  5, 12, 16, 22, 24, 26, 28, 152
Paul, —— 357
Paxton, James 169
Pennington, Dennis 12
Pepper, Abel C 14
Periet, Father 123
Perkins, Samuel E 14, 199, 200
Pierce, Henry D 15
Pinckney, Charles 73, 74
Pinet, Father 123
Pirtle, Henry 197, 199
Plasket, William 284, 285
Polk, Josiah F 173
Polke, William 12
Poole, Jo. 15, 44, 48
Porter, John R 13
Posey, Gen. Thomas 348
Pratt, Daniel D 13
Prescott, Wm. H 31
Prichet, Mrs 331
Prince, William 210
Prior, Moses 332, 333, 346
Prior, Mrs. Moses 332, 333, 346
Proctor, Rev. David 162
Pryor. (See *Prior*.)
Putnam, Prof. F. W 222

Quarles, W 13, 169, 171

Ralston, Alexander 155
Randolph, Benjamin 330
Randolph, Joseph 359
Rapp, Frederick 153
Rapp, George 237
Rariden, James 13, 199
Raridon —— 319
Rasles, Father 123, 131
Ray, Gov. James B 153, 210
Ray, James M .. 13, 30, 31, 34,
    35, 38, 39, 42, 158, 163
Raymond, Charles H 15
Reed, Joseph 158

INDEX OF NAMES.

Reeder, Daniel.............. 286
Reeder, David.............. 286
Reeder, Jacob.............. 286
Reeder, Joseph 286
Reeder, Stephen 286
Reynolds, Jonah 267
Reynolds, Wm. F............ 14
Reynolds, ——.............. 319
Ribourde, Father 123
Rice, Rev................... 274
Ridenour, J. M......15, 61, 62, 63
Riley, John................. 286
Rittenhouse, —— 343
Ritter, Levi.............15, 44
Roache, Addison L.,
 14, 38, 39, 42, 43, 44, 46, 49, 51, 61
Rorison, Brainard........... 15
Ross, Morris M............. 15
Rugg, Samuel L............. 14
Russell, Alexander W........ 170

St. Clair, Gov. Arthur.151, 275,
 287, 288, 289, 290, 291, 292, 294,
  295, 296, 313, 345
St. Clair, Arthur (the younger) 13
Schoolcraft, Henry R........ 238
Scott, Gen. Charles,
 262, 286, 287, 288, 335, 348
Scott, James.....12, 16, 19, 22, 208
Scott, Rev. James:........... 164
Scott, Lucius H............. 211
Scudder, Caleb..........156, 162
Scudder, K. A........156, 169, 170
Sergeant, Winthrop 134
Shaler, Prof. N. S........... 222
Sharpe, Ebenezer............ 174
Sharpe, Thomas H........13, 170
Shanks, J. P. C..........15, 62
Sheets, Wm............13, 30, 31
Shelby, Evan................ 256
Shoemaker, Daniel........... 256
Simonson, John S............ 15
Simpson, Ephraim 341
Slaughter, Wm. B............ 13
Sloan, George W............. 15
Smalley, Wm....295, 296, 297,
 298, 299, 300, 301, 302, 303,
 304, 305, 306, 307, 308, 309,
  310, 311, 330
Smith, Ballard.............. 14
Smith, George 156
Smith, Hamilton..........14, 38
Smith, Rev. John.339, 341, 356, 362
Smith, John................. 286
Smith, Oliver H......13, 192, 199

Smith, Samuel 13
Smith, Capt. Wm. B.......... 75
Smith, ——.................. 319
Snyder, D. E................ 14
Soward, John 264, 265
Soward, Ziba............264, 265
Spencer, Col. Oliver,
  286, 322, 323, 324
Spencer, O. M...321, 322, 323, 324
Sparks, Jared 29
Stapp, Milton 12, 16, 36
Stephens, John L............ 31
Stevens, J. F............... 14
Stevens, S. C............... 12
Stevens, T. M............... 15
Stewart, James H............ 14
Stickney, Benjamin F........ 137
Stites, Maj. Benjamin.....252, 253
 254, 255, 256, 257, 261, 262, 266, 354
Stites, Benjamin, Jr ..255, 256, 340
Stites, Elijah.....255, 261, 275, 276
Stites, Hezekiah,
  256, 259, 260, 262, 266
Stites, Jonathan............ 256
Stites, Nehemiah............ 255
Stites, Rhoda 261, 274
Story, Joseph 29
Stout, Elihu................ 37
Stowe, Calvin E 31
Strange, John............... 163
Strong, Col............283, 284
Sullivan, Jeremiah...10, 13, 17, 29
  30, 31, 35, 37, 199, 208
Sullivan, T. L..........13, 35, 37
Sweetser, Philip............ 12
Symmes, John Cleves,
  253, 255, 258, 276

Talbott, R. C............... 14
Tanner, Gordon.............. 14
Taylor, Walter 152
Taylor, Zachary......157, 178, 179
Terrell, Gen. W. H. H.,
  6, 15, 62, 63, 64, 65
Test, Charles H.,
  15, 59, 60, 61, 63, 64
Thomas, Daniel.............. 16
Thomas, Jesse B............. 152
Thompson, John H............ 13
Thompson, Richard W........ 199
Thompson, W. P............. 198
Thornton, Henry P......9, 13, 16
Tiffin, Edward 135
Tingley..................... 286
Tipton, John......13, 153, 154, 179

Todd, Charles N............. 15
Torbet, Oliver B 14, 245, 329
Torry, Ensign................. 347
Trueman, Maj. Alexander.295, 296
  297, 298, 299, 300, 301, 302, 305, 330
Tucker, Henry 341, 342, 343
Tuttle, E. C................. 15

Underhill, Robt. W........... 14
Upfold, Rt. Rev. George...14, 38

Van Hyse................314, 315
Vanness, Garret..........359, 360
Van Vorhis, F. J.............. 16
Vigo, Francis................ 18
Vivier, Father 132
Volney, Francis, Count....... 134

Wade, Thomas C..........256, 257
Wagner, G. D 14
Walker, L. F...............15, 62
Wallace, David.............10, 13
Wallace, John W............. 269
Walpole, Luke............... 168
Walters, Thomas.........359, 360
Washington, George 86
Wayne, Gen.Anthony..296, 317,
  318, 324, 325, 326, 327, 328, 329,
  330, 335, 336, 341, 345, 347, 348,
         351, 352, 355, 356
Webb, John..............313, 314
Welch, James........319, 320, 321

Wheeling, ——............... 344
Whitcomb, James...10, 13, 17,
  18, 19, 22, 23, 27, 28, 34, 35, 36,
                   184, 194, 211
White, Albert S.............. 13
White, Daniel A.............. 29
White, Capt. Jacob...329, 333, 334
White, R. K..........194, 196, 197
Wick, Wm. W..13, 27, 158, 159, 169
Wickerham................... 291
Wildman, James A........... 15
Wiley, Delany............... 15
Wilkinson, Gen. James...262,
  287, 288, 292, 293, 295, 296, 348
Willard, Ashbel P............ 14
Williams, Jesse L............ 14
Willson, S. C....15, 44, 47, 49. 199
Wilson, D. W................ 198
Wilson, John R.............. 16
Wilson, Robert Anderson.231, 234
Wineman, ——............... 154
Winthrop, Thomas L......... 29
Wolfe, Nathaniel............. 198
Wood, Aaron................ 14
Wood, Henry C.............. 198
Woodruff, Allen............. 256
Woollen, Wm. Wesley..16, 64, 65
Wright, Joseph A..........14, 199
Wylie, Andrew,
       18–20, 21, 28, 79, 80

Yandes, Simon..15, 43, 46, 170, 199

www.ingramcontent.com/pod-product-compliance
Lightning Source LLC
Chambersburg PA
CBHW031424230426
43668CB00007B/424